International Or

International Relations scholars typically expect political communities to resemble one another the more they are exposed to pressures of war, economic competition and the spread of hegemonic legitimacy standards. However, historically it is heterogeneity, not homogeneity, that has most often defined international systems. Examining the Indian Ocean region – the centre of early modern globalization – Andrew Phillips and J. C. Sharman explain how diverse international systems can emerge and endure.

Divergent preferences for terrestrial versus maritime conquest, congruent traditions of heteronomy and shared strategies of localization were factors which enabled diverse actors including the Portuguese Estado da Índia, Dutch and English company sovereigns and mighty Asian empires to co-exist for centuries without converging on a common institutional form. Debunking the presumed relationship between interaction and homogenization, this book radically revises conventional thinking on the evolution of international systems, while deepening our understanding of a historically crucial but critically understudied world region.

ANDREW PHILLIPS is an Australian Research Council Discovery Early Career Research Award Fellow and Associate Professor in International Relations and Strategy in the School of Political Science and International Studies at the University of Queensland.

J. C. SHARMAN is a Professor in the Centre for Governance and Public Policy at Griffith University.

Cambridge Studies in International Relations: 137

International Order in Diversity

Cambridge Studies in International Relations is a joint initiative of Cambridge University Press and the British International Studies Association (BISA). The series aims to publish the best new scholarship in international studies, irrespective of subject matter, methodological approach or theoretical perspective. The series seeks to bring the latest theoretical work in International Relations to bear on the most important problems and issues in global politics.

Cambridge Studies in International Relations

136 *Ole Jacob Sending, Vincent Pouliot and Iver B. Neumann*
Diplomacy and the making of world politics

135 *Barry Buzan and George Lawson*
The global transformation
History, modernity and the making of international relations

134 *Heather Elko McKibben*
State strategies in international bargaining
Play by the rules or change them?

133 *Janina Dill*
Legitimate targets?
Social construction, international law, and US bombing

132 *Nuno P. Monteiro*
Theory of unipolar politics

131 *Jonathan D. Caverley*
Democratic militarism
Voting, wealth, and war

130 *David Jason Karp*
Responsibility for human rights
Transnational corporations in imperfect states

129 *Friedrich Kratochwil*
The status of law in world society
Meditations on the role and rule of law

128 *Michael G. Findley, Daniel L. Nielson and J. C. Sharman*
Global shell games
Experiments in transnational relations, crime, and terrorism

127 *Jordan Branch*
The cartographic state
Maps, territory, and the origins of sovereignty

Series list continues after index

International Order in Diversity

War, Trade and Rule in the Indian Ocean

ANDREW PHILLIPS AND J. C. SHARMAN

CAMBRIDGE
UNIVERSITY PRESS

CAMBRIDGE
UNIVERSITY PRESS

University Printing House, Cambridge CB2 8BS, United Kingdom

Cambridge University Press is part of the University of Cambridge.

It furthers the University's mission by disseminating knowledge in the pursuit of education, learning and research at the highest international levels of excellence.

www.cambridge.org
Information on this title: www.cambridge.org/9781107446823

First published 2015

Printed in the United Kingdom by Clays, St Ives plc

A catalogue record for this publication is available from the British Library

Library of Congress Cataloguing in Publication data
Phillips, Andrew, 1977–
International order in diversity : war, trade and rule in the Indian Ocean / Andrew Phillips, J. C. Sharman.
pages cm. – (Cambridge studies in international relations ; 137)
ISBN 978-1-107-08483-4 (hardback)
1. Indian Ocean Region – Relations. 2. Geopolitics – Indian Ocean Region. I. Sharman, J. C. (Jason Campbell), 1973– II. Title.
DS341.P55 2015
327.09182′4–dc23

2014044743

ISBN 978-1-107-08483-4 Hardback
ISBN 978-1-107-44682-3 Paperback

Contents

Maps

Tables

Acknowledgements

This book reflects our shared fascination with empires, and a related longstanding interest in the role of military power in the rise of the West. From the outset we were united in our frustration at two disconnects within International Relations scholarship. The first was the still widespread tendency to banish empires to the distant, irrelevant past, and to base theories of international systems almost exclusively on the experience of today's global sovereign state monoculture. The second was the field's tacit reliance on an outdated triumphalist historiography, which both exaggerates and elongates the period of Western global military supremacy. This misreading of history mistakes the sovereign state's contemporary triumph as somehow reflecting the logical end-point of centuries of continuous interaction and competition. Our intuition was that history was far messier and more meandering, and that making sense of durably diverse international systems, where neither the sovereign state nor the West had been predominant, would provide a useful corrective.

In focusing on the Indian Ocean, we were motivated by our desire to contribute to an exciting body of scholarship that is now seeking to recast International Relations on less Eurocentric foundations. But as political scientists based in Australia (itself a product of extra-European Western hegemony) our interests have also been shaped by our country's preoccupation with the dawn of a purportedly 'Asian century'. For while Australians increasingly ponder the challenges of navigating an increasingly post-Western world, a popular historical understanding of how international relations worked in maritime Afro-Asia before Western dominance has until now remained elusive. Without this historical understanding, it remains difficult to contextualize or prepare for the transformations that are now reshaping the global order. Beyond our theoretical ambitions, then, we hope that this book will also help to expand readers' historical horizons, enabling them to more confidently engage a world where non-Western powers are reclaiming their earlier centrality.

Anyone who writes a book incurs many debts along the way, and we are no exception. We would especially like to thank Alex Cooley, Luke Glanville, Seb Kaempf, Peter Katzenstein and Chris Reus-Smit for their thoughtful and detailed feedback on an early version of the main argument. Similarly valuable was a panel ('Globalization's Cradle: International Relations Theory and the Indian Ocean') at the 2013 International Studies Association annual conference, featuring Amitav Acharya, Charles Butcher, Ryan Griffiths, Peter Katzenstein, Manjeet Pardesi, Shogo Suzuki and Bill Thompson. We have also presented our main thesis at Griffith University, the University of Queensland and the Australian National University, and we are grateful for the feedback we received in these fora. Likewise, we also appreciated the valuable feedback we received from presentations of the argument at the 2011 International Studies Association Asia-Pacific Regional Section Inaugural Conference, the 2012 Oceanic Conference on International Studies and the Woolloongabba Writers' Collective. We are especially grateful to Janice Bially Mattern, who provided excellent suggestions for refining the argument in her capacities as chair and discussant of our ISA Asia-Pacific Regional Section panel. We would also like to thank Cathy Moloney and Ben Walter for their terrific research assistance. Sharman would like to thank his current and former colleagues at Griffith who provided comments – in particular Luke Glanville, Ian Hall, Hun Joon Kim, TongFi Kim, Andrew O'Neil, Frank Smith, Pat Weller and Wes Widmaier. Likewise, Phillips would like to thank University of Queensland colleagues who provided constructive feedback on the book's main argument, in particular Stephen Bell, Richard Devetak, Tim Dunne, Heather Rae, Chris Reus-Smit, Emily Tannock and all other participants in the St Lucy's International History Reading Group. We are very appreciative of the detailed and helpful feedback provided by the anonymous reviewers and the time and effort that this represents.

We gratefully acknowledge the financial support provided by the Australian Research Council grants DE130100644, DP120100937 and FT120100485, and the University of Queensland Early Career Researcher Award grant 2011002322. Lastly, Andrew Phillips would like to thank his parents for their unending support and encouragement, while J. C. Sharman would like to thank Bilyana for putting up with his frequent absences, both physical and mental.

Introduction

We live in an unusual age. For most of history, international systems have consisted of a bewildering diversity of political units, ranging from city-leagues through to feudal monarchies, confederacies and sprawling imperial realms. By contrast, ours is an insistently homogeneous era, the diversity of an earlier time now succeeded by a global monoculture of sovereign states. The sovereign state's universal triumph in the post-World War II era is too often seen as evidence of an inexorable historical logic, by which greater interaction between the world's political communities inevitably compelled a convergence in polity forms. The conviction that political communities will increasingly resemble one another as interaction between them rises is deeply ingrained in mainstream International Relations (IR) theories, even if scholars differ as to why this nexus between interaction and homogenization supposedly exists. From the vantage point of today's sovereign state monoculture, this equation of increased interaction with unit homogenization seems plausible. Against the wider backdrop of world history prior to 1945, however, it seems hopelessly parochial, ignoring the persistent heterogeneity in polity forms that has characterized global politics for the greater part of the modern era.

How can we account for the emergence, operation and persistence of durably diverse international systems? This is the central research puzzle we address in this book. Focusing specifically on the Indian Ocean region from 1500 to 1750 – the cradle of what has been dubbed 'oriental globalization' – we seek here to explain how and why interaction reinforced heterogeneity during the early modern era.[1] Already the flywheel of trade between Africa, Asia and Europe from the middle of the first millennium of the common era, from the late fifteenth century onwards the Indian Ocean region saw a marked increase in

[1] J. Hobson, *The Eastern Origins of Western Civilization* (Cambridge University Press, 2004), p. 36.

both the diversity of its polity types, and the scale and frequency of interaction between them. Portuguese crusaders, sent by their king to find spices and Christian allies in the East; vast Mughal cavalry armies from Central Asia, their leaders proudly claiming direct descent from Genghis Khan; the Dutch and English East India Companies – the forerunners of today's multinational corporations and the vanguards of the West's eventual conquest of Asia – each differed radically from one another in their cultural outlooks, institutional forms and political and economic goals.

Against many International Relations theorists' expectations of interaction driving convergence, however, these different polity forms co-existed for centuries alongside one another, together constituting a richly diverse and durable international system. Concentrating on these examples of statist, imperial and corporate polity forms, we establish in this study how this diversity first emerged, and explain why competition failed to produce convergence towards a common polity form. We further explain how heterogeneous actors successfully stabilized their relations with one another without the benefit of possessing shared norms and common cultural understandings. Finally, we demonstrate how this historical heterogeneity continued to profoundly structure the international politics of the Indian Ocean region even following the advent of full-blown Western colonialism from the late eighteenth century.

Mainstream International Relations theories – beholden to the view that increased interaction should call forth a greater uniformity in polity forms over time – anticipate that the centuries-long process of global integration dating from the sixteenth century should have corresponded with a progressive convergence towards a common polity form. But with the very late exception of the state's universalization after the collapse of European colonial empires from the late 1940s to the mid 1970s, the historical record firmly contradicts such expectations. Considering the first 'wave' of globalization in particular – marked by the European conquest of the Americas, the rise of the transatlantic slave trade and the growth of European maritime expansion in Asia – we see not homogenization, but rather a reinforcement of pre-existing diversity.[2]

[2] On the three 'waves' of globalization, located respectively in the sixteenth century, the nineteenth century and the post-1945 era, see generally R. Robertson, *The Three Waves of Globalization: A History of a Developing Global Consciousness* (London: Zed Books, 2003).

The historical prevalence of heterogeneous international systems is deeply disorienting for most International Relations theorists. Such systems appear by their very existence to confound some of the discipline's most basic assumptions about what international politics is and how international systems should work. Traditionally preoccupied with the problem of securing order among like units dwelling in anarchy, IR scholars have paid less attention to the challenges presented by hierarchical international systems, and less still to heteronomous systems governed neither by an exclusive logic of anarchy nor hierarchy.[3] The assumption that international politics is the domain of relations between functionally equivalent like units – sovereign states – has absolved IR scholars from having to explain the processes of interaction between unlike units. At critical points in global history, functionally dissimilar polities co-existed without the stabilizing ballast of either the conventions of a sovereign state system or the commands of an imperial international order. Far from being a transient symptom of disorder, a diversity of polity forms in fact helped to constitute order within such systems. But with a few exceptions, the field has remained generally silent on how we are to make sense of international relations within the heterogeneous international systems that have predominated for most of world history.[4]

[3] Recently, a profusion of studies have begun to redress IR's prior neglect of hierarchy in international politics. See, for example, A. Cooley and H. Spruyt, *Contracting States: Sovereign Transfers in International Relations* (Princeton University Press, 2009); T. Dunne, 'Society and Hierarchy in International Relations', *International Relations* 17:3 (2003), pp. 303–20; D. C. Kang, 'The Theoretical Roots of Hierarchy in International Relations', *Australian Journal of International Affairs* 58:3 (2004), pp. 337–52; D. A. Lake, *Hierarchy in International Relations* (Ithaca, NY: Cornell University Press, 2009); and J. C. Sharman, 'International Hierarchies and Contemporary Imperial Governance: A Tale of Three Kingdoms', *European Journal of International Relations* 19:2 (2013), 189–207. By contrast, heteronomy remains extremely understudied, barring John Ruggie's seminal discussion of the medieval to modern transition in Western Europe. See J. G. Ruggie, 'Territoriality and Beyond: Problematizing Modernity in International Relations', *International Organization* 47:1 (1993), pp. 139–74.

[4] One of the best early studies on heterogeneous international systems remains Y. H. Ferguson and R. W. Mansbach, *Polities: Authority, Identities, and Change* (Columbia: University of South Carolina Press, 1996). For an excellent recent argument for heterogeneity as a routine feature of international systems, see J. Mulich, 'Microregionalism and Intercolonial Relations: The Case of the Danish West Indies, 1730–1830', *Journal of Global History* 8:1 (2013), pp. 72–94.

The very messiness of heterogeneous international systems has encouraged the field either to neglect such systems entirely or to relegate them to a remote and incomprehensible past, casting them as idiosyncratic and transient preludes to the 'real' international politics that emerged after 1945. This relegation stems in part from the field's natural preoccupation with making sense of contemporary puzzles in global politics, where assumptions of unit homogeneity can be taken as a constant. This analytic bias is, however, reinforced by a frequently unacknowledged normative bias among many IR scholars, which identifies institutional and cultural homogeneity as synonymous with international order, and institutional and cultural heterogeneity with disorder. This bias for monocultures over mixed international systems is prevalent to varying degrees of self-consciousness across many theoretical traditions: classical realist nostalgia for *ancien régime* Europe's ideological unipolarity; liberal prescriptions for international integration through universal marketization and democratization; English School apprehensions over the post-colonial 'revolt against the West'; even many constructivist claims that international order is rooted in common constitutional values and institutional practices. All implicitly reject the idea of order in diversity, seeing mixed international systems as either way-stations to a more ordered and homogeneous future or as symptoms of the fragmentation and decline of international orders.[5]

This refusal to confront the typical and defining untidiness of past international systems – and to therefore establish how diversity rather than uniformity might work to constitute order between political communities – is problematic for two main reasons. First, constricting our frame of reference to sovereign state systems (or occasionally to imperial hierarchies) is fundamentally harmful for purposes of theory-building. A neglect of heterogeneous international systems encourages us to mistake contingent outcomes (e.g. Europe's post-medieval convergence towards the sovereign state) as evidence of supposedly universal relationships (e.g. interaction causes convergence). In so doing, it forecloses consideration of alternative ways in which order might be maintained between political communities.

[5] An excellent overview and critique of assumptions in international thought equating homogeneity with order can be found in F. Halliday, 'International Society as Homogeneity: Burke, Marx, Fukuyama', *Millennium: Journal of International Studies* 21:3 (1992), pp. 435–61.

Second, a failure to adequately theorize the dynamics of heterogeneous international systems leaves scholars unable to make sense of international relations as played out in the crucial centuries following the post-1500 first wave of globalization. From the early sixteenth to the late eighteenth century, expanding webs of military, economic and cultural exchange knitted the populations of the Old and New Worlds together on a historically unprecedented scale.[6] This surge in interaction occurred in an age fundamentally different from our own, when neither the West nor the sovereign state was dominant. That successive waves of truculent Westerners were able to inveigle their way into Asia's bazaars and palaces – despite lacking either decisive military or institutional advantages over their originally far wealthier hosts – is a crucially important puzzle for understanding how the present global international order came to be. It is nevertheless one that International Relations theory remains unable to address without a framework for comprehending the dynamics of heterogeneous international systems.

The concerns driving this book are thus both theoretical and historical in nature. Theoretically, we aim to correct the conviction that increased interaction capacity within international systems will inevitably drive a convergence in polity forms over time. We take 'interaction capacity' to refer to 'the level of transportation, communication and organization capability in the unit/system that determines what types and levels of interaction are possible'.[7] Existing theories expect that military or economic competition will promote convergence through processes of Darwinian competition and Lamarckian institutional learning, or that convergence will result as polities increasingly conform to common standards of legitimacy. Against these mechanisms of competition, learning and conformity, we propose an alternative perspective to account for the puzzle of persistent diversity.

While existing International Relations theories conventionally assume a functional equivalence among polities, our story of the Indian Ocean starts from the proposition that different polities (sovereign states, empires or chartered company sovereigns like the Dutch and English East India Companies) want different things and go about

[6] On this point, see A. G. Hopkins, 'Introduction: Globalization – An Agenda for Historians', in A. G. Hopkins (ed.), *Globalization in World History* (London: Pimlico, 2002), pp. 4–5.

[7] B. Buzan and R. Little, *International Systems in World History: Remaking the Study of International Relations* (Oxford University Press, 2000), p. 441.

getting them in different ways. These differences in ends and means may enable different polity types to potentially escape the zero-sum competitive logic that frequently defines relations between functionally equivalent like units. But if diversity is favoured when polities are sufficiently *different* from one another as to avoid symmetrical zero-sum competition, it can be made more durable when they possess sufficient *congruences* in compatible beliefs concerning the organization of political authority, and when actors are willing to reconcile these congruent beliefs through reciprocal processes of localization. Thus, even though the Mughals and the Dutch and English company sovereigns came from different mental universes, both could accept shared and overlapping authority claims according to which two rulers would hold different sovereign prerogatives over the same territory. Both engaged in practices of localization to legitimize and stabilize the resulting accommodations. These three conditions of different preferences, congruent beliefs grounded in heteronomous conceptions of political authority, and practices of localization, explain how a durably diverse international system composed of unlike units can arise and endure.

We illustrate this argument through an examination of the international relations of the Indian Ocean international system from *c.* 1500 to 1750. It is through the in-depth study of this region that we hope to make a substantive historical contribution. Already host to key trans-continental trading routes linking Africa, Europe and Asia from as far back as the seventh century,[8] from 1500 the Indian Ocean emerged as simultaneously the primary site of European–Asian military and diplomatic interaction, the locus of early modern trade between Africa, Asia and Europe, and the world's premier civilizational 'turntable' of cross-cultural exchange.[9] Global historians increasingly acknowledge the Indian Ocean international system as 'ground zero' for early modern globalization.[10] Its crucial historical importance notwithstanding, International Relations has almost totally neglected the Indian Ocean.

[8] K. N. Chaudhuri, *Trade and Civilisation in the Indian Ocean: An Economic History from the Rise of Islam to 1750* (Cambridge University Press, 1985).

[9] P. J. Katzenstein, 'A World of Plural and Pluralist Civilizations: Multiple Actors, Traditions and Practices', in P. J. Katzenstein (ed.), *Civilizations in World Politics* (London: Routledge, 2007), p. 35.

[10] K. N. Chaudhuri, *Asia Before Europe: Economy and Civilization of the Indian Ocean from the Rise of Islam to 1750* (Cambridge University Press, 1990); M. Pearson, *The Indian Ocean* (London: Routledge, 2003).

Beyond merely recovering regional particularity, however, the broader historical contribution lies in our challenge to a Eurocentric view of global history that remains implicit but pervasive throughout much of the field.[11] Notwithstanding their key differences, most International Relations theories remain informed by a historical narrative grounded in three claims. First, late medieval Latin Christendom is viewed as having been unusually politically fragmented relative to other civilizational centres.[12] Second, this exceptional political fragmentation subsequently created a space for the modern sovereign state's early emergence that supposedly did not exist in other Old World societies, especially the major empires of South and East Asia. Third, the West's precocious modernity, and specifically its early development of the sovereign state, allowed it to then coercively remake the world's polities along Western lines through imperialism and then decolonization.

Against this conventional Western exceptionalism, we demonstrate that heteronomy was neither confined to the medieval period, nor was it specific to Western Europe. Instead, it was the very existence of culturally different but structurally congruent beliefs about the legitimacy of heteronomous institutions and practices that allowed Western insinuation into the Indian Ocean international system. Enjoying military advantages only in the naval realm, vanguard agents of Western expansion such as the Portuguese Estado da Índia were dwarfed in wealth and power by Asian behemoths such as the Mughal Empire. For the Portuguese, as for the Dutch and English who succeeded them, this unfavourable balance of material capabilities ensured that ingratiation and insinuation predominated over imposition as the primary means of expanding their influence within the richer and more populous societies they encountered in Asia.

Drawing from the work of specialist international legal historians who have established the ubiquity of legal pluralism in the early modern world, we stress the importance of shared traditions of heteronomy, brought into rough alignment through improvised practices of localization, in enabling Europeans to establish an enduring toehold

[11] On IR's persistent and entrenched Eurocentrism, see generally J. M. Hobson, *The Eurocentric Conception of World Politics: Western International Theory, 1760–2010* (Cambridge University Press, 2012).

[12] Ruggie, 'Territoriality and Beyond', pp. 148–9.

along Asia's maritime margins.[13] This approach departs radically from the traditional triumphalist 'rise of the West' historiography that has typically informed IR interpretations of the modern global international system's evolution. This view has stressed Western institutional innovation, rather than Afro-Eurasian institutional congruence, in explaining the dynamics of Western expansion.[14] According to the conventional Eurocentric perspective, the rise of the West in the early modern Indian Ocean region was driven by the material advantage provided by superior European military technology, and the institutional advantage provided by the sovereign state. The evidence presented in this book shows the first to be marginal and the second illusory.

The argument summarized

How can we explain the proliferation and survival of diverse, unlike units in an environment of increasing interaction? How does a heteronomous international system work? And how does a better understanding of such a system deepen our knowledge of European engagement with the wider world in the centuries before Western dominance? The temporal starting point for our argument is the arrival of new actors in the Indian Ocean: the Portuguese from around the Cape of Good Hope after 1497; the Mughals from Central Asia in 1526; and the Dutch and English East India Companies from the early 1600s. Our opening claim here is that these actors were indeed diverse, representing contrasting statist, imperial and corporate forms, and that their entry and subsequent relations represented a step-level increase in

13 For a recent synthesis of the literature on legal pluralism and early modern history, see L. A. Benton and R. J. Ross (eds.), *Legal Pluralism and Empires, 1500–1850* (New York University Press, 2013).

14 Prominent examples of the 'rise of the West' genre include V. D. Hanson, *Why the West Has Won: Carnage and Culture from Salamis to Vietnam* (London: Faber & Faber, 2002); E. Jones, *The European Miracle: Environments, Economies and Geopolitics in the History of Europe and Asia* (Cambridge University Press, 2003); W. H. McNeill, *The Rise of the West: A History of the Human Community* (University of Chicago Press, 2009); and G. Parker, *The Military Revolution: Military Innovation and the Rise of the West, 1500–1800* (Cambridge University Press, 1996). In fairness, McNeill retreats significantly from Eurocentrism in later editions of *The Rise of the West,* without completely abandoning a hypothesis of Western power resting primarily on Western institutional superiority.

interaction within an already densely interconnected world region. Our second task is to explain how this interaction actually reinforced diversity. We address these matters systematically in the following chapters, but foreshadow these two successive components of our main argument – the emergence of diversity and its subsequent perpetuation – briefly below.

Establishing diversity

What were the dominant polity types in the early modern Indian Ocean, and how were they distinguishable from one another? Let us begin with the Portuguese Estado da Índia, the polity that most closely resembled the modern sovereign state. The king of Portugal established the viceroyalty of the Estado da Índia in 1505. After an extraordinarily rapid period of conquest in the next decade, the Portuguese controlled a network of forts and ports from Mozambique to the Persian Gulf, to Malacca and the Spice Islands, with further trading posts in China and Japan. All of these entrepôts, and the whole Indian Ocean, were claimed for the Portuguese king, to be ruled by his representative in Goa. Although not matching the ideal-type of the modern sovereign state, the resulting structure has nevertheless been described as 'precociously statist'.[15]

Specifically, the Portuguese favoured a centralized structure of authority that flowed directly down from the king to the governor of the Estado da Índia, and then to his subordinate officials, and extended in scope to military and commercial as well as administrative affairs.[16] The strict vertical, unified chain of command, the pattern of direct appointment from the administrative centre, and the public control of military and economic prerogatives gave the Estado da Índia a modern statist cast that is conspicuously lacking from either the imperial or corporate sovereign models. Despite the consensus about the state being the best-adapted institutional form to survive the rigours of

[15] J. E. Wills Jr., 'Was There a Vasco da Gama Epoch? Recent Historiography', in A. Disney and E. Booth (eds.), *Vasco da Gama and the Linking of Europe and Asia* (Oxford University Press, 2000), p. 354.

[16] A. R. Disney, *A History of Portugal and the Portuguese Empire* (Cambridge University Press, 2009); S. Subrahmanyam, *The Portuguese Empire in Asia 1500–1700* (London: Blackwell-Wiley, 2012); M. N. Pearson, *Port Cities and Intruders: The Swahili Coast, India and Portugal in the Early Modern Period* (Baltimore, MD: Johns Hopkins University Press, 1998).

international military and commercial competition, the Estado da Índia was never the region's dominant polity form, eventually being marginalized by the company sovereigns that succeeded it.

Certainly the most powerful units in the Indian Ocean region after 1500 were continental empires, especially the Safavids (from 1501), the Ottomans (after their conquest of Egypt in 1517) and the Mughals (from 1526). Because it was the most central to the region's development, we focus on the Mughal Empire, though historians have noted close similarities in the political forms of these three empires.[17] The Mughals emerged from Central Asia after 1526 to conquer most of South Asia. While never completely dominant throughout the entire subcontinent, the Mughals rapidly established their hegemony across the Indo-Gangetic plain. This laid the foundation for a power formation of truly prodigious proportions. By 1600, the Mughal Empire included more people (approximately 100 million) and greater fiscal and military resources than every polity in Christian Europe combined.[18] This preponderance of material power ultimately allowed the Mughals to set the terms of European engagement with much of the Indian Ocean international system for most of the early modern period. The layered and heteronomous conception of authority in the Mughal Empire was critical in allowing Europeans' entry into the Indian Ocean world, and in enabling the growth of hybrid European–Asian authority arrangements.

The empire was a hierarchical but at the same time polyglot agglomeration. The imperial court relied extensively on local intermediaries to uphold its rule. The empire's constituent communities were furthermore bound to the centre through customized compacts that varied significantly in their allocation of privileges and responsibilities.[19] This

[17] See, for example, D. E. Streusand, *Islamic Gunpowder Empires: Ottomans, Safavids, and Mughals* (Boulder, CO: Westview Press); S. Bose, *A Hundred Horizons: The Indian Ocean in the Age of Global Empire* (Cambridge, MA: Harvard University Press); S. Subrahmanyam, 'A Tale of Three Empires: Mughals, Ottomans, and Habsburgs in a Comparative Context', *Common Knowledge* 12:1 (2006), pp. 66–92.

[18] M. N. Pearson, 'Merchants and States', in J. D. Tracy (ed.), *The Political Economy of Merchant Empires: State Power and World Trade 1350–1750* (Cambridge University Press, 1990), p. 52.

[19] C. A. Bayly, *Imperial Meridian* (London: Longman, 1989); D. H. Nexon and T. Wright, 'What's at Stake in the American Empire Debate', *American Political Science Review* 101:2 (2007), p. 253.

reliance on local clients and 'heterogeneous contracting'[20] empowered emperors to extend their primacy over a huge number of subordinate polities, allowing them to tap deep reserves of agricultural and commercial wealth in the process. This primacy was, however, much more fluid and territorially uneven in its application than contemporary sovereign statist authority.[21] The sharp domestic/foreign distinction that is fundamental to modern conceptions of state sovereignty was alien to the Mughal mind-set. Further departing from Westphalian conceptions of state sovereignty, the Mughals refused to acknowledge any international equals. Instead, they maintained that their rightful authority extended without any limit. Lastly, while enjoying access to formidable military power resources, the Indian Ocean region's early modern emperors neither sought nor attained a monopoly of legitimate violence within their borders. Thus, in Mughal India, local elites and hereditary tax-farmers for the Mughal administration collectively retained autonomous command of over 300,000 horsemen at the height of Mughal power in the mid-seventeenth century.[22]

In completing our survey of the most prominent of the diverse polities of the Indian Ocean regional system, we come finally to the company sovereigns, the Dutch East India Company (Vereenigde Oost-Indische Compagnie or VOC) and the English East India Company (EIC). These entities were neither sovereign states themselves, nor were they mere extensions of their respective home states. Instead, they were hybrid actors without twenty-first-century equivalents. The VOC and the EIC were private, profit-maximizing joint stock enterprises that also enjoyed key sovereign prerogatives and wielded extensive armed force. Thus, the EIC was invested with powers including the right to administer civil and criminal justice within its factories, the right to maintain armies and a navy, and the prerogative to enforce its monopoly against European and

[20] D. H. Nexon, *The Struggle for Power in Early Modern Europe: Religious Conflict, Dynastic Empires, and International Change* (Princeton University Press, 2009), p. 72.

[21] L. A. Benton, *A Search for Sovereignty: Law and Geography in European Empires, 1400–1900* (Cambridge University Press, 2010), p. 31.

[22] C. B. Asher and C. Talbot, *India before Europe* (Cambridge University Press, 2006), p. 128; D. M. Peers, 'Revolution, Evolution or Devolution: The Military and the Making of Colonial India', in W. Lee (ed.), *Empires and Indigenes: Intercultural Alliance, Imperial Expansion and Warfare in the Early Modern World* (New York University Press, 2011), p. 98.

Asian interlopers by force.[23] Similarly, the VOC could sign international treaties, declare war, make peace and maintain military and naval forces. Their enjoyment of these quintessentially sovereign prerogatives notwithstanding, both the VOC and the EIC were also very definitely private companies, owned by shareholders and run for profit.[24]

Company sovereigns were comprised of networks of trading outposts stretched throughout the Indian Ocean littoral, relying for their maintenance upon the companies' accommodations with a plethora of local political actors.[25] The companies neither desired nor attempted to assert a monopoly on legitimate violence across their jurisdictions. Instead, EIC and VOC factors continuously cultivated local vassals, hired mercenaries and rendered tribute to the Mughal emperor to secure their factories from attack. The result was entities comprised of multiple overlapping structures of authority, which projected their jurisdictional claims unevenly across a networked archipelago of entrepôts. By imbricating themselves within local political systems in this manner, not only did the companies thus instantiate diversity themselves, they also promoted it in others.

Thus while the Portuguese Estado da Índia was a reasonable, though hardly perfect, approximation of the sovereign state, each of the other two forms generally did not have criteria held to define the sovereign state: unqualified domestic jurisdictional supremacy; clearly demarcated territorial exclusivity; relations with external actors on the basis of sovereign equality; and the claim to a domestic monopoly on legitimate violence.

Stabilizing diversity

How can the Indian Ocean's durable diversity of polity forms be explained, particularly in light of the continuous and accelerating interaction between these polities that marked the early modern period?

23 P. Lawson, *The East India Company: A History* (New York: Longman, 1993), p. 29.

24 N. Steensgaard, *Carracks, Caravans and Companies: The Structural Crisis in the European–Asian Trade in the Early 17th Century* (Lund: Studentlitteratur, 1973); D. C. North, *Institutions, Institutional Change and Economic Performance* (Cambridge University Press, 1990).

25 P. Stern, *The Company-State: Corporate Sovereignty and the Early Modern Foundations of the British Empire in India* (Oxford University Press, 2011), p. 208.

The heart of the argument presented in this book is that diversity in the Indian Ocean international system was a product of three interacting factors: first, the existence of different goals and preferences distinguishing the region's European intruders from local African and Asian polities; second, the presence of culturally distinct but structurally congruent commitments to heteronomy among European and indigenous elites; and third, a shared willingness among European and local polities to adapt through practices of localization. Different goals meant that zero-sum competition was the exception rather than the rule between Europeans and local polities. Common commitments to heteronomous authority structures allowed different actors to improvise governance arrangements that allowed for different kinds of authority claims over the same territory. Practices of localization stabilized these arrangements, through both symbolic legitimation and the forging of alliances of convenience between European and local actors.

Rulers' differing cultural orientations profoundly shaped the purposes they pursued following their entry into the Indian Ocean world. Beginning with the Portuguese, Europeans pursued wealth and power through adherence to an oceanic – or thalassocratic – vision of empire that sharply distinguished them from the Asian land-based empires and the other African and Asian polities. Europeans sought monopolistic control over oceanic spaces, rather than territory.[26] Under the thrall of early modern mercantilist thought, the Portuguese, but also to a degree the Dutch and English, sought to establish political control over huge maritime areas in order to gain a stranglehold over major trading routes linking Europe to the wider world.[27] Within the Indian Ocean (and to a lesser extent, littoral East Asia), Europeans aimed to realize this goal by establishing far-flung networks of fortified trading entrepôts along the maritime fringes of the most wealthy and powerful polities.

The Mughals differed in their land-based strategic orientation. Simply stated, the Mughals were to a very large degree uninterested in maritime affairs: 'The whole mind-set of the Mughal emperors and their nobles was land-based. Prestige was a matter of controlling vast areas on which were located fat, meek peasants. Glory was to be won

26 E. Mancke, 'Early Modern Expansion and the Politicization of Oceanic Space', *Geographical Review* 89:2 (1999), p. 226.

27 Benton, *A Search for Sovereignty*, p. 106.

by campaigns on land.'[28] Given their vast wealth and a structural trade surplus with the rest of the world, the Mughals could afford to be nonchalant about European dominance of the seas.[29] The Mughals' land-based orientation derived from their origins as horse-borne pastoralists who traced their lineage to previous steppe conquerors including Genghis Khan and Timur (otherwise known as Tamerlane).[30] Importantly, this reticence to project political power into the maritime domain was not exclusive to the Mughals. On the contrary, 'there is evidence of a coherent ocean-space construction that governed the region until disrupted by the Europeans at the end of the fifteenth century'.[31] Across Indian Ocean littoral societies, Afro-Asian rulers perceived the sea as 'a non-territory, a space not suitable for control or even influence, but rather one that existed solely as a transport surface'.[32] This attitude contrasted profoundly with the thalassocratic visions informing the European intruders.[33] It was this dissonance in oceanic perceptions and political preferences that created space for an enduring accommodation between European interlopers and Afro-Asian hosts.

As the exception that supports the rule, it is notable that the most conspicuous instance of zero-sum conflict within the early modern Indian Ocean system was between the Portuguese and the Dutch VOC in the period 1600–50. This was precisely because they had similar goals

[28] Pearson, 'Merchants and States'; S. Subrahmanyam, 'Holding the World in Balance: The Connected Histories of the Iberian Overseas Empires 1500–1640', *American Historical Review* 112:5 (2007), p. 1373.

[29] J. Gommans, *Mughal Warfare: Indian Frontiers and the High Road to Empire 1500–1700* (London: Routledge, 2002), p. 163; J. F. Richards, *The Mughal Empire* (Cambridge University Press, 1996), p. 2.

[30] This is not to suggest that the Mughal lack of interest in maritime affairs was absolute. Particularly from the 1570s, with the conquest of the maritime sultanates of Gujarat and Bengal, customs revenues occupied an increasing proportion of Mughal taxation receipts, while Mughal officials at times involved themselves in a private capacity in maritime trade. This caveat notwithstanding, receipts from taxation of agricultural production nevertheless remained the overwhelming source of Mughal income for the empire's duration. On this point, see C. Lefevre, 'Europe–Mughal India–Muslim Asia: Circulation of Political Ideas and Instruments in Early Modern Times', in A. Fluchter and S. Richter (eds.), *Structures on the Move: Technologies of Governance in Transcultural Encounter* (Heidelberg: Springer, 2012), p. 139.

[31] P. E. Steinberg, *The Social Construction of the Ocean* (Cambridge University Press, 2001), p. 41.

[32] *Ibid.*, p. 46. [33] *Ibid.*, p. 75.

of imposing a monopoly on Indian Ocean trade through controlling networks of key ports and sea lanes. Directly contradicting Eurocentric narratives positing the irresistible rise of the sovereign state, the corporate enterprise of the Dutch was very much the victor in this struggle.

If the existence of different but compatible preferences between Europeans and Afro-Asians constitutes the first pillar of the explanation for durable diversity, the second pillar relates to heteronomy. Heteronomy, the existence of multiple, overlapping and fluid authority structures within the same territory, was a practice that had long proved critically important in enabling long-distance trade and cross-cultural exchange.[34] Pre-existing traditions of heteronomy, which had initially evolved in part to accommodate self-governing trading diasporas, provided a niche for Europeans from the sixteenth century onwards. The common experience Europeans and Asians shared in navigating layered and multiple authority structures within their own cultural milieux enabled them to improvise hybrid heteronomous governance arrangements for mutual co-existence.

In contrast to conventional narratives that invoke European institutional exceptionalism explaining Western expansion into the early modern Indian Ocean littoral, our account instead stresses institutional congruence between European and local African and Asian polities. This emphasis on institutional commonalities, combined with our focus on the variations in European and local polities' purposes and preferences, goes a long way towards explaining the puzzle of the durable diversity in the Indian Ocean international system.

The third pillar of the argument foregrounds the creative agency actors exerted in constructing and legitimating the heteronomous arrangements that regulated interaction between Europeans and host communities. The legitimization of such authority arrangements occurred through complex negotiations between Europeans and locals. These negotiations entailed the symbolic legitimation of the European presence, reinforced by parallel self-interested military and commercial alliances of convenience. We dub this process 'localization'. First coined by historian O. W. Wolters and introduced to International Relations by Amitav Acharya, localization initially referred to the reciprocal processes through which local actors shape, adapt and

[34] P. D. Curtin, *Cross-Cultural Trade in World History* (Cambridge University Press, 1984).

adopt foreign ideas about authority and legitimacy to fit in with existing beliefs and norms.[35] Here we adapt this concept to capture the more interactive process through which Europeans insinuated their way into local polities, acting alternatively as vassals, partners or suzerains depending on locally prevalent cultural scripts. Yet this localization did not yield any deep intersubjective consensus between Europeans and Asians and Africans concerning the nature or purpose of their relationship to one another. Friction, chauvinism and mutual condescension remained constants from the Europeans' arrival until the nineteenth-century advent of full-blown colonialism. But the parties' subscription to culturally distinct but structurally similar notions of shared and layered sovereignty did create enough common ground for them to legitimize and sustain a variety of heteronomous arrangements. These in turn stabilized and expanded endemic diversity in the region.

Our primary focus is on the durably diverse international system that emerged and endured in the Indian Ocean before the era of Western colonial dominance. Yet if our coverage were to end at 1750, how would we characterize the regional order that took hold after this date? Did the region simply belatedly conform to the European master template of universal convergence towards the sovereign state, albeit with a two-and-a-half-century lag? On the contrary, the postscript to our story in the later eighteenth and nineteenth centuries is that, rather than replicating the European sequence of heteronomy to sovereign states in an anarchical system, the Indian Ocean came to be defined by a hierarchical arrangement of European colonial empires that overlaid rather than erased regional heteronomy. British domination of South Asia and Dutch dominance of archipelagic South-East Asia rested on a multitude of differentiated arrangements with subordinate polities. In this way, the region's characteristic diversity endured all the way down to the mid-twentieth century, albeit with heteronomous arrangements overlaid by colonial hierarchy following the West's rise to global hegemony.

This book has an expansive remit, covering the area from the Swahili Coast of East Africa to the South-East Asian archipelagos over three or

[35] O. W. Wolters, *History, Culture, and Region in Southeast Asia* (Singapore: Southeast Asia Program Publications, 1982); A. Acharya, *Whose Ideas Matter? Agency and Power in Asian Regionalism* (Ithaca, NY: Cornell University Press, 2009).

four centuries. The theoretical claims advanced are equally ambitious. But because no one project can realistically aim to do everything, it is important to make clear the scope and limits of the book from the outset. Empirically, this study is squarely focused on the Indian Ocean region, with other regions of the world considered only in passing. Similarly, the focus is primarily historical rather than the already well-ploughed field of post-1945 international politics. The theoretical goal is to explain how one durably diverse international system emerged and persisted. We do not assert that our explanation reveals the only way such systems may arise and endure. There may well be diverse pathways to diverse international systems. Given this position, we do not advance our thesis in the form of necessary conditions, which in any case seem problematic if agency, contingency and equifinality (the possibility that there may be more than one cause of the same outcome) have any role in the social world. We advance our argument to demonstrate how International Relations scholars can account for durably diverse international systems, and to hopefully inspire further study of the broad range of mixed international systems that have predominated for most of world history.

Plan of the book

Our analysis begins in Chapter 1 with an elaboration of our central research question: explaining why persistent diversity within international systems is a puzzle for International Relations scholars. We establish that the presumption that interaction promotes sameness is common, though not universal, across a broad range of otherwise antagonistic theoretical traditions, in particular realism, rationalism and constructivism. These beliefs are ultimately anchored in mechanisms of competition, for realists and rationalists, or conformity, for the closely related strands of constructivism and sociological institutionalism. The growing weight of evidence highlighting the historical preponderance of durably diverse international systems confirms the inadequacy of these approaches, and creates the space for our alternative explanation.

We then introduce the Indian Ocean international system to establish the larger historical backdrop of our argument. We seek to familiarize readers with an international system that International Relations scholars have almost totally neglected, but that global historians now acknowledge as being critically significant as the cradle of early modern globalization. We situate the Indian Ocean international system within a larger Old World context encompassing the societies of Europe, Africa and Asia. A bewildering diversity of polity forms co-existed within this larger milieu, but institutions and practices of heteronomous accommodation were common throughout.

Our empirical chapters establish that polity diversity increased rather than diminished as military, commercial and cultural interaction between them grew. Engaging the puzzle of persistent diversity thematically and chronologically, we first explain how polity diversity first increased with rising interaction in the sixteenth century. The next task is to show why competition between the region's Western polities (the established Estado da Índia and the parvenu English and Dutch East India Companies) failed to produce convergence on a single polity form in the seventeenth century, despite continuous increases in interaction. We then analyse how the region's diverse European and Asian polities were able to co-exist and eventually even partially intermesh, despite the absence of common norms or shared cultural understandings. Finally, we demonstrate how the region's experience of heteronomy shaped its international politics following the shift towards Western colonial hierarchy from the late eighteenth century.

Chapter 2 explains how a durably diverse international system emerged in the Indian Ocean following the entry of new European and Central Asian players into the region from the late fifteenth century. Specifically, we look at the arrival of the statist Portuguese Estado da Índia in the Indian Ocean, and contrast this form with the Mughals as a classic empire. The focus of our comparison is on variations between these polities' internal structures of authority, their mode of relating to external actors and their organization of military power. A key conclusion is that European entry to the region was facilitated through the existence of contrasting but compatible European and Afro-Asian preferences, rather than by any decisive European military or institutional superiority. While the Europeans sought to build maritime networks, major land-based local empires derived power, wealth and prestige from the control of sedentary populations. These divergent preferences for oceanic versus land-oriented modes of aggrandizement allowed the Portuguese to co-exist – however uneasily – with local powers, laying the foundations for the durably diverse international system that thereafter evolved in the region.

Chapter 3 examines the further expansion and consolidation in polity diversity that attended the entry of the chartered company sovereigns from 1600, specifically the English and Dutch East India Companies. Here we explain the company sovereigns' unique nature and origins, as well as their success in trading and fighting from one side of the region to the other. In particular, we account for the companies' eclipse of the Portuguese, who, despite most closely approximating what is conventionally regarded as the best-adapted unit, the sovereign state, were increasingly marginalized in the seventeenth century. Thanks to similar maritime, mercantilist goals among the Europeans, competitive dynamics were at work among the interlopers in the Indian Ocean region, just as they were in the state system that was by then emerging in Western Europe. But crucially, unlike in Europe, it was the statist form rather than its competitors that lost out in the Indian Ocean. This outcome, the marginalization (though not elimination) of the statist form by rival polities, is incongruous from the perspective of mainstream International Relations. This intra-European rivalry illustrates how competition worked to consolidate the region's existing heterogeneity.

Progressing from the focus on the origins and consolidation of a heterogeneous Indian Ocean international system in the sixteenth and seventeenth centuries, Chapter 4 examines the operation of that system, concentrating specifically on the stabilization of relations between the region's European and non-Western polities. If different preferences between land-based local powers and maritime Europeans facilitated the West's entry, diversity was stabilized through the existence of culturally different but complementary beliefs concerning the legitimacy of heteronomous institutions of authority, and accompanying practices of localization. As an empire, the Mughals shared authority with subordinate polities that acknowledged their supremacy. Smaller 'galactic polities' in South-East Asia and elsewhere in the region likewise routinely paid tribute to more than one overlord as part of a layered, gradated structure of authority.[36] Sharing a world-view that

[36] Throughout this inquiry, we periodically refer to 'galactic polities'. We draw this concept from anthropologist Stanley Tambiah's work on traditional South-East Asian polities, which he characterized as being organized around the model of the *mandala*, a framework which fused cosmology with political geography, and where power was seen to radiate outwards from the capital and the ruler in steadily diminishing circles of influence. Tambiah described galactic polities'

emphasized divisible, non-exclusive sovereignty, the English and Dutch imbricated themselves by alternately playing overlord and subordinate to local polities. In so doing, they further expanded and entrenched heteronomy. The stabilization of relations between diverse polities occurred without the benefit of shared norms or cultural standards uniting Europeans with Asians and Africans. There was a congruence of beliefs and practices, rather than any thick intersubjective consensus.

Although our primary goal is to explain the origins, consolidation and operation of the Indian Ocean international system from 1500 to 1750, it is also essential to address what came after this point. Consequently, Chapter 5 examines the reconfiguration of regional polity diversity that occurred with the transition to a Western-dominated imperial hierarchy from the late eighteenth century. As noted, rather than following the European sequence of heteronomy to sovereign states under anarchy, the Indian Ocean system was defined by colonial empires until after World War II. In this chapter we examine the relative importance of changing military dynamics versus ideational factors in accounting for this transition. The prior existence of a heteronomous international system conditioned and constrained Western imperialists in their shift towards improvised empire after 1750. Rather than witnessing an end to relations governed by beliefs in shared, overlapping sovereignty and practices of adaptation, the rise of colonial empires instead saw a reconfiguration of these ideas and practices in a more explicitly hierarchical form down to the final dissolution of these empires after World War II.

We conclude by first briefly testing the extension of our findings beyond the Indian Ocean context, before finally articulating the

political geography as follows: 'This conception of territory as a variable space, control over which diminished as royal power radiated from the center, is integral to the schematic characterization of the traditional polity as a mandala composed of concentric circles, usually three in number. This concentric circle, representing center–periphery relations, was ordered thus: In the center is the king's capital and the region of its direct control, which is surrounded by a circle of "provinces" ruled by princes or "governors" appointed by the king, and these again are surrounded by tributary polities more or less independent.' S. Tambiah, 'The Galactic Polity: The Structure of Traditional Kingdoms in Southeast Asia', *Annals of the New York Academy of Sciences* 293:1 (1977), pp. 74–5. Though Tambiah's framework derived from studies of South-East Asian polities, the 'galactic' structure was in fact common throughout many smaller Indian Ocean littoral polities, and this is reflected in our usage throughout the text.

principal theoretical and historical implications of our study. Even a cursory consideration of other regions reinforces the need for theories of diverse international systems, and illuminates also the corresponding dangers of seeking to build purportedly general International Relations theories on the experience of one atypical region. Taken-for-granted assumptions and institutions, from the idea of sovereign states as the natural building blocks of international systems to the presumption of homogeneous preferences, to the universal relevance of power-balancing, are shown to be highly contingent and parochial. Conversely, a broader perspective offers the opportunity to set aside the discipline's Eurocentric blinkers. More positively, it also reinforces existing calls within the field for a more genuinely international International Relations, that is more attuned to the rich diversity of histories and experiences in Europe and elsewhere that have cumulatively contributed to the evolution of today's global order.

1 *The puzzle of durable diversity in International Relations*

On 20 December 1999, the Portuguese-administered territory of Macau formally reverted to Chinese rule. Macau's reincorporation into China passed with little fanfare outside East Asia, attracting far less global media scrutiny than the handover of Hong Kong two years previously. And yet it marked the end of a critically important era of world history, signifying the end of one of the last vestiges of the diversity of political arrangements that had attended Western expansion into Asia. While Beijing will govern Macau as a Special Administrative Region until 2049, the Macau transfer constituted a final pre-millennial instance of the sovereign state's universal triumph over empire, and with it the apparent vindication of scholars who anticipate that interaction promotes global convergence in polity forms.

Considering the first three centuries of large-scale Western participation in the Indian Ocean regional international system, we contest the view that interaction always promotes sameness between political communities. This chapter proceeds in four sections. We begin by examining conventional theories of the presumed nexus between interaction and homogenization. Focusing especially on realism, rationalism and closely related constructivist and sociological institutionalist accounts, we demonstrate that these approaches each predominantly rely on causal mechanisms whereby interaction produces a convergence on a common polity form via some combination of competition or conformity. The primary problem with such accounts is the historical prevalence of diverse international systems, but there are also conceptual weaknesses in each of these perspectives. In the second section, we briefly contrast these claims against a growing literature that establishes diversity, rather than uniformity, as the default condition of most international systems throughout history. Notwithstanding their predominant focus on explaining homogeneity and convergence, the third section shows that these major theoretical traditions do nevertheless contain implicit theories of diverse international systems. Diversity might reflect the difficulty of power projection, asymmetrical alliances, economic specialization, the contracting out of sovereign prerogatives between unequal powers, or stratification between diverse units under normative regimes of unequal entitlement. This section compares and contrasts these subordinate theories of diversity with the main thesis of this book, and also defines our notion of an international system. The chapter concludes by introducing the Indian Ocean in terms of its four sub-regions of South Asia, the Middle East, South-East Asia and East Africa.

Interaction and presumptive convergence in International Relations theories – a survey and critique

Three mechanisms of convergence: military Darwinism, economic competition and normative socialization

Our first main goal is to establish the basic theoretical puzzle driving this book: International Relations theory is over-supplied with mechanisms explaining convergence, even though most international systems have been defined by durable diversity. The belief in the power of interaction to promote sameness is deeply entrenched within mainstream theories. Realists and rationalists, generally subscribing to a logic of competition, privilege war and trade as the primary mechanisms through which weaker and less efficient institutional forms are winnowed and international systems are progressively made more homogeneous. In contrast, sociological institutionalists and constructivists invoke a logic of conformity in arguing that increased interaction produces convergence. For these theorists, war and trade play a subordinate role to ideational processes, specifically the diffusion of common standards of legitimacy and conceptions of rightful authority, in pulling polities towards a common mean. We present the mechanisms of military Darwinism, institutional learning through economic competition and normative socialization separately for analytical clarity. In practice, however, most scholars generally invoke them in combination, assigning them varying weights according to their theoretical orientation. Although these mechanisms have generally been invoked to explain the rise of the modern sovereign state, even in the absence of the state, the logic of each requires convergence on the most powerful, efficient or legitimate type of unit in the system. As noted, the objection to these theories of convergence is at bottom an empirical one, yet it is also important to raise some important conceptual shortcomings with each explanation.

Realism and Darwinian military competition

Realism posits that military competition and elimination constitute the greatest stimulus for institutional adaptation, and with it a long-term convergence in polity forms. Innovations that enhance polities' survival prospects (e.g. the growth of mass conscript armies) are expected to diffuse rapidly, encouraging a more homogeneous international system over time, as 'winners' increasingly resemble one another while 'losers' (i.e. those unable or unwilling to adopt innovations) are culled through their conquest by more adaptable adversaries.[1] Kenneth Waltz is the most famous exponent of this view in International Relations theory, speaking of how, thanks to systemic survival pressures, maladapted units 'fall by the wayside'.[2] The strong expectation is that the diversity of polities within an international system will diminish over time. In his study of military emulation, Resende-Santos asserts: 'Whether firms in the market or states in the system, units in competitive realms are continually pressed to ensure they are internally well organized and equipped to thrive and survive.'[3] Fazal notes more generally that this view of the elimination of maladapted units via military competition is a vital, but often only implicit, plank of the realist position.[4] Military Darwinism of the kind most realists favour regards institutional convergence as the result of the winnowing effects of war between units engaged in a ceaseless quest for survival. Engaged in a zero-sum competition for power, weaker and maladapted forms are said to be doomed to eventual assimilation or extinction as they are conquered and absorbed by their stronger, better-adapted neighbours.

[1] B. R. Posen, 'Nationalism, the Mass Army, and Military Power', *International Security* 18:2 (1993), pp. 80–124.
[2] K. Waltz, *Theory of International Politics* (New York: McGraw Hill, 1979), p. 118.
[3] J. Resende-Santos, *Neorealism, States, and the Modern Mass Army* (Cambridge University Press, 2007), p. 6.
[4] T. M. Fazal, *State Death: The Politics and Geography of Conquest, Occupation and Annexation* (Princeton University Press, 2007), pp. 60–1.

This realist military Darwinism accords with a major body of literature in historical sociology that credits war as the primary engine of state formation in late medieval and early modern Europe.[5] The gradual establishment of Western military supremacy over the rest of the world in the nineteenth century ostensibly further supports the realist position, with the early modern 'military revolution' and the later birth of industrial warfare supposedly providing Europe with the coercive wherewithal necessary to incorporate other societies into a Europe-dominated international system.[6] For realists, 'war made the state and the state made war' in the hothouse of late medieval and early modern Europe.[7] The ensuing military revolution eventually enabled the West to 'out-gun' the rest, and thereby compel global conformity with Western political forms.[8] This realist mechanism of competition constitutes what Hendrik Spruyt has dubbed a 'strong form selection perspective' on international politics: 'Such selection ... reduces the variation in adaptive forms to only a few types, perhaps even to the point of singularity.'[9]

Rationalists and Lamarckian economic competition

In contrast to the emphasis on war as the chief mechanism promoting convergence in unit forms, rationalists put economic factors centre-stage. They place greater weight on rational emulation, deliberate adaptation and learning, rather than elimination, in linking increased interaction with homogenization. Rationalists thus subscribe to an

5 C. Tilly, *Coercion, Capital and European States, AD 990–1992* (Oxford: Blackwell, 1992); B. Downing, *The Military Revolution and the Political Change: Origins of Democracy and Autocracy in Early Modern Europe* (Princeton University Press, 1992); T. Ertman, *Birth of the Leviathan: Building States and Regimes in Medieval and Early Modern Europe* (Cambridge University Press, 1997).

6 G. Parker, *The Military Revolution: Military Innovation and the Rise of the West, 1500–1800* (Cambridge University Press, 1988), p. 4.

7 C. Tilly, 'Reflections on the History of European State-making', in C. Tilly (ed.), *The Formation of National States in Western Europe* (Princeton University Press, 1975), p. 42.

8 McNeill, *The Rise of the West*; Parker, *The Military Revolution*.

9 H. Spruyt, 'Diversity or Uniformity in the Modern World? Answers from Evolutionary Theory, Learning and Social Adaptation', in W. R. Thompson (ed.), *Evolutionary Interpretations of World Politics* (New York: Routledge, 2001), p. 116.

evolutionary theory of a more Lamarckian than Darwinian cast, even while sharing with realists an overarching conception of international politics that privileges competition. For rationalists, while military prowess may be a proximate cause of success in war, the economic determinants of military power – and especially the institutional foundations either supporting or inhibiting sustained economic growth – are key in shaping the evolution of international systems.[10]

Thus for North and Thomas: 'Efficient economic organization is the key to growth; the development of an efficient economic organization in Western Europe accounts for the rise of the West.'[11] Increasing volumes of trade and efficient institutions reinforced one another.[12] Subsequently, 'international competition provided a powerful incentive for other countries to adapt their institutional structures to provide equal incentives for economic growth'.[13] North's later work is devoted in part to explaining the persistence of inefficient institutions,[14] but nevertheless he maintains: 'Polities and economies struggled, not only inside Europe for hegemony but also in the growing empires of the rest of the world, where competition played the critical role . . . of inducing increased efficiency.'[15]

Though Spruyt's sophisticated explanation of why states won out over trading leagues and city-states relies in some measure on each of the three mechanisms of military Darwinism, rationalist institutional adaptation and normative socialization, there are pronounced similarities with North. States enjoyed key advantages over city-states and city-leagues in preventing free-riding and lowering transaction costs in domestic and foreign exchanges. At this point 'War did not work as an evolutionary process that selected among types of units, but it did indicate to political elites and social groups which type of social organization was the more efficient, and they subsequently adopted the

[10] D. C. North, 'Institutions, Transaction Costs, and the Rise of Merchant Empires', in Tracy, *The Political Economy of Merchant Empires*, p. 24; H. Spruyt, *The Sovereign State and its Competitors* (Princeton University Press, 1994), pp. 21, 157–8, 178.

[11] D. C. North and R. P. Thomas, *The Rise of the Western World: A New Economic History* (Cambridge University Press, 1973), p. 1.

[12] North, *Institutions, Institutional Change and Economic Performance*, p. 127.

[13] North and Thomas, *The Rise of the Western World*, p. 157.

[14] D. C. North, 'A Transactions Cost Theory of Politics', *Journal of Theoretical Politics* 2:4 (1990), pp. 355–67.

[15] North, *Institutions, Institutional Change and Economic Performance*, p. 26.

most competitive institutional form.'[16] In emphasizing the importance of learning and self-conscious adaptation to environmental pressures, rationalist expectations of convergence ostensibly grant greater agency to actors in accounting for institutional change than realism. But this alternative view of competition nevertheless assumes the primacy of centripetal dynamics over durable diversity.

Constructivism, sociological institutionalism and normative socialization

In contrast to realists' and rationalists' common privileging of competition in driving the evolution of international systems, sociological institutionalists and constructivists instead emphasize conformity through normative socialization in promoting convergence on a system of like units. Socialization in this context refers to organizations looking to enhance their legitimacy via mimicry of perceived leaders or models. Units are said to adapt themselves to more closely resemble appropriate or valorized forms and thereby bolster their prestige and self-esteem, even potentially at the expense of military effectiveness or economic efficiency. Perhaps the most explicit exponents of ideationally driven convergence have been the new institutional sociologists.[17] These scholars are generally looking to explain institutional similarities in much smaller units than whole polities, but nevertheless their arguments can and have been applied to the development of international systems.

In the main, they explicitly reject the notion that sameness is driven by either military or economic efficiency, even in instances like Meiji Japan's modernization.[18] The most important scholar in this tradition is David Strang, who argues that the worldwide expansion of the European state system from 1415 onwards was primarily explained

[16] Spruyt, *The Sovereign State and its Competitors*, p. 178.

[17] J. W. Meyer and B. Rowan, 'Institutionalized Organizations: Formal Structure as Myth and Ceremony', *American Journal of Sociology* 83:2 (1977), pp. 340–63; P. J. DiMaggio and W. W. Powell, 'The Iron Cage Revisited: Institutional Isomorphism and Collective Rationality in Organizational Fields', *American Sociological Review* 48:2 (1983), pp. 147–60; J. G. March and J. P. Olsen, *Rediscovering Institutions: The Organizational Basis of Politics* (New York: The Free Press, 1989); J. W. Meyer *et al.*, 'World Society and the Nation-State', *American Journal of Sociology* 103:1 (1977), pp. 144–81.

[18] P. J. DiMaggio and W. W. Powell, *The New Institutionalism in Organizational Analysis* (University of Chicago Press, 1991), p. 70.

by legitimacy concerns because the 'cultural framework of the international system shapes state action'.[19] Strang argues that the state is a product of a selection process, but that it is above all a cultural process. Sovereign states constituted by mutual recognition were exempted from the military struggle for survival, while non-Western polities not enjoying the same recognition were fair game for conquest and colonization. Non-states are progressively eliminated while states survive, leaving the system ever more dominated by states.

Constructivist studies of the evolution of the international system share with sociological institutionalists an emphasis on the power of normative socialization to produce conformity. They are nevertheless distinctive in their more sustained effort to understand the genesis of the norms that sociological institutionalists favour as the chief drivers of unit convergence. Constructivists such as John M. Owen and Daniel Philpott have examined how the rise of revolutionary conceptions of individual and collective rights drove transformations of political community in the West that then subsequently diffused globally.[20] These ideational shifts are credited with effecting a long-term systemic shift away from international orders grounded in either heteronomy or imperial hierarchy, and towards a sovereign state monopoly. This focus on the transformative impact of revolutionary ideas on polity forms complements sociological institutionalists' stress on normative selection mechanisms promoting unit convergence. But as constructivists' analysis of the dynamics of post-war decolonization illustrates, it does accord indigenous actors greater agency than in the more structuralist sociological institutionalist accounts.[21] These actors may be able to harness systemic norms to advance their own political ends.

Sociological institutionalist and constructivist expectations of convergence, grounded as they are in a logic of conformity rather than competition, rely on different mechanisms to account for the presumed trend towards homogeneity within international systems. Specifically,

[19] D. Strang, 'Anomaly and Commonplace in European Political Expansion: Realist and Institutional Accounts', *International Organization* 45:2 (1991), p. 146.

[20] J. M. Owen IV, *The Clash of Ideas in World Politics: Transnational Networks, States, and Regime Change, 1510–2010* (Princeton University Press, 2010); and D. Philpott, *Revolutions in Sovereignty: How Ideas Shaped Modern International Relations* (Princeton University Press, 2001).

[21] Philpott, *Revolutions in Sovereignty.*

Table 1.1 ***Interaction capacity and unit convergence in mainstream International Relations theories***

Theoretical tradition	Overarching logic	Expected outcome of increased interaction capacity	Mechanism of convergence	Type of social interaction promoting convergence
Realism	Competition	Convergence	Convergence through elimination	Military competition
Rationalism	Competition	Convergence	Convergence through rational emulation	Economic interaction (especially increased trade)
Sociological institutionalism	Conformity	Convergence	Convergence through socialization	Spread of common standards of legitimacy
Constructivism	Conformity	Convergence	Convergence through socialization	Spread of common standards of legitimacy

these models foreground processes of socialization and mimicry to produce institutional convergence. Polities adapt to internationally prevalent standards of legitimacy, adopting a 'chameleon strategy' to secure recognition and acceptance from other politics.[22] Different theoretical viewpoints vary in the weight they assign to external pressure versus genuine internalization in characterizing the mimesis said to produce homogenization. The 'productive power'[23] of international legitimacy standards in generating strong pressures towards convergence is another important theme in these accounts.[24]

Having presented these general accounts of convergence, for ease of reference the key points are summarized in Table 1.1.

[22] Spruyt, 'Diversity or Uniformity in the Modern World?' p. 121.

[23] M. Barnett and R. Duvall, 'Power in International Politics', *International Organization* 59:1 (2005), pp. 48–9.

[24] See, for example, generally, Philpott, *Revolutions in Sovereignty*.

Conventional mechanisms of convergence – a theoretical critique

Before we deal with the empirical problems of assuming convergence is the historical master trend in international systems, it is important to at least briefly consider some conceptual shortcomings of these various mechanisms.

Taking the last considered first, the homogeneity of the current international system appears to vindicate constructivist claims about normative socialization, institutional mimicry and unit convergence. But underpinning these claims lies a fairly demanding set of assumptions that limits the scope of this explanation. International legitimacy standards must be codified, prevailing conceptions of legitimacy should mandate uniformity in polity forms rather than heterogeneity, and 'receiver' polities have to be sufficiently malleable to yield to these pressures towards conformity. The historical predominance of heterogeneous international systems over monocultures casts doubt on how often these assumptions hold. For example, early modern Europeans accepted a plethora of polity forms, both in Europe and overseas. The 'composite monarchies'[25] that later evolved into sovereign nation-states inhabited 'an early modern world filled with a variety of corporate bodies politic and hyphenated, hybrid, overlapping and composite forms of sovereignty'.[26] More monistic and territorially exclusive conceptions of state sovereignty began to take decisive hold in Europe only from the mid-eighteenth century, and became globally entrenched in Western-dominated international law only in the nineteenth century.[27] And, even then, the 'standard of civilization', which lingered well into the twentieth century, explicitly legitimized hierarchical differentiation between unlike units. To the extent that ideational factors are considered primary in shaping international systems, then, the historical evidence indicates diversity and differentiation over uniformity as the historical norm.

The idea that economic competition will produce convergence on a common unit form similarly depends on some demanding assumptions. Rationalists assume in the face of environmental changes that it is easy

[25] J. H. Elliott, 'A Europe of Composite Monarchies', *Past and Present* 37:1 (1992), pp. 48–71.

[26] Stern, *The Company-State*, p. 3.

[27] See, generally, A. Anghie, *Imperialism, Sovereignty and the Making of International Law* (Cambridge University Press, 2007); and Benton, *A Search for Sovereignty*.

for actors to learn, that they will learn the same lessons from exposure to the same environmental changes, and that they will apply these lessons in the same ways, thus producing institutional convergence. Each of these claims is contestable.[28] Within social orders as complex as international systems, pressures towards convergence deriving from increased interaction may be too diffuse and too ambiguous to force agents to revise existing institutional arrangements. Even where environmental pressures do spur change, different actors might seek to achieve the same ends via different means in different ways. The literature on the persistence of 'varieties of capitalism' shows how diversity is compatible with a perceived common need for greater competitiveness in a globalized economy, while also highlighting the 'stickiness' of institutions in the face of environmental pressures.[29]

Lastly, turning to realism, Spruyt convincingly argues that realist adherents of strong form selection misread evolutionary theory, which in fact anticipates variation rather than uniformity in response to environmental changes. But strong form selection perspectives underestimate the inertia of pre-existing institutions and social coalitions in inhibiting adaptation to shifting environmental pressures.[30] Evolutionary survival pressures may favour disparate rather than common adaptations among polities, analogous to a situation where climate change might induce one species to evolve a capacity for seasonal variation while compelling changes in another species' migratory patterns.[31] The claim that continuous Darwinian military competition ineluctably leads to the elimination of 'unfit' forms is therefore problematic. Others have noted that for elimination to be an efficient mechanism of change in promoting like units, the rate of extinction of these units needs to be much higher than that observed in most international systems, especially the contemporary one.[32]

[28] March and Olsen, *Rediscovering Institutions*; J. Elster, 'Rational Choice History: A Case of Excessive Ambition', *American Political Science Review* 94:3 (2000), 685–95.

[29] P. A. Hall and D. W. Soskice, *Varieties of Capitalism: The Institutional Foundations of Comparative Advantage* (Oxford University Press, 2001).

[30] Spruyt, 'Diversity or Uniformity in the Modern World?', p. 114.

[31] *Ibid.*

[32] R. H. Jackson, *Quasi-States: Sovereignty, International Relations and the Third World* (Cambridge University Press, 1990); Strang, 'Anomaly and Commonplace in European Political Expansion'; T. M. Fazal, *State Death: The Politics and Geography of Conquest, Occupation, and Annexation* (Princeton University Press, 2007).

More generally, perhaps the core problem these theories share is that their preoccupation with explaining current homogeneity has sustained a common failure to specify the scope conditions under which interaction should either drive unit convergence or alternatively stimulate increasing polity diversity. Continuous military competition *can* produce unit convergence through elimination, as China's experience during the Period of Warring States demonstrates.[33] But it need not always do so. Likewise, military and commercial competition *can* promote convergence through self-conscious processes of institutional learning and adaptation.[34] Again, however, the relationship between competition, learning and convergence is complex and contingent rather than universal. Finally, socialization pressures and resulting mimicry *can* yield convergence through conformity.[35] But pressures to conform may just as easily promote hierarchy and differentiation. As discussed in the third section of the chapter, the claim that increased interaction drives unit convergence is not universal among these schools. Subordinate or implicit strands of thought within each tradition can be harnessed to explain the nature and dynamics of heterogeneous international systems. Nevertheless, there is a general perception that interaction drives convergence. The immediate priority, however, is to now present some evidence for the previous claims that international systems populated by unlike rather than like units are indeed the predominant historical form.

Problematic diversity – heterogeneity as the norm in international systems

Because most International Relations scholars are most concerned with comprehending the dynamics of international politics of today's sovereign state monoculture, they take homogeneity as the norm and heterogeneity as the exception within international systems. Yet important recent International Relations scholarship indicates that diversity has historically been the rule rather than the exception. Even in relation to

[33] V. Tin-bor Hui, *War and State Formation in Ancient China and Early Modern Europe* (Cambridge University Press, 2005).

[34] Spruyt, *The Sovereign State and its Competitors*.

[35] Strang, 'Anomaly and Commonplace in European Political Expansion'; Philpott, *Revolutions in Sovereignty*.

the Peace of Westphalia in 1648 – the so-called 'majestic portal' marking the shift from medieval heteronomy to sovereign anarchy[36] – revisionist scholars have 'defined Westphalia down'[37] by emphasizing the persistent diversity of polity forms in West-Central Europe.[38] The original contribution in this study therefore does not lie in identifying this heterogeneity as a commonplace characteristic of international systems. This fact has already been demonstrated by others, even if it is only now beginning to reshape the mainstream. Rather, the goal is to provide a general explanation as to how and why this heterogeneity might persist under conditions of increased interaction. Before we present this explanation in detail, below we briefly review the prevalence of heterogeneous systems in world history, from ancient times to the twentieth century.

Heterogeneous systems were the norm in the ancient world. For both Roman and Chinese empire-builders, the immense diversity of the peoples and polities over which they held sway was inescapable. Rome claimed suzerainty not only over sedentary commercial societies (e.g. the ancient Greek city-states), but also over sparsely populated territories inhabited by peoples subscribing to various forms of tribal rather than state-like political organization (e.g. Gaul, ancient Britain).[39] Vassal polities were tied to Rome through a host of idiosyncratic and often highly mutable contractual arrangements, while the fluid frontier between the empire and 'barbarian' peoples formed a zone of military, commercial and cultural exchange between dissimilar polities.[40] Likewise, China's original unification under the western

36 L. Gross, 'The Peace of Westphalia', *American Journal of International Law* 42:1 (1948), p. 28.

37 Nexon, *The Struggle for Power in Early Modern Europe*, p. 277.

38 S. D. Krasner, 'Westphalia and All That', in J. Goldstein and R. Keohane (eds.), *Ideas and Foreign Policy: Beliefs, Institutions and Political Change* (Ithaca, NY: Cornell University Press, 1993), pp. 235–64; Nexon, *The Struggle for Power in Early Modern Europe*; A. Osiander, *Before the State: Systemic Political Change in the West from the Greeks to the French Revolution* (Oxford University Press, 2007); B. Teschke, *The Myth of 1648: Class, Geopolitics, and the Making of Modern International Relations* (London: Verso, 2003).

39 For an excellent survey of historiography that emphasizes heterogeneity over uniformity as the defining characteristic of the Roman Empire, see R. Hingley, 'Cultural Diversity and Unity: Empire and Rome', in S. Hales and T. Hodos (eds.), *Material Culture and Social Identities in the Ancient World* (Cambridge University Press, 2009), pp. 54–75.

40 *Ibid.*, p. 59.

state of Qin in 221 BCE fused together a constellation of state-like entities that had been fighting among themselves for supremacy for the preceding five centuries. The unification of China's warring states did not, however, produce universal homogeneity in East Asia. Instead, China remained the centre of a diverse international system that encompassed Confucian satellite kingdoms (e.g. Korea, Vietnam) as well as shifting tribal confederacies on the Asian steppe.[41]

The medieval period saw no decline in the diversity of polities populating the Old World, despite the fact that the period saw a dramatic increase in commercial and cultural interaction throughout Europe, Asia and Africa.[42] In Europe, the eleventh-century revival of long-distance trade spurred the growth of a range of different polities – sovereign states, city-states and city-leagues – that co-existed uneasily under the umbrella of the papal–imperial diarchy.[43] Medieval Europe was unique in its specific combination of separate religious and temporal authority structures each claiming universal authority. But the existence of multiple, layered and overlapping authority structures comparable to those found in Latin Christendom was general throughout the Old World. Within South Asia, the emergence of smaller polities consolidated the power of local political and scribal elites without completely dislodging earlier imperial agglomerations.[44] South-East Asia's political geography at this time was similarly heteronomous. Powerful empires such as Angkor and Majapahit shared with smaller counterparts the character of being 'galactic polities', in which cosmic and political power was said to radiate from the centre to the periphery with diminishing intensity.[45] It was not uncommon for subordinate galactic polities to simultaneously pay tribute to multiple suzerains.

Islam's emergence and spread from the seventh century saw not only the arrival of Arab political power throughout the Middle East and

41 J. H. Bentley, *Old World Encounters: Cross-Cultural Contacts and Exchanges in Pre-Modern Times* (New York: Oxford University Press, 1993), pp. 35–6. See also, for Tang Dynasty China in particular, Z. Wang, *Tang China in Multipolar Asia: A History of Diplomacy and War* (Honolulu: University of Hawaii Press, 2013).

42 Bentley, *Old World Encounters*, p. 114.

43 Spruyt, *The Sovereign State and its Competitors*.

44 S. Pollock, *The Language of the Gods in the World of Men: Sanskrit, Culture and Power in Premodern India* (Berkeley: University of California Press, 2006), p. 380.

45 Tambiah, 'The Galactic Polity', pp. 71–5.

North Africa, but also a rise in interregional commerce throughout the Indian Ocean littoral.[46] The thirteenth-century advent of a Pax Mongolica throughout most of Eurasia had likewise sparked a surge in interregional commerce that ultimately outlived Genghis Khan's evanescent empire.[47] Far from diminishing after 1500, the early modern period saw the reinforcement of an established pattern in which growing military, commercial and cultural interaction spawned the multiplication of diverse, unlike polity forms. From the sixteenth century, we observe a pattern of imperial consolidation, commercial expansion and increasing polity diversity repeat itself.[48] The rise of large land-based Islamic empires (the Ottomans, Mughals and Safavids), the Western conquest of the Americas, and the growth of European maritime empires in Asia jointly knitted the world together in ever denser and broader webs of commercial activity, without this greater interconnectivity producing homogeneity.[49] Western and Asian imperialists after 1500 struck customized compacts with local power-holders. With the exception of pandemic-driven collapse in the Americas, however, subordinate polities were generally incorporated rather than eliminated. The result was either the preservation of existing diversity or its expansion. New empires overlaid rather than eradicated earlier polity forms, and new institutional structures arose to meet the distinct challenges of conveying authoritative commands and coordinating market transactions across continents.[50]

After 1750, the rough balance of power between Europeans and non-Europeans in the Old World that had prevailed from the sixteenth century yielded to an age of asymmetry in which Western power became almost universally ascendant. But underlying continuities

[46] Chaudhuri, *Trade and Civilisation in the Indian Ocean.*

[47] J. L. Abu-Lughod, *Before European Hegemony: The World System A.D. 1250–1350* (Oxford University Press, 1989).

[48] See, generally, C. A. Bayly, *Imperial Meridian: The British Empire and the World, 1780–1830* (London: Routledge, 1989), ch. 1.

[49] Subrahmanyam, 'Holding the World in Balance', p. 1359.

[50] While we focus in this book on the role of company sovereigns in spearheading the West's infiltration into Asia, company sovereigns and other forms of chartered authority were also important in driving the European conquest of the Americas. On this see, generally, L. Roper and B. Ruymbeke (eds.), *Constructing Early Modern Empires: Proprietary Ventures in the Atlantic World, 1500–1750* (Leiden: Brill, 2007).

persisted across this break. Western imperialists generally continued to favour various methods of indirect rule that built upon rather than erased local diversity. In British India, for example, 693 'princely states' comprising 41 per cent of the Raj's territory remained subject to indirect rule rather than direct control from Calcutta.[51] A similar arrangement existed in the Dutch East Indies, where Batavia dominated the archipelago in partnership with indigenous rulers who retained aspects of sovereignty in 282 'native states' not directly subject to Dutch rule.[52] In Africa, likewise, Lord Lugard's pioneering advocacy of 'indirect rule' through tribal intermediaries proved more representative of European colonialism in that continent than the more direct methods of colonial administration employed by the French.[53] The Belgian Congo – a territory approximately the size of Western Europe with a population of 30 million – remained King Leopold II's private fiefdom (the Congo Free State) until 1908, further indicating the persistence of diverse non-state forms of political authority within the international system down to the twentieth century.[54]

The overriding point here is that there remains a fundamental discrepancy between what many International Relations theorists expect and what historians, historical sociologists and some more historically inclined revisionist International Relations scholars have actually observed in the majority of international systems prior to the mid-twentieth century. Fortunately, the dominant theoretical traditions we have considered do contain subordinate or implicit accounts for making sense of the puzzle of durable diversity.

[51] L. Benton, 'From International Law to Imperial Constitutions: The Problem of Quasi-Sovereignty, 1870–1900', *Law and History Review* 26:3 (2008), p. 601.

[52] R. Cribb, 'Legal Pluralism and Criminal Law in the Dutch Colonial Order', *Indonesia* 90 (2010), p. 63.

[53] On the contrast between British and French methods of colonial over-rule in the African context, see, generally, M. Crowder, 'Indirect Rule: French and British Style', *Africa* 34:3 (1964), pp. 197–205. On the early influence of practices of indirect rule pioneered in British India for the British Empire's subsequent methods of organizing diversity within its imperium, see, generally, M. H. Fisher, 'Indirect Rule in the British Empire: The Foundations of the Residency System in India (1764–1858)', *Modern Asian Studies* 18:3 (1984), pp. 393–428.

[54] See, generally, M. Ewans, *European Atrocity, African Catastrophe: Leopold II, the Congo Free State and its Aftermath* (London: RoutledgeCurzon, 2002).

Implicit theories of diversity – towards a conceptual framework for accounting for durably diverse international systems

Although as discussed extensively in the first section the dominant theories are heavily premised on interaction leading to convergence, it is nevertheless important not to ignore the fact that some elements of each of these rich and varied schools of thought can accommodate the notion of international systems comprised of diverse units. As such, it is important not to caricature these approaches or assume some sort of monolithic consistency within them. Here we engage in three main tasks. First, we revisit realism, rationalism and constructivism in turn to examine how each one might make sense of heterogeneous systems like those sketched out in the preceding section, or like the early modern Indian Ocean international system. Second, having done so we then compare and contrast with the main thesis of this book to highlight points of similarity and difference. Our third and final task prior to presenting a synoptic survey of the Indian Ocean in the final section is to clearly explain what we mean by the concept of international system, and to justify its post-1500 application to the Indian Ocean.

Realist accounts for diversity within international systems

The realist bias towards convergence through competition is most conspicuous in Waltz, for whom notions of unit differentiation drop out entirely.[55] But other realist works do hint at the possibility of diversity. Realism presumes that military competition should produce convergence over time, as 'losing' polity forms are culled and 'winning' polity forms diffuse throughout an international system. The crucial caveat in this causal sequence is 'over time'. That competition should *eventually* produce convergence does not preclude the possibility that this convergence might be preceded by a period of competition between diverse units.

A realist theory of heterogeneity might begin with environmental changes – for example, the emergence of new forms of military technology – that spur a wave of speciation as polities respond in diverse

[55] Waltz, *Theory of International Politics*, pp. 95–7.

ways to the security challenges brought about by these changes. The rise of disruptive military innovations like the stirrup or gunpowder weapons has traditionally spawned the rise of 'hopeful monsters', a diverse array of polity forms that organize themselves around different modes of warfare in order to maximize their survival chances.[56] The best-known example of such speciation is Tilly's examination of the coercion-intensive, capital-intensive and capitalized coercion paths to state formation in late medieval and early modern Europe. There, a host of environmental changes (only some of which were military) spurred mutations in polity forms, as rulers forged new modes of war-making and developed new forms of extractive institutions to assure their survival chances amid increased geopolitical competition.[57] Unlike many of his later imitators, Tilly stresses the resulting diversity of political units arising from geopolitical competition: 'The long survival and co-existence of all three types [city-states, urban federations and national states] tells against any notion of European state formation as a single, unilinear process, or of the national state – which, indeed, did eventually prevail – as an inherently superior form of government.'[58] Less well known but equally important are the 'mixed' international systems that formed on the Asiatic steppe and on the internal frontiers of sub-Saharan Africa, where predominantly cavalry-based polities continually abraded against their more sedentary counterparts.[59]

The concept of 'loss of strength' gradients offers another path to explain how diversity might persist, by temporarily muting the selection effects of military competition. Realists have long recognized that the potency of military power typically diminishes with distance.[60] Seen through this lens, technological and geographical limitations on

[56] On the concept of 'hopeful monsters' and its attempted transference from evolutionary biology to international politics, see W. J. Brenner, 'In Search of Monsters: Realism and Progress in International Relations Theory after September 11', *Security Studies* 15:3 (2006), p. 520.

[57] Tilly, *Coercion, Capital and European States*, p. 21.

[58] *Ibid.*

[59] See, for example, T. J. Barfield, 'The Shadow Empires: Imperial State Formation along the Nomad–Chinese Frontier', in S. Alcock (ed.), *Empires: Perspectives from Archaeology and History* (Cambridge University Press, 2001), pp. 13–16; and R. A. Oliver and A. Atmore, *Medieval Africa, 1250–1800* (Cambridge University Press, 2001), pp. 8–9.

[60] See, for example, K. E. Boulding, 'Towards a Pure Theory of Threat Systems', *American Economic Review* 53:2 (1963), p. 431.

polities' ability to harm or destroy one another could work to preserve polity diversity, especially between continents.

Further hints of a realist explanation of diversity lie in recent work on contracting in mediating security relations between unequal allies. That actors might pursue self-help through alliance formation is a core realist insight. The historical prevalence of protectorate arrangements and subsidiary alliances between dominant and weaker actors prior to the twentieth century illustrates that marginal actors can find methods of self-preservation that involve alienating portions of their sovereignty to stronger polities without being completely absorbed by them.[61] Polity diversity could thus be extended and preserved by a proliferation of these protectorate-type arrangements.[62]

These possibilities aside, realists' explanatory model ultimately remains wedded to a conception of institutional evolution driven by war, in which the systems effects of selection through military victory and defeat should eventually push towards convergence. Given this bedrock conviction that war will eventually produce convergence as the strong prosper and the weak are eliminated, realism generally struggles to explain how and why polity diversity might persist and even expand where systemic military interaction between unlike units is continuously increasing over a period of centuries.

Rationalist accounts for diversity within international systems

While competition and convergence remain master concepts within the rationalist frame, the tradition encompasses also ideas of specialization, complementarity and contracting that can be integrated into an account of durably diverse international systems. A starting point is rationalists' broad acknowledgement that system-wide forces (e.g. a dramatic growth or contraction in volumes of international trade) may exert widely varying impacts on patterns of domestic cleavage and coalition within polities, according to actors' differing factor endowments and capacities for

61 C. Newbury, 'Patrons, Clients and Empire: The Subordination of Indigenous Hierarchies in Africa and Asia', *Journal of World History* 11:2 (2000), pp. 227–63.

62 On the phenomenon of relational contracting and asymmetric alliances in the contemporary state system, see, generally, D. A. Lake, 'Anarchy, Hierarchy and the Variety of International Relations', *International Organization* 50:1 (1996), pp. 1–33.

political and social mobilization.[63] This insight provides the starting point for Spruyt's pioneering explanation of the emergence of city-states, city-leagues and sovereign states in the wake of the medieval commercial revolution. Spruyt explains late medieval polity diversity in part by arguing that differences in the nature of trade shaped actor preferences in ways that yielded divergent social coalitions. This produced differing polity forms as a consequence. Thus, in northern Italy, a regional focus on low-volume, high-value trade in luxury goods encouraged merchants to pursue monopolistic strategies that favoured the rise of city-states.[64] The nature of the Baltic trade – focused on high-volume, low-value commodity goods – instead favoured oligopolistic arrangements in the form of city-leagues.[65]

Spruyt's insights notwithstanding, his narrative of European political development ultimately endorses the dominant interaction–convergence nexus. A late medieval epoch of speciation and variation eventually progresses to an early modern phase of selection, as mechanisms of mutual empowerment and the inherent functional advantages of the sovereign state see it prevail over city-states and city-leagues. The bias towards eventual convergence thus remains strong, despite Spruyt's sophisticated account of initial variation following the environmental change of the early modern commercial revolution. A much more structural economic account of enduring diversity premised on European expansion in the sixteenth and seventeenth centuries is Immanuel Wallerstein's World Systems Theory.[66] Famously Wallerstein argues that the dynamics of a capitalist system first globalized by the Dutch entrenched small initial differences to form an enduring system of the economic core, periphery and semi-periphery.

More recent work by Cooley and Spruyt demonstrates that the hierarchical transfer of sovereignty functions between nominally equal states through practices of incomplete contracting remains prevalent

[63] See, generally, R. Rogowski, *Commerce and Coalitions: How Trade Affects Domestic Political Alignments* (Princeton University Press, 1990); and Spruyt, *The Sovereign State and its Competitors*.

[64] Spruyt, *The Sovereign State and its Competitors*, p. 76.

[65] *Ibid.*

[66] I. Wallerstein, *The Modern World System*, vol. I: *Capitalist Agriculture and the Origins of the European World-Economy in the Sixteenth Century* (New York: Academic Press, 1974); I. Wallerstein, *The Modern World System*, vol. II: *Mercantilism and the Consolidation of the European World-Economy, 1600–1750* (New York: Academic Press, 1980).

today.[67] This raises the possibility that polity diversity might be perpetuated through a range of customized compacts between unlike units. This possibility is potentially even more fruitful when applied to the early modern world, where sovereign territoriality was not a system-wide constitutive rule, and where agents consequently enjoyed even greater latitude for allocating sovereign prerogatives among multiple parties.

Surveying the rationalist tradition, we can therefore reconstruct a plausible explanation for durably diverse international systems. This explanation would focus on concepts of economic specialization producing initial polity variation, followed by economic complementarities and asymmetric contracting then working to preserve and institutionalize polity diversity. But even a reconstructed rationalist theory of durable diversity remains incomplete in at least two respects. First, with respect to the process of initial specialization and polity variation, rationalists (and even more so scholars like Wallerstein) typically treat actor preferences as arising straightforwardly from the interaction between their economic interests and capabilities and systemic environmental changes (e.g. increases in trade volumes). Yet reducing preferences to material interests alone is problematic. For preferences (e.g. European maritime versus Asian terrestrial orientations in the Indian Ocean) are frequently unintelligible outside the distinct cultural contexts out of which they form. Second, the same can be said for the arrangements through which sovereign prerogatives are spliced and shared between different actors through mechanisms of asymmetric contracting. Both preference formation and practices of asymmetric contracting – factors rationalists respectively favour for explaining the emergence and entrenchment of polity diversity – cannot be understood outside their conditioning cultural contexts. For this reason, our discussion now turns to the constructivists, who share with us a stress on ideational factors as being fundamental to polity diversity within international systems.

Constructivist accounts of durable diversity within international systems

Scholars stressing the primacy of ideational forces in structuring world politics are the most agnostic in their acceptance of the

[67] A. Cooley and H. Spruyt, *Contracting States: Sovereignty Transfers in International Relations* (Princeton University Press, 2009).

interaction–convergence nexus. There is a presumption that a logic of conformity will compel growing unit homogeneity. Yet constructivists in particular are potentially well equipped to explain both how diverse polity forms are first generated, and then how relations between unlike units are then subsequently perpetuated.

Constructivists recognize that polities are constituted through historically and culturally specific understandings of collective identity, and by equally contingent norms prescribing the moral purposes of political authority. This basic insight provides a promising starting point for explaining the initial emergence of diverse polities within international systems. Constructivists are on more difficult ground when trying to explain the persistence of polity diversity under conditions of rapidly increased interaction, however. This problem is particularly apparent when examining international systems dominated by empires. Empires throughout history have embodied inegalitarian visions of the good, matched by hierarchy among diverse and functionally unlike units. For example, the classic 'standard of civilization' – resting on a tripartite distinction between 'civilized', 'barbarous' and 'savage' polities – constituted the ideological glue integrating a nineteenth-century global order marked by unprecedented interaction between diverse political units.[68] *Conformity* within this system to an imposed Western standard of legitimacy by no means implied an accompanying *uniformity* of polity forms. On the contrary, within imperial orders defined by 'regimes of unequal entitlement',[69] conformity instead entailed polities' subscription to one of a number of clearly defined roles and identities, each bringing with it its own distinct bundle of privileges and responsibilities.[70]

Proceeding from this basis, a constructivist account of durably diverse international systems might focus on 'regimes of unequal entitlement' mediating relations between unlike units to explain durable diversity. Seen through this lens, constructivists might argue that durably diverse international systems may persist when different polities conform to prevailing system-wide regimes of unequal entitlement. This conformity might be sustained as a result of genuine broad-based consensus around

[68] G. Gong, *The 'Standard of Civilization' in International Society* (Oxford: Clarendon Press, 1984).

[69] C. Reus-Smit, 'Struggles for Individual Rights and the Expansion of the International System', *International Organization* 65:2 (2011), p. 217.

[70] *Ibid.*

shared standards of legitimacy. Alternatively, it could also be the result of weaker actors' coercive socialization into these regimes. In either instance, however, constructivists would likely explain stable heterogeneity as derivative of system-wide normative constitutional structures, which institutionalize a differential allocation of privileges and responsibilities among a diverse range of political actors.

We present below a stylized representation of the subordinate strands theorizing the emergence and perpetuation of durably diverse international systems (Table 1.2). These insights demonstrate the potential within existing theoretical paradigms for explaining how heterogeneous international systems emerge and endure. Nevertheless, none of the existing theories are sufficient by themselves to account for how diversity emerged and endured in the Indian Ocean international system.

Explaining durable diversity in the Indian Ocean international system – a theoretical framework

As previewed in the Introduction, our explanation of durable diversity in the Indian Ocean international system hinges on three elements. First, that different actors held compatible preferences that dampened or eliminated the zero-sum competition which is too often taken to be a constant in international politics. The most important example is the Islamic empires' primarily terrestrial orientation in contrast to the Europeans' mainly maritime ambitions. Second, African, Asian and European actors held culturally distinct but institutionally congruent beliefs concerning heteronomy, holding that sovereign authority could be legitimately shared and spliced, rather than parcelled out within sharply defined borders in a mutually exclusive manner. Finally, Asians, Africans and Europeans exercised agency through strategies of localization, which facilitated Europeans' insinuation into local polities through a combination of symbolic legitimation and the forging of alliances of convenience between European and indigenous actors.

It bears repeating that both realist and rationalist accounts considered above may be able to account for diversity within international systems over the short or medium term, but they are much less suited to explaining why increasing interaction produces greater diversity over a period of centuries. More conceptually, the centrality of compatible

Table 1.2 ***Explaining the emergence and persistence of durably diverse international systems – insights from existing approaches***

Theoretical tradition	Default logic of convergence through interaction	Explanation for initial emergence of polity diversity	Explanation for stabilization of polity diversity
Realism	Convergence through military competition and Darwinian elimination of 'unfit' units	Asymmetric military specialization, different modes of warfare yield different polities	(1) Loss of strength gradient temporarily insulates a diversity of polity forms of varying 'fitness' (2) Patron–client alliances lock diverse unequal sovereigns into asymmetric relations of protection and obedience
Rationalism	Convergence through economic competition and Lamarckian institutional learning and adaptation	Changes in volume and composition of trade encourage economic specialization, producing diverse social coalitions, and with them diverse polities	(1) Economic complementarities between unlike units provide motive for preserving diversity (2) Incomplete contracting between unlike units provides institutional mechanism for preserving diversity
Constructivism	Convergence through conformity to shared standards of legitimacy	Different visions of the good yield different polity forms	Polity diversity preserved through collective conformity to regimes of unequal entitlement, underpinned by either: (1) system-wide consensus on constitutional values and institutions that should mediate inter-polity relations; or (2) hegemonic enforcement of preferred vision of the good

preferences and congruent ideas and institutions sets our explanation of diversity apart from theories that primarily focus on instrumental action to satisfy materially defined preferences. For realists, the priority is actors' quest to maximize security through either building up their own military resources or allying with stronger powers. For rationalists, it is the search for increased economic efficiency to maximize wealth. Realist and rationalist treatments of contracting as a mechanism for perpetuating polity diversity, either through protectorate arrangements or in line with economic specialization, are purely instrumental. What is missing is an account of the derivation of preferences that is attentive to the cultural contexts in which these preferences are constituted. Similarly absent is an account of the congruent beliefs and practices through which contracting occurs and is institutionalized. For this reason, a renewed engagement with theoretical traditions such as constructivism, which has stressed ideas as constitutive of actors' preferences and institutional practices, is important.

Our thesis is closer to the constructivist explanation of diverse international systems than the other two. Yet even when constructivists sever the presumed link between conformity and institutional convergence, there is still a residual emphasis on the logic of conformity that privileges a conception of international systems as social orders underwritten by 'thick' sets of constitutional values and accompanying fundamental institutions. This presumption accords well with some international orders, such as Latin Christendom or the East Asian Sinosphere.[71] But it accords far less well in international systems such as the early modern Indian Ocean system, where no such commonalities obtained. It was *congruence* and *localization*, rather than *consensus* and *conformity* to common standards of legitimacy, that instantiated and preserved the Indian Ocean system's durable diversity. Explaining how this process unfolded brings us to our theoretical framework, which centres on the three core themes of compatible preferences, congruent ideas and institutions, and a common commitment to two-way practices of localization.

[71] A. Phillips, *War, Religion and Empire: Transformation of International Orders* (Cambridge University Press, 2011).

Compatible preferences

As noted in the previous section, rationalists in particular have argued that compatible preferences and accompanying economic specialization can generate and sustain heterogeneous international systems. Our main point of differentiation lies in our characterization of the nature of actors' preferences. Rationalists generally take preferences as the artefact of polities' internal distribution of factor endowments, or as the result of social bargaining between rival coalitions pursuing their economic interests. In contrast, we argue that actors' preferences in the Indian Ocean international system were conditioned by strong cultural orientations, not reducible to the straightforward expression of material interests. The balance of compatible interests between European thalassocracies and indigenous empires was not foreordained by their respective material endowments. On the contrary, the thalassocratic vision of empire that drove first the Portuguese and then later the Dutch and English into the Indian Ocean system was peculiar to Europeans, having no local analogues. Equally, the land-based orientation of Asia's steppe conquerors did not stem from technological incapacity, but rather a disinclination to emulate the Europeans' oceanic strategy.

An understanding of the contingent and ideational foundations of the region's balance of interests helps to explain the reconfiguration of diversity that occurred with the rise of European colonial empires after 1750, covered in Chapter 5. The changes in European preferences from a maritime to a territorial orientation, and from a preference for divisible to indivisible forms of sovereignty, served as a catalyst for the hierarchical reordering of diversity under colonial empires. Compatible interests thus were crucial in enabling the initial expansion of diversity and its persistence, but also for anticipating its demise.

Congruent ideas and institutions

Congruent ideas and institutions between Europeans and non-Europeans provided a crucial second condition for maintaining durable diversity in the Indian Ocean system. Their vast differences notwithstanding, Europeans and host communities shared congruent beliefs regarding heteronomy and the divisible nature of sovereignty, conceived as a bundle of prerogatives that could be shared among multiple actors occupying the same territory. For example, Europeans and host communities both had extensive prior experience managing resident trading diasporas through customs of commercial extra-territoriality. Throughout the Old World, 'foreign merchants were granted the privilege of living under and of settling their disputes according to their own laws. This was not seen as an infringement on the sovereignty of the local ruler, but rather as a means of attracting commerce without losing control over it.'[72]

European and host communities' conceptions of political authority were far from identical. The proprietary constitutionalism that underpinned the European company sovereigns, for example, was grounded in a firmly rights-based discourse.[73] This contrasted with the sacerdotal ideologies of universal kingship constituting South and South-East Asia's 'galactic polities'.[74] These differences in ideational content aside, European and non-European conceptions of sovereignty remained similar in form. These correspondences were crucial in lubricating locals' acquiescence to a permanent, armed European trading presence along the Indian Ocean littoral. The ideational congruence between European and host polities' conceptions of sovereignty enabled both to imagine the possibility of permanent European entrenchment in the Indian Ocean system. A shared familiarity with legal pluralism and customs of commercial extra-territoriality provided the institutional means for making this possible. Explaining precisely how Europeans and locals interacted to enable this insinuation brings us to the third pillar of our framework – localization.

Localization

Despite the existence of compatible interests and ideational and institutional congruences conducive to their insertion, outsiders could not

[72] J. Fisch, 'Law as a Means and as an End: Some Remarks on the Function of European and Non-European Law in the Process of European Expansion', in W. J. Mommsen and J. A. De Moor (eds.), *European Expansion and Law: The Encounter of European and Indigenous Law in 19th and 20th Century Africa and Asia* (Oxford: Berg, 1992), p. 23.

[73] V. Hsueh, *Hybrid Constitutions: Challenging Legacies of Law, Privilege and Culture in Colonial America* (Durham, NC: Duke University Press, 2010), p. 2.

[74] Tambiah, 'The Galactic Polity'. On the application of the concept of 'galactic polities' to the Mughal Empire, see S. J. Tambiah, 'What did Bernier Actually Say? Profiling the Mughal Empire', *Contributions to Indian Sociology* 32:2 (1998), p. 380.

effortlessly slot into ready-made enclaves in Indian Ocean polities. Both Europeans and Mughals, for example, had to legitimate their participation in local political and economic systems, and forge self-interested alliances of convenience with indigenous partners. Locals frequently aimed to co-opt them into their polities to strengthen indigenous authority and wealth. Recruiting and adapting a concept already familiar to International Relations scholars, we characterize this double-sided process of accommodation as one of localization, a concept first coined by the historian of South-East Asia O. W. Wolters and then introduced to the field by Amitav Acharya.[75]

Amitav Acharya defines localization as 'the active construction (through discourse, framing, grafting and cultural selection) of foreign ideas by local actors, which results in the former developing significant congruence with local beliefs and practices'.[76] Acharya explores localization within the contemporary context of South-East Asian security diplomacy. The historians like Wolters who introduced the notion of localization used it to capture indigenous initiative in appropriating foreign (mainly Indian) religious and political ideas to bolster medieval South-East Asian rulers' power and legitimacy.[77] Here, we invoke localization to stress the creative synthesis of foreign and local ideas and practices that European and indigenous actors improvised to accommodate differences after 1500. We also favour localization over other possible formulations (e.g. customization or hybridization) because local participation reflected indigenous actors' beliefs that such collaboration would strengthen their wealth and power.

Localization stabilized diversity presence through two processes – symbolic legitimation and the forging of more instrumentally motivated alliances of convenience. Entities such as the company sovereigns manifested their power in radically different ways across the Indian Ocean, adapting their symbolic repertoires and alliance-building strategies to the demands of local contexts. These repertoires and strategies were agency-centred. But they could not have succeeded without the prior existence of compatible interests and congruent ideas and institutions. Through the interaction of interests, ideas and institutions, and practices of localization, polity diversity emerged and was consolidated

[75] Wolters, *History, Culture, and Region in Southeast Asia*, p. 55.
[76] Acharya, 'How Ideas Spread', p. 245.
[77] Wolters, *History, Culture and Region in Southeast Asia*, p. 55.

in the Indian Ocean. Before we explore how this process played out, however, we must first delineate the nature, history and parameters of the Indian Ocean international system itself.

Defining an international system

The theoretical discussion so far has focused on the presence or absence of variation between units in international systems. But what counts as an international system? International Relations scholars have advocated several conceptions of what is meant by the term.[78] Bull and Watson speak of multiple centres of political authority engaged in sufficiently regular interaction such that 'the behaviour of each is necessary in the calculations of others'.[79] Tilly adopts a very similar definition: 'States form systems to the extent that they interact, and to the degree their interaction significantly affects each party's fate.'[80]

We follow these precedents in defining international systems as geographically extensive networks of social relations, populated by multiple units of political authority that routinely interact with one another across the full range of sectoral domains (i.e. cultural, economic, military and political), and exhibit an awareness of their social environment as a coherent and integrated field of strategic interaction. Our definition of international systems combines emphases on interaction capacity and strategic interdependence that are already prevalent within the literature. Beginning with interaction capacity, we maintain that interactions between polities must be routine and manifest across a wide range of sectoral domains to constitute an international system.[81] This is because it is only within such an environment that one could reasonably expect 'system effects' – notably unit homogenization through competition or socialization – to be present.[82] The insistence

[78] B. Buzan and R. Little, 'The Idea of "International System": Theory Meets History', *International Political Science Review* 15:3 (1994), p. 231.

[79] H. Bull and A. Watson (eds.), *The Expansion of International Society* (Oxford: Clarendon Press, 1984), p. 1.

[80] Tilly, *Coercion, Capital and European States*, p. 4.

[81] Our emphasis on interaction across a range of sectoral domains as a key constitutive characteristic of 'system-ness' draws from Buzan and Little, *International Systems in World History*, pp. 72–7.

[82] On 'system effects' as a feature of complex social systems, see, generally, R. Jervis, *System Effects: Complexity in Political and Social Life* (Princeton University Press, 1997).

on strategic interdependence as a requirement for 'system-ness' privileges economic and especially military interaction, because we wish to retain a definition of international system narrow enough only to include social environments whose major actors are sufficiently interconnected that their actions can affect one another's key interests. This restrictive focus on military competition as a defining feature of international systems is necessary to avoid an overly expansive definition that might otherwise include cases where polities were linked by nothing more than episodic commercial and cultural contact. Defining international systems in this way also has the advantage of pre-empting the realist objection that polity diversity is merely the transient by-product of technological limitations that temporarily mute the homogenizing effects of military competition.

On what grounds can the Indian Ocean be classified as an international system? As discussed in greater detail in the fourth section below, we argue that the Indian Ocean region became an international system from around 1500. This transition reflected not only a sharp rise in trade flows, diplomacy and cultural interactions across the region, but also a shift in agents' thinking, as actors began conceiving of the region as a single, unified field of operations. Thus, for example, in the sixteenth century the struggle between the Portuguese and the Ottomans reached from East Africa and the Red Sea to the coast of South Asia and all the way to Aceh. This recognition of the region's fluid and evolving nature reflects an understanding of 'system-ness' as a variable condition rather than an absolute attribute.[83] If region and sub-region are arguably more objective geographical terms, international system is thus a much more intersubjective concept, which reflects social agents' perceptions and strategies as much as the material context in which they interact.[84]

So far this chapter has covered much ground. We began by surveying the major International Relations theories to illuminate their common bias equating growing interaction between polities with their increasing

[83] On system-ness as a variable rather than absolute condition, see G. Therborn, 'Globalizations: Dimensions, Historical Waves, Regional Effects, Normative Governance', *International Sociology* 15:2 (2000), p. 157.

[84] And even with this caveat, it is worth noting that even the most taken-for-granted geographical concepts are frequently the product of socially and historically contingent constructions. See, generally, M. W. Lewis and K. E. Wigen, *The Myth of Continents: A Critique of Metageography* (Berkeley: University of California Press, 1997); and Steinberg, *The Social Construction of the Ocean.*

homogenization. We then countered this presumption by canvassing the scholarship demonstrating the countervailing tendency for interaction to be associated with a growth rather than a reduction in polity diversity over time. We next revisited major International Relations theoretical traditions to recover subordinate themes that could help make sense of durably diverse international systems, before then contrasting this with the main argument of this book.

We now turn finally to an overview of the Indian Ocean region. The Indian Ocean was from antiquity the principal flywheel for Afro-Asian long-distance trade. A vast maritime region constituted by high levels of commercial and cultural exchange between South Asia, South-East Asia, the Middle East and East Africa, the Indian Ocean was then overlaid by dense military and political interaction after 1500, following the direct entry of European thalassocracies and the consolidation of powerful Islamic empires along its littoral. This history of long-standing and accelerating interaction across multiple domains makes it an ideal setting for examining the effects of increasing interaction on polity composition, and thus for explaining durable diversity within international systems.

The world's flywheel: an overview of the Indian Ocean region

In the past two decades, inspired by Braudel's studies of the Mediterranean, historians have increasingly embraced frameworks that conceive world-historical regions around major oceans.[85] Historians' rationale for doing so is straightforward. Before the railway age, transportation on rivers and seas constituted the cheapest and most efficient way of moving people and goods over large distances.[86] Contrary to realists' emphasis on the 'stopping power' of water, for most of history the world's seas and oceans more often served as bridges than barriers to interaction between political communities. Limitations in navigational and ship-building technologies admittedly impeded large-scale interactions across the huge expanses of the Atlantic and the Pacific before 1500. By contrast, the Indian Ocean – combining a continuous littoral stretching

[85] See, for example, P. Butel, *The Atlantic* (London, Routledge, 1999); M.-L. Hinkkanen and D. Kirby, *The Baltic and the North Seas* (London: Routledge, 2000); D. B. Freeman, *The Pacific* (London: Routledge, 2009).

[86] Buzan and Little, *International Systems in World History*, p. 193.

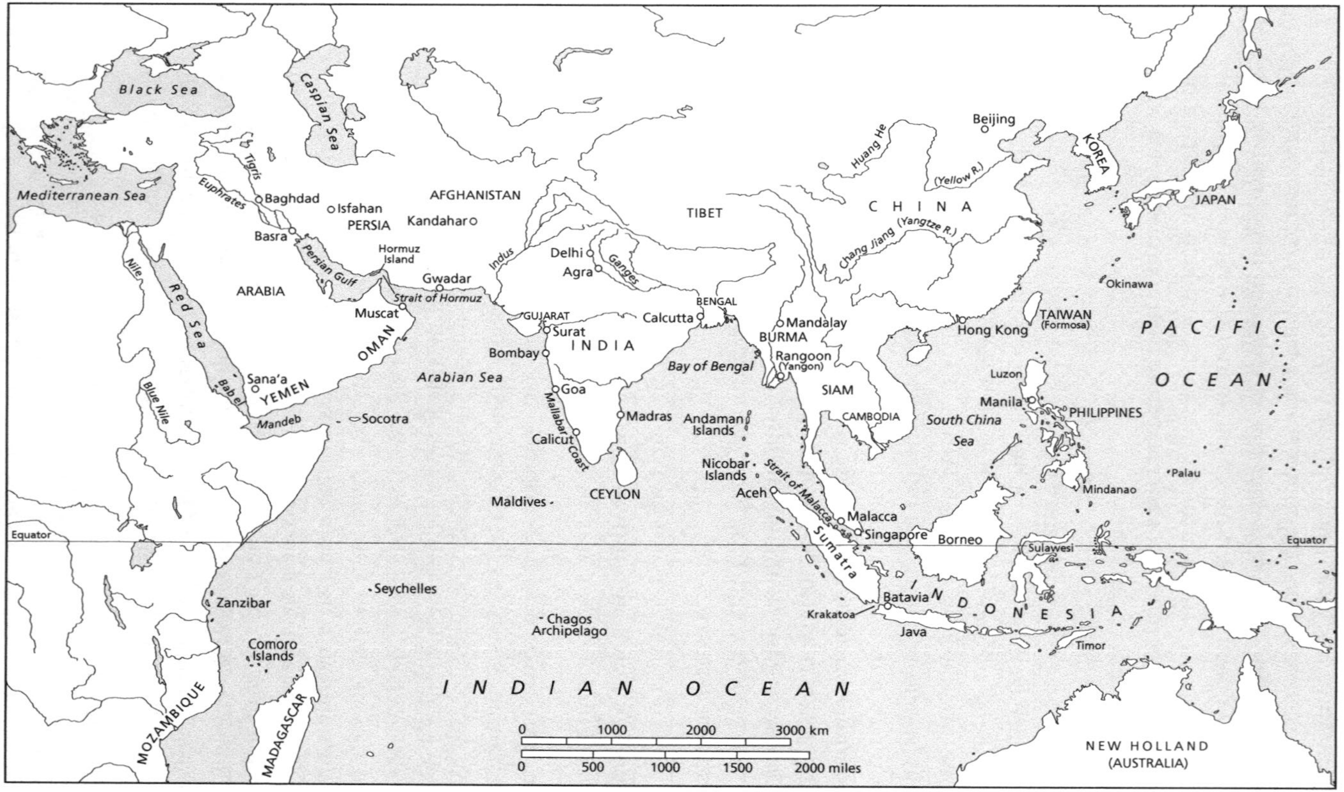

Figure 1.1 The Indian Ocean international system.

from East Africa to South-East Asia with the climatic regularity of the monsoon winds – provided an ideal medium for inter-polity exchange.

The Indian Ocean possesses features that favoured its early growth as an arena of cultural and commercial interaction. Geographically, it is an 'embayed ocean', substantially enclosed on three sides by the coastlines of East Africa, South and South-East Asia and Western Australia.[87] With a continuous littoral stretching from the southern tip of Africa through the Arabian Peninsula, and then along the Indian coast and down to the Malay Peninsula, the Indian Ocean abuts most of Afro-Eurasia's key population centres, while connecting East Asia with the rest of Eurasia through the Straits of Malacca.[88] From antiquity onwards, maritime traders were able to hug the Indian Ocean coast, moving people, goods and ideas throughout the Old World with short-legged ships that would never have crossed the vastness of the Atlantic or the Pacific.[89] Prior to the steamship era, the predictable seasonal winds of the Asian monsoon (a term that came into English from the Arabic for 'season' via the Portuguese) were crucial in allowing traders to maintain transcontinental commercial networks.[90] Finally, the ecological variability of littoral Indian Ocean societies ensured the production of a diverse range of agricultural goods, strengthening specialization and further spurring incentives for long-distance trade.[91]

Geographically, the Indian Ocean was a 'goldilocks' phenomenon – big enough to encompass an ecological diversity sufficient to make long-distance trade desirable and profitable among littoral societies, but small enough to remain easily navigable, in contrast to the forbidding expanses of the Atlantic and the Pacific. Already a focal point of intercontinental contacts stretching back millennia, the Indian Ocean's status as the world's great interconnector burgeoned further from the seventh century, following the Tang Dynasty's re-establishment of central rule in China (618 CE) and Islam's near-synchronous rise (622 CE). These developments brought political stability at opposite ends of Eurasia, boosting opportunities for long-distance trade.[92]

[87] S. R. Prange, 'Scholars and the Sea: A Historiography of the Indian Ocean', *History Compass* 6:5 (2008), p. 1382.
[88] *Ibid.*
[89] J. H. Bentley, 'Seas and Ocean Basins as Frameworks of Historical Analysis', *Geographical Review* 89:2 (1999), p. 219.
[90] Prange, 'Scholars and the Sea', p. 1382. [91] *Ibid.*
[92] Chaudhuri, *Trade and Civilisation in the Indian Ocean*, p. 34.

Islam's later regional spread meanwhile provided common cultural reference points for various merchant diaspora communities, again promoting integration.[93] By then, however, regional patterns of exchange between the region's four main sub-regions – South Asia, the Middle East, South-East Asia and East Africa – were already well established.

South Asia's combination of demographic weight, commercial might and geographic centrality puts it at the heart of the Indian Ocean region. Along with China, India constituted the global centre of agricultural production and manufacturing (mainly textiles) before the industrial revolution.[94] A 'metallurgical black hole' from Roman times, Indian markets sucked in precious metals (mainly gold) from Africa and Central Asia, exporting textiles and spices in return.[95] Economically self-sufficient except for precious metals and horses (the latter a militarily vital commodity sourced mainly from the Asian steppe and the Middle East), the subcontinent remained politically divided between land-oriented competitive empire-builders in the interior, and a constellation of relatively autonomous trade-oriented port cities strung along the coast.[96] These entrepôts sourced Indian textiles and other products from the interior via the subcontinent's extensive river systems.[97] The cyclical nature of the monsoonal winds, combined with the tendency for critical tributaries to dry up in the summer months, nevertheless lent these port settlements a distinctly seasonal character.[98] Historian Tirthankar Roy stresses their provisional character, and the itinerant and cosmopolitan nature of the self-governing merchant communities that inhabited them.[99] Originating a pattern that would be replicated across the Indian Ocean littoral, these port

93 See, for example, G. D. S. Sood, 'Circulation and Exchange in Islamicate Eurasia: A Regional Approach to the Early Modern World', *Past and Present* 212:1 (2011), pp. 116–17.

94 Chaudhuri, *Asia before Europe – Economy and Civilisation of the Indian Ocean from the Rise of Islam to 1750*, p. 297.

95 S. Dale, 'India under Mughal Rule', in D. Morgan and A. Reid (eds.), *The New Cambridge History of Islam*, vol. III: *The Eastern Islamic World, Eleventh to Eighteenth Centuries* (Cambridge University Press, 2010), pp. 288–9.

96 A. Reid, 'Islam in Southeast Asia and the Indian Ocean Littoral, 1500–1800: Expansion, Polarisation, Synthesis', in Morgan and Reid, *The New Cambridge History of Islam*, vol. III, p. 431.

97 T. Roy, *India in the World Economy: From Antiquity to the Present* (Cambridge University Press, 2012), p. 9.

98 *Ibid.*, p. 10. 99 *Ibid.*

cities would form the primary connective tissue linking not only the interior to the ocean, but also the Indian Ocean's constituent sub-regions to one another.[100]

Besides its economic importance, India exported many intellectual, cultural and ideological innovations that influenced other societies throughout the Indian Ocean and beyond. So pervasive and profound were these influences that historian Linda Shaffer has dubbed them 'Southernization', drawing a deliberate parallel with the much later processes of 'Westernization' that the West spearheaded globally following the industrial revolution.[101] Sanskritic and Buddhist high cultures originating from India spread throughout the Indian Ocean in the middle centuries of the first millennium BCE. Extending as far afield as north-eastern Asia, these influences substantially reshaped conceptions of both religious and political authority in recipient societies. Likewise, the later centuries of the first millennium CE saw a significant cultural and religious 'Indianization' of polities in Indo-China and the Malay archipelago.[102] The spread of Indian mathematics to the Arab world and China meanwhile stimulated important scientific breakthroughs in both, while pioneering Indian successes in cultivating sugar and cotton transformed agricultural production throughout much of the Old World.[103]

Whereas China enjoyed successive periods of imperial unity (interspersed with eras of dynastic decline), plurality and political fragmentation generally predominated in India prior to the Mughal intrusion in the sixteenth century. Such centralization as occurred in the subcontinent before the Mughals took place on a more modest scale than in China, and compounded rather than reduced the sub-region's extant diversity. In the north, from the twelfth century Turkic invaders extended Islamic influence without erasing local cultural differences, which if anything grew more pronounced in the late medieval period.[104] In the south, meanwhile, the Vijayanagara Empire (established in 1336) checked Islam's advance all the way down to the

[100] Reid, 'Islam in Southeast Asia and the Indian Ocean Littoral', p. 431.
[101] L. Shaffer, 'Southernization', *Journal of World History* 5:1 (1994), p. 1.
[102] L. Shaffer, *Maritime Southeast Asia to 1500* (New York: M. E. Sharpe, 1996), p. 24.
[103] Shaffer, 'Southernization', p. 7.
[104] Asher and Talbot, *India before Europe*, p. 52.

mid-sixteenth century.[105] The result was a fragmented and fluid political landscape, where no single ruler exercised hegemony.

While South Asia remained the Indian Ocean region's politically divided and permeable core, its littoral necklace of port cities enmeshed it deeply within adjacent sub-regions. The most established connection was arguably the trade ties linking India to the Middle East. These trade ties mediated the spread of important innovations between these two sub-regions.[106] The commercial and cultural traffic between the two sub-regions was hardly one-way. For the Middle East had from the dawn of the agricultural revolution been a primary hub of commerce and culture in its own right. This trend accelerated notably following Islam's rise in the seventh century, after which time this new religion gradually provided a thin skein of cultural commonality spanning the region in its entirety.

As Islam's cradle, the Middle East provided the Indian Ocean region with fundamental cultural scaffolding enabling expanded cross-regional exchange. As early as the eighth century CE, Islamic warriors implanted Islam in the subcontinent through the conquest of Sind.[107] Far more important for the region as a whole, however, was the peaceful spread of Islam through maritime commerce. Arab traders initially brought Islam to the coasts of western India and East Africa.[108] Gujarati merchants subsequently helped transmit Islam to South-East Asia from the fourteenth century. Islam's uptake by local rulers strengthened their authority, while its acceptance by cosmopolitan trading diasporas also accelerated commercial integration through the spread of Islamic law and financial practices.[109]

Through both commerce and conquest, Islam was thus progressively established as a ubiquitous presence throughout the region. So significant was the spread of Islam in drawing the region's constituent sub-regions together that historians have characterized the Indian Ocean as an 'Islamic sea' prior to the advent of large-scale European regional involvement.[110] Nevertheless, it would be wrong to reduce the Middle

[105] *Ibid.*, p. 54. [106] Shaffer, 'Southernization', p. 7.

[107] J. F. Richards, 'The Islamic Frontier in the East: Expansion into South Asia', *South Asia: Journal of South Asian Studies* 4:1 (1974), p. 92.

[108] M. Pearson, 'Islamic Trade, Shipping, Port States, and Merchant Communities in the Indian Ocean, Seventh to Sixteenth Centuries', in Morgan and Reid, *The New Cambridge History of Islam*, vol. III, pp. 330–1.

[109] Sood, 'Circulation and Exchange in Islamicate Eurasia', pp. 138–9.

[110] P. Beaujard, 'The Indian Ocean in Eurasian and African World Systems before the Sixteenth Century', *Journal of World History* 16:4 (2005), p. 451.

East's significance to the wellspring of Islam alone, and so neglect the thickening commercial ties that linked it to the wider region. These ties had ancient origins, dating back from the trade between Mesopotamia and the Indus river valley civilization in the first millennium BCE.[111] Following the Abbasid caliphate's collapse in the mid-thirteenth century, however, Middle Eastern trading routes became even more oriented towards the Indian Ocean, as trade shifted from its traditional focus around Baghdad and Damascus towards southerly routes focused instead on Aden and Fustat.[112] This maritime connection would continue into Ottoman times, the Porte maintaining an elaborate 'soft empire' of commercial and diplomatic networks throughout the region well into the sixteenth century.[113]

South-East Asia formed the Indian Ocean region's third sub-region. Here, it was the magnetic lure of the spice trade that drew Indian traders into South-East Asia over a millennium before the Europeans. Together with indigenous Malay sailors, Indian merchants helped establish a buoyant international market for luxury spices by the late fourth century CE.[114] Until 1621, the Moluccan Islands were the only places in the world where cloves, nutmeg and mace could be grown in commercial quantities.[115] The inherent scarcity of these spices ensured their status as low-bulk, high-value commodities, sustaining a flourishing long-distance trade with other Indian Ocean sub-regions from this time, and also with China.[116] The spice trade stimulated sustained contact between India and South-East Asia, contributing to the latter's substantial cultural and religious 'Indianization' towards the end of the first millennium.[117] By dint of its geographic position, South-East Asia also formed a highly porous frontier zone between the Indian Ocean region and the Sinosphere. Below, we argue that the Ming Dynasty's formal withdrawal from the Indian Ocean after 1433 marked an end to Chinese authority claims in the 'Great Southern Ocean', warranting a delineation between the Indian Ocean region and the Sinosphere as distinct regional orders. Nevertheless, substantial commercial ties continued to link the East Asian littoral with the Indian Ocean, and South-East Asia formed the primary meeting point for these contacts.

111 Roy, *India and the World Economy*, pp. 20–1.
112 Chaudhuri, *Trade and Civilisation in the Indian Ocean*, p. 58.
113 G. Casale, *The Ottoman Age of Exploration* (Oxford University Press, 2011), p. 125.
114 Shaffer, 'Southernization', p. 6. 115 *Ibid.* 116 *Ibid.* 117 *Ibid.*

We conclude our survey of the Indian Ocean region with the polities of East Africa. These polities were collectively referred to as the *Zanj* by the Arab traders with whom they were connected through trade even before the rise of Islam.[118] Trade ties had likewise linked East Africa with India as far back as the beginning of the Common Era.[119] Stretching from the Limpopo River in the south through what is now Somalia in the north, East Africa formed an integral part of the Indian Ocean region. Ivory, gold, slaves and aromatic spices from the interior formed the primary commodities tying East Africans into a larger Indian Ocean trading system. The leading import was Indian cloth and textiles.[120] A regular triangular trade between East Africa, the Middle East and the west coast of India has led Michael Pearson to refer to this half of the Indian Ocean region as the 'Afrasian Sea'.[121] As was the case throughout the Indian Ocean, interregional commercial networks crystallized primarily around an 'archipelago of towns',[122] with coastal entrepôts such as Kilwa, Zanzibar, Mombasa and Mogadishu (the latter two visited by Zheng He's huge Chinese fleet in the early fifteenth century) forming the main urban pivots linking the African interior to the larger global economy.[123] These city-states were ruled by Muslim sultans and predominantly populated by Islamicized Bantus referred to as Swahili ('coastal dwellers' in Arabic).[124] These ports were open to maritime traders from all across the region. These coastal cities depended on the inland areas, and there was a regular exchange of goods and people along the major valley systems like the Zambezi, as well as via overland trade routes, but the peoples of the hinterland remained largely unconverted by the Swahili Muslims.[125] Though powerful kingdoms and confederacies arose in areas like the Zimbabwe Plateau and further north in Christian Abyssinia, East Africa did not host major empires on the scale that the Mughals, Ottomans and Safavids established in South Asia and the Middle East. East Africa was a vital sub-region within the larger Indian

[118] Pearson, 'Islamic Trade, Shipping, Port States and Merchant Communities in the Indian Ocean', pp. 330–1.
[119] *Ibid.* [120] *Ibid.*, p. 332. [121] Pearson, *Port Cities and Intruders*, p. 9.
[122] M. Vink, 'From Port City to World-System: Spatial Constructs of Dutch Indian Ocean Studies, 1500–1800', *Itinerario* 28:2 (2004), p. 59.
[123] Pearson, *Port Cities and Intruders*, p. 20. [124] *Ibid.*
[125] *Ibid.*, pp. 20–1.

Ocean, and would remain so as the latter evolved from a trading zone to a fully fledged international system after 1500.

From region to system: the Indian Ocean in an age of transition

What most distinguished the Indian Ocean region from others prior to 1500 was not the presence of heteronomous tendencies per se, but the extent to which heteronomy predominated over alternative principles of political organization. What rendered the region most significant was its status as Afro-Eurasia's 'great connector', linking not only its constituent sub-regions, but also more distant areas, most notably Latin Christendom, the Central Asian steppe and East Asia. The over-land caravan trade had also linked these regions since antiquity through the Silk Road, which at various periods connected China, South-East and Central Asia with the Middle East and the Mediterranean.[126] In an ancient precursor of a problem that was to trouble Europeans in the early modern period, the Roman Empire had suffered a persistent drain of gold in order to pay for Chinese luxuries (including but not limited to silk) traded along this route.[127] As well as linking buyers and sellers, the Silk Road had also fostered the spread of religions, from Nestorian Christianity and Judaism to Buddhism and Islam.[128] Indeed, in part, it was the growing political instability along the Silk Route after the collapse of the Mongol Empire that stimulated European maritime expansion, as both Christopher Columbus and Vasco da Gama sought new access to the East.[129] But the growth of direct maritime Indian Ocean trade did not close the older Silk Road route, even as it first supplemented and then surpassed it as the primary locus of European interactions with Asia after 1500.

From the early centuries of the second millennium CE, the Indian Ocean saw a surge in trade that progressively knitted its sub-regions together in ever more dense webs of commercial and cultural exchange.

126 X. Liu, 'The Silk Road: Overland Trade and Cultural Interactions in Eurasia', in M. Adas (ed.), *Agricultural and Pastoral Societies in Ancient and Classical History* (Philadelphia: Temple University Press, 2001), p. 155.

127 *Ibid.*

128 See, generally, R. Foltz, *Religions of the Silk Road: Premodern Patterns of Globalization* (London: Palgrave Macmillan, 2010).

129 Abu-Lughod, *Before European Hegemony*, p. 362.

So significant was this growth in trade that some historians have posited the existence of an 'Indian Ocean Trading Ecumene' extending all the way from southern Africa through to the Sea of Japan.[130] Given the existence of a distinct and separate hierarchical international system in the East Asian Sinosphere, we find this notion too broad as a signifier of an international system per se. Trading connections abounded between the Indian Ocean and the East Asian Sinosphere, and we acknowledge them throughout our analysis, but we maintain that the two remained distinct and separate as international systems. The Indian Ocean's distinctiveness from the East Asian Sinosphere is further confirmed by the fact that the Chinese themselves routinely distinguished littoral East Asia (the 'Eastern Sea'), over which they claimed suzerainty, from the Indian Ocean littoral societies (the 'Western Sea'), over which they generally did not claim political authority.[131] This qualifier aside, the idea of an 'Indian Ocean Trading Ecumene' extending from Zanzibar to Nagasaki, if perhaps too expansive to describe an international system, does, however, convey the breadth of Indian Ocean trading networks before 1500, and their extensions into other regions. Importantly, it also highlights the centripetal influence Indian Ocean commerce exerted in drawing representatives from different regions into closer contact with one another.

Conventional accounts of globalization date its emergence at the earliest from the sixteenth century, with the onset of direct European participation in Asia's maritime trade and the coercive integration of the Americas into a nascent global capitalist order.[132] This characterization, while accurately capturing the threshold when the Indian Ocean transformed from a trading region to a fully fledged international system, nevertheless unjustly downplays the increasing interconnectedness that Indian Ocean maritime commerce had already

[130] See, for example, H. R. Clark, 'Maritime Diasporas in Asia before Da Gama: An Introductory Commentary', *Journal of the Economic and Social History of the Orient* 49:4 (2006), pp. 385–94.

[131] Steinberg, *The Social Construction of the Ocean*, p. 48. The main exception to this Chinese distinction between the 'Eastern Sea' and the 'Western Sea' emerged during the Yuan Dynasty, which, as we will see, broke from Chinese tradition and unsuccessfully asserted expansive authority claims in the Indian Ocean as well as East Asia.

[132] See, for example, D. O. Flynn and A. Giraldez, 'Born with a "Silver Spoon": The Origin of World Trade in 1571', *Journal of World History* 6:2 (1995), pp. 201–21.

stimulated before 1500. In the eastern Mediterranean, for example, the lure of long-distance trade with Asia had by the thirteenth century fuelled the rise of powerful maritime republics that sought to monopolize the Europe–Asia trade through their domination of key trade routes and the establishment of a networked series of fortified trading entrepôts.[133]

The early centuries of the second millennium also saw increased direct Chinese participation in the Indian Ocean region. Chinese diaspora merchant communities were active in the Indian Ocean from as early as the eleventh century, and by the thirteenth century advances in Chinese ship-building technology had enabled Chinese merchants to sail directly to Indian ports in Chinese-made ships, and to dominate the India–China maritime trade by the fourteenth century.[134] Coincident with the growth of private Chinese maritime activity in the Indian Ocean, the Yuan and Ming Dynasties likewise witnessed increased Chinese diplomatic activism within the region. Under Kublai Khan, the Yuan Dynasty sought to claim direct hegemony over large swathes of the subcontinent.[135] Early Ming encroachments on the region were less intrusive, although no less universal in intent. Successive naval missions to the subcontinent and beyond sought to secure local rulers' submission to the Chinese emperor, consistent with the Neo-Confucian ideology of the Great Unified Empire.[136] The Ming court's abrupt abandonment of interest in the Indian Ocean after 1433 thus marked an important departure from preceding centuries. But it did nothing to sever the deep connections linking Chinese trading diasporas to the region.

While the rise of Ottoman power restricted Christians' eastern Mediterranean access to the Indian Ocean, and Ming policy meanwhile circumscribed China's official engagement in the region, both Central Asia and the Atlantic powers of Latin Christendom were on the cusp of far more direct involvement from 1500. Central Asian pastoralists had profoundly influenced the Indian subcontinent from as far back as the

[133] P. Curtin, *Cross-Cultural Trade in World History* (Cambridge University Press, 1984), p. 138.
[134] T. Sen, 'The Formation of Chinese Maritime Networks to Southern Asia, 1200–1450', *Journal of the Economic and Social History of the Orient* 49:4 (2006), p. 446.
[135] *Ibid.*, p. 447. [136] *Ibid.*, pp. 436–8.

Turkic invasions in the twelfth century.[137] In the lead-up to 1500, however, pastoralists' ability to marry their traditional mastery of cavalry warfare with emerging advances in gunnery equipped them with the capacity to launch renewed offensives aimed at capturing the vast agricultural wealth of the Indo-Gangetic plain.[138]

Like representatives from the other regions considered, Western Europeans were also drawn into participation in Indian Ocean maritime commerce from the late medieval period. More so even than the eastern Mediterranean powers, however, Western Europeans were constrained by distance, their geographic ignorance and limited navigational skills, and the blocking power of the rising Ottoman giant. In the approach to *c.* 1500, however, improvements in ship-building techniques, navigational skills and naval warfare provided first the Portuguese with an ability to overcome these traditional obstacles to participation in the Indian Ocean region.[139] These innovations would ultimately facilitate the West's arrival in the commercial hub of the Old World, extending a trend towards increasing interaction and growing polity diversity that was by then already well established.

By the beginning of the sixteenth century, the Indian Ocean was thus already becoming an arena of commercial and cultural exchange not only among its constituent sub-regions, but between virtually all of Afro-Eurasia's major power centres. Crucially for our account, as these actors continued to converge after 1500, military and diplomatic exchange – a prerequisite for the emergence of a fully fledged international system – increased in parallel. Had it been sustained, Ming China's maritime thrust might have brought an Indian Ocean international system into being almost a century before the arrival of the Portuguese. Ming China certainly possessed the technological capacity to maintain a robust naval presence there, with Chinese treasure ships of the fifteenth century vastly exceeding local shipping in size.[140] China's commercial connections with the Indian Ocean region were also longstanding, and provided an additional motive to assert Chinese authority there.[141] As it was, fears of invasion from steppe pastoralists

137 Asher and Talbot, *India before Europe*, p. 52. 138 *Ibid.*, p. 115.

139 F. Fernández-Armesto, *Pathfinders: A Global History of Exploration* (New York: W. W. Norton, 2007), pp. 142–3.

140 Pearson, 'Islamic Trade, Shipping, Port Cities and Merchant Communities in the Indian Ocean', p. 320.

141 Sen, 'The Formation of Chinese Maritime Networks', pp. 446–7.

helped convince the Ming court to abandon further long-range maritime expeditions, leaving the Indian Ocean open for the Europeans' later intrusion.[142] If they were premature, Ming fears of steppe invaders were far from misplaced. For alongside the European thalassocracies, steppe invaders would substantially reshape the early modern world after 1500.

Surveying the Indian Ocean, historian Anthony Reid argues: 'The key political institution of the Indian Ocean trade in the fifteenth century had been the city-state, a cosmopolitan autonomous polity dedicated to trade and dependent on it.'[143] From 1500, the port city networks of the Indian Ocean region were increasingly sandwiched between two new entrants – the Europeans from the sea and expanding Central Asian steppe conquerors.[144] From modest beginnings, the European maritime networks would come to mediate a twenty-five-fold increase in the volume of Europe–Asia trade along the Cape route in the three centuries from 1500, consolidating the Indian Ocean's integration as an international system.[145]

Roughly coincident with the entry of the first of these thalassocracies, the Portuguese, into the Indian Ocean, the region was further pulled together through the rise of powerful land-based Islamic empires. The Ottomans' conquest of first Egypt in 1517, and then the Arabian Peninsula soon after, drew them directly into the Indian Ocean maritime world, while the Mughal conquests exerted a similarly tectonic impact on northern India.[146]

As we enter the sixteenth century, then, we observe a region with longstanding if diffuse commercial and cultural ties rapidly morphing into an international system, marked by routine military and diplomatic as well as commercial and cultural exchange between its polities. Far from ending the port city networks that connected the Indian Ocean littoral, European thalassocracies would enmesh themselves within them, harnessing the existing practices of legal pluralism and

[142] J. Grygiel, *Great Powers and Geopolitical Change* (Baltimore, MD: Johns Hopkins University Press, 2011), pp. 150–1. See also R. Finlay, 'The Treasure Ships of Zheng He: Chinese Maritime Imperialism in the Age of Discovery', *Terrae Incognitae* 23:1 (1991), p. 4.

[143] Reid, 'Islam in Southeast Asia and the Indian Ocean Littoral', p. 431.

[144] *Ibid.*, p. 434.

[145] J. de Vries, 'The Limits of Globalization in the Early Modern World', *Economic History Review* 63:3 (2010), p. 718.

[146] Reid, 'Islam in Southeast Asia and the Indian Ocean Littoral', p. 434.

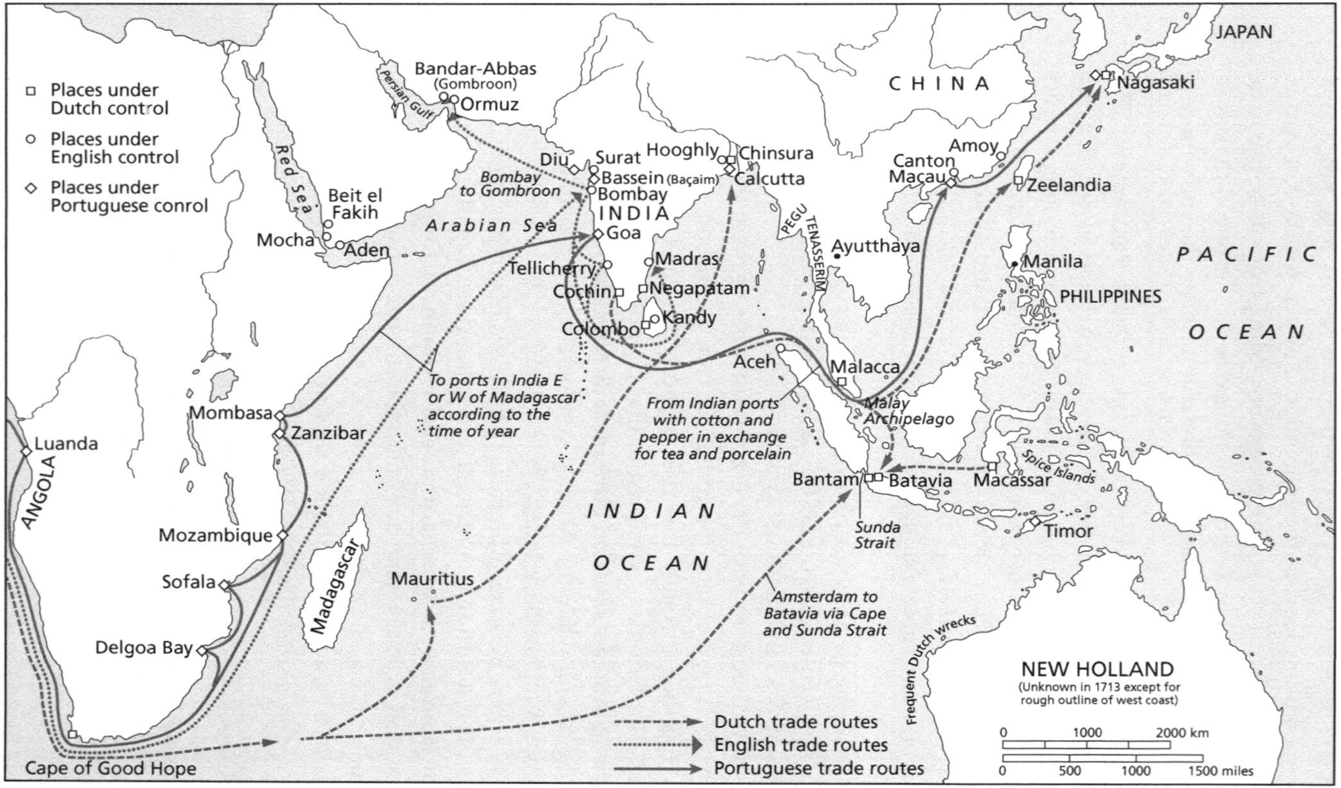

Figure 1.2 European trading routes and networks in the Indian Ocean, 1500–1750.

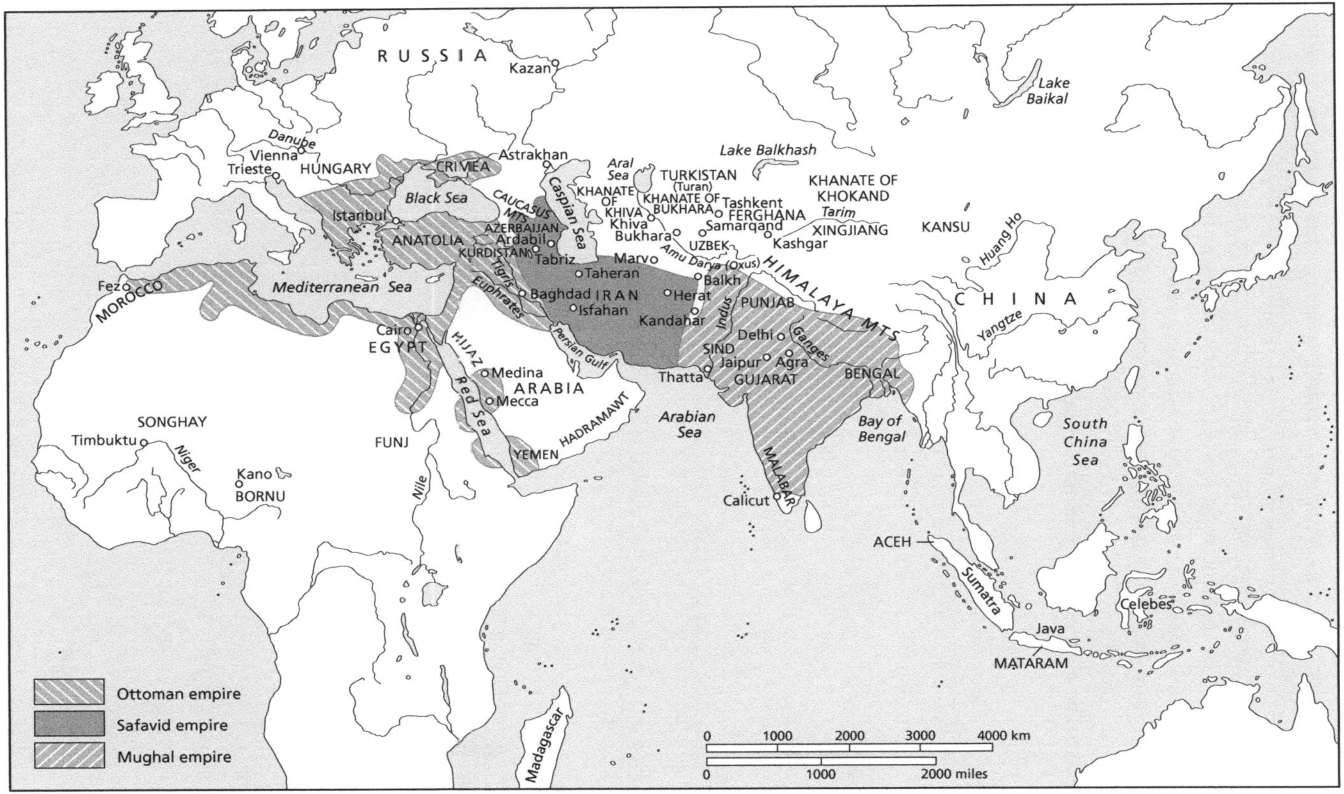

Figure 1.3 Islamic land-based empires around the Indian Ocean, *c.* 1700.

commercial extra-territoriality to do so. Simultaneously, expanding empires such as the Mughals' would overlay this maritime world through loose suzerain arrangements, eventually partially incorporating European intruders in the process. The entry of new actors into the Indian Ocean, producing a dramatic increase in military competition, commercial activity and cultural exchange, saw the birth of the Indian Ocean international system. Against expectations, however, this system was defined by its durable diversity. How and why this proved the case is the subject of the remaining chapters.

2 *The initial growth of diversity, 1500–1600*

In establishing the expanding diversity of the Indian Ocean system in the 1500s, two polity forms are central to our argument. The first is the statist model represented by the Portuguese, who first entered the Indian Ocean when Vasco da Gama's expedition rounded the Cape of Good Hope in December 1497 as part of the king's strategy to find Christian allies and spices in the East. The Portuguese quickly carved out a maritime domain that was subordinated to royal authority in Lisbon through a viceroy (based in Goa) who governed all the far-flung Portuguese possessions in the East.

The second is the realm created by the Mughals after their push south into India from Central Asia from 1526. A superpower of their day, the Mughals governed a huge and vastly wealthy territory that was organized along classically imperial lines. As such, like the Safavid and Ottoman Empires further to the west, the Mughals adopted a layered, gradated political structure, in which important sovereign prerogatives were delegated to subordinate rulers, and authority was conceived in terms of proximity or distance from the person of the emperor.

While it is a fundamental tenet of today's sovereign state system that none is entitled to command and none obliged to obey, this presumption of equality is very much the exception rather than the rule in historical terms, given the past prevalence of empires and heteronomous international systems. In the Indian Ocean system, and indeed in most others, it was entirely unremarkable for many, perhaps even most, actors within that system to acknowledge in some way the authority of some superior polity. In this way more minor polities are also part of our story, like the tributary sultanates of the East African Swahili Coast, the subordinate polities owing fealty to the Mughal emperor, or the 'galactic' polities of South-East Asia. In particular, the relations between subordinate polities and the principal statist, imperial and corporate actors are vital for illustrating the manner in which culturally different but structurally similar conceptions of authority both facilitated European entry to the region, and entrenched and extended heteronomy. The importance of these subordinate polities notwithstanding, our focus on the Portuguese and Mughals in this chapter, and the Dutch and English company sovereigns in the next, reflects Waltz's dictum that 'international political structures are defined in terms of the primary units of the era, be they city-states, empires or nations'.[1]

Against the conventional expectation that this diversity would have been reduced to one form (or at least that differences between them would have narrowed) via the mechanisms reviewed in the last chapter, polity diversity proved to be durable in the Indian Ocean international system. Indeed, it was further expanded by the arrival of the trading companies a century later. How and why did this diversity endure? How can we explain the establishment and survival of the initial European bridgehead in the region? How did the Portuguese and the Mughal Empire relate to each other? Here we begin to marshal historical evidence in support of the argument put forward previously in more abstract terms. Two features in particular were crucial, relating to the different preferences held by the Portuguese in contrast to local polities, discussed in this chapter, and the possibilities of heteronomous accommodations, touched upon here, but covered in more detail in Chapters 3 and 4. The third component part of our main thesis, improvised practices of localization, is explained in Chapter 4.

Co-existence between the Europeans and local powers was crucially dependent on the contrasting maritime goals of the Portuguese (and later the Dutch and English) versus the terrestrial orientation of the Mughals and other important local actors, like the Safavid Empire. The Portuguese strategy was almost entirely premised on the control of key ports and sea lanes, and the accompanying seaborne flow of spices and other goods. With rare exceptions on the Zimbabwe Plateau and in Ceylon, the Portuguese seldom sought to take over territory beyond the littoral. In contrast, as a result of their Central Asian origins, the nature of their fiscal and military organization, their huge wealth, their enjoyment of a structural trade surplus with the rest of the world, but above all their land-oriented mind-set, the Mughals were largely indifferent to the conduct of seaborne trade. They did not conceive of such trade or key sea lanes as something they would exert themselves to control, or

[1] Waltz, *Theory of International Politics*, p. 91.

deny to others. Though there was certainly variation, the smaller polities at the western and eastern extremities of the region shared the Mughals' rather laissez-faire approach to maritime trade, which was seen as a private affair of merchants, rather than something to be fought over or subjected to the political authority of the ruler. In this sense, the European conception of sea lanes and trade routes as a goal of strategic competition was novel and foreign.

This claim that European entry into and survival within the Indian Ocean region was first and foremost the result of contrasting world-views and cultures conflicts with the thesis that European military or institutional superiority was the decisive factor. We argue that the Portuguese, and later the Dutch and the English, did not enjoy any substantial technological advantage in land warfare over local powers in the Indian Ocean in the first two and a half centuries of European presence. In particular, they were hopelessly out-matched by the Mughal armies. Europeans did enjoy a significant though not insurmountable advantage in fortifications, not so much in any superior resistance to cannon fire but through their ability to allow defenders to use flanking fire against attackers through the *trace italienne* fortress design.[2] Most importantly, however, the intruders enjoyed a substantial naval advantage in cannon-armed sailing ships. Even here, however, we argue that this material superiority itself reflected underlying cultural orientations that shaped each polity's goals.

A final point of note that spans this chapter as well as the next is the highly uneven performance of the polity form which conventional wisdom holds should have been dominant: the sovereign state. Although the Portuguese Estado da Índia did not conform exactly to the model of a state, taking into account the tendency to cultivate subordinate tributaries and suzerainties, it was much closer to this form than the other major actors in the region. Given this close similarity, it is the strong expectation of conventional International Relations scholarship – based on the contemporaneous Western European experience – that this near-state-like form[3] should out-compete its rivals, which would either fall by the wayside or copy this institutional model. As the historical record clearly demonstrates, however, if anything the opposite was the case.

[2] T. Andrade, *Lost Colony: The Untold Story of China's First Great Victory over the West* (Princeton University Press, 2011).

[3] We thank an anonymous reviewer for this term.

Not only did the Estado da Índia remain singular in the region, it was eclipsed, though never eliminated, by rival polity forms.

This chapter proceeds as follows. The first section introduces the Portuguese Estado da Índia, delineates its constitution and purposes, and justifies its characterization as the polity form most closely approximating the sovereign state in the Indian Ocean in the early modern period. The second section then contrasts the Estado da Índia with the region's other main entrant at this time, the Mughal Empire. By far the region's most powerful polity, the Mughals warrant consideration both as exemplars of empire as a polity form, and also because they more than anyone else conditioned the terms of European entry into the region. The third and fourth sections then engage the dynamics of European–local relations in the region as they played out from the 1500s. The third section critiques conventional claims asserting Western institutional (especially military) superiority as the key to European expansion, noting instead the centrality of culturally conditioned Western maritime and local terrestrial orientations in affording the West entry into the region. The final section further develops this argument, stressing the centrality of compatible interests as an enabling condition for stable polity diversity to flourish in the Indian Ocean international system.

The Portuguese Estado da Índia

In the 1400s, the Portuguese steadily expanded the range of their exploration, trade and naval presence to incorporate the Atlantic islands of Madeira and the coastal fringes of Guinea.[4] By the 1480s they had alternately fought and traded nearly all the way down the Atlantic coast of Africa. Driving successive Portuguese monarchs on further, especially King Manuel I, was not just the idea of trade and accumulation, but a geopolitical crusading imperative. Like their Spanish counterparts, the Portuguese aristocracy had come of age fighting Muslim foes in the Iberian Peninsula and then in North Africa.[5] By sailing around the southern tip of Africa to the Indies beyond, the Portuguese king aimed to gain powerful Christian allies with whom to challenge Muslim

[4] F. Fernández-Armesto, *Before Columbus: Exploration and Colonization from the Mediterranean to the Atlantic, 1229–1492* (Philadelphia: University of Pennsylvania Press, 1987), pp. 219–20.

[5] *Ibid.*

domination of the Holy Lands, as well as valuable spices to finance this campaign.[6]

Manuel ultimately aspired to be crowned emperor after having captured Jerusalem with the aid of hoped-for allies like the fabled powerful Christian king Prester John, an achievement that was thought might bring about the second coming of Christ.[7] Vasco da Gama's mistaken initial impression that the Hindus he met in Calicut were Christians only bolstered this impression (believing that Krishna was Christ and that local temple paintings of various Hindu gods were strange representations of Christian saints; in turn, many Hindus thought the Portuguese were some kind of Muslims).[8] Though more of a pragmatist, Afonso de Albuquerque, the main architect of Portuguese strategy in the region, shared this broad goal. He aimed at one point to conquer Arabia, burn down Mecca, and take the body of the Prophet to be held for ransom.[9] A subsequent appreciation of how scarce Christian or other suitable allies in the East actually were, and the failure of attempts to convert the Mughal emperor and the Safavid shah to Christianity, necessarily made the Portuguese somewhat more realistic, though an underlying hostility towards 'the Moors' remained a constant.[10] More recent historiography has, however, taken issue with earlier Northern European historians' value-laden judgements deriding the Catholic Portuguese as 'pre-modern', in contrast to their Protestant Dutch and English competitors.[11] Particularly in East Africa, the Portuguese crusading impulse did not prevent close cooperation with local Muslims, including many marriages.

[6] A. R. Disney, *A History of Portugal and the Portuguese Empire*, vol. II (Cambridge University Press, 2009), p.126.

[7] A. J. R. Russell-Wood, *The Portuguese Empire, 1415–1808: A World on the Move* (Baltimore, MD: Johns Hopkins University Press, 1992), p. 11; S. Subrahmanyam and Luís Filipe F. R. Thomaz, 'Evolution of Empire: The Portuguese in the Indian Ocean During the Sixteenth Century', in Tracy, *The Political Economy of Merchant Empires*, p. 301; Disney, *History of Portugal*, p. 126.

[8] Disney, *History of Portugal*, pp. 124–5.

[9] Pearson, *Port Cities and Intruders*, p. 144; Disney, *The Portuguese Empire*, p. 133.

[10] S. Subrahmanyam, 'Taking Stock of the Franks: South Asian Views of Europeans and Europe', *Indian Economic and Social History Review* 42:1 (2005), pp. 69–100.

[11] Subrahmanyam, 'A Tale of Three Empires'; S. Subrahmanyam, *Mughals and Franks: Explorations in Connected History* (Oxford University Press, 2012).

From 1580 to 1640 Portugal became part of a personal union with the Spanish Habsburgs as Philip II of Spain became Philip I of Portugal. Officially Portugal and Spain were governed separately, and in practice there was little coordination in their respective extra-European ventures. The union worsened Portugal's diplomatic situation, however, by loosening its traditionally close ties with the English, and especially by attracting the enmity of the Dutch. A nobles' revolt in 1640 ended the union, but not before the Dutch had begun to undercut Portuguese power in Asia.

Very quickly after their arrival in the Indian Ocean region, the Portuguese set up a network of small fortified bases from which to trade and maintain their ships. These were located all around the region, from the Swahili Coast of East Africa, to Hormuz in the Persian Gulf, Goa in the west of India, Malacca and the Spice Islands, and even further east with smaller trading posts in Macau and Deshima in Japan. Only seven years after Vasco da Gama first reached India, the king of Portugal established the viceroyalty of the Estado da Índia in 1505. The Estado da Índia became 'a complex of territories, establishments, goods, persons, and administrative interests in Asia and East Africa, generated by or subordinate to the Portuguese crown, all of which were linked together as maritime network'.[12] The overwhelmingly maritime nature of this domain was confirmed by one early seventeenth-century Portuguese writer, who observed that: 'the king our lord does not have more than twenty leagues of land in all Asia, from Macau to the Cape of Good Hope'.[13] The Portuguese outposts built upon the medieval innovation of the factory (*feotoria*), a crown institution that had upheld the commercial interests of Portuguese merchant communities resident in European entrepôts such as Bruges. These factories were organized in a notably hierarchical and centralized fashion, with heads of individual *feotorias* reporting to the viceroy in Goa, and then via the viceroy to Lisbon itself.[14] Here there is some evidence that the Portuguese were following Venice's early example of a

12 Subrahmanyam and Thomas, 'Evolution of Empire', p. 304.

13 Quoted in Z. Biedermann, 'Portuguese Diplomacy in Asia in the Sixteenth Century: A Preliminary Overview', *Itinerario* 29:2 (2005), p. 13.

14 S. Subrahmanyam, 'Written in Water: Designs and Dynamics in the Portuguese *Estado da India*', in S. E. Alcock (ed.), *Empires: Perspectives from Archaeology and History* (Cambridge University Press, 2001), p. 51.

centralized, statist thalassocracy committed to the monopolization of strategic Europe–Asian trading routes.[15]

Complementing the Portuguese strategy of controlling key maritime choke-points like Hormuz in the west and Malacca in the east, was a claim to dominion over the whole ocean as a *mare clausum* ('closed sea'), including a monopoly on all seaborne trade. The hope was that in combination these measures would force local rulers to become 'vassals and tributaries' of the Portuguese king, put the Venetians who co-operated with Muslim spice traders out of business, and raise revenue to wage successful wars against the Ottomans.[16] The Portuguese sought to exercise this claim of a monopoly on all Indian Ocean trade via a system of passes (*cartaz*) required by all ships trading in the region. Although the exact provisions changed over time, the *cartaz* mandated a customs payment to Portuguese authorities, prohibited private trade in goods on which the crown claimed a monopoly, and forbade those holding the *cartaz* from trading with enemies of the Portuguese. As with most aspects of the Estado da Índia, there was almost always a yawning gap between Portuguese aims and pronouncements and what they actually managed to implement and enforce. During the sixteenth century there were only around 10,000 Portuguese spread across the whole region.[17] In theory, the monopoly claim on trade was upheld by Portuguese warships confiscating or sinking any ship not carrying a pass, and in practice this did sometimes happen, especially off the west coast of India. To the extent that the system was enforced, it constituted a classic case of Tilly's analogy between state-making and a protection racket. Rulers created a threat, and then charged private third parties in return for protection from this threat.[18]

Trade to Europe was governed in a similarly *dirigiste* manner. The great Portuguese *nao* or carrack ships of around 1,600 tons carried up to 700 passengers and the all-important merchandise on the eighteen-month

[15] L. Benton, 'Legal Spaces of Empire: Piracy and the Origins of Ocean Regionalism', *Comparative Studies in Society and History* 64:4 (2005), p. 713.

[16] J. D. Tracy. 'Introduction', in Tracy, *Political Economy of Merchant Empires*, p. 6.

[17] G. V. Scammell, 'Indigenous Assistance in the Establishment of Portuguese Power in Asia in the Sixteenth Century', *Modern Asian Studies* 14:1 (1980), p. 8.

[18] C. Tilly, 'War Making and State Making as Organized Crime', in P. Evans *et al.* (eds.), *Bringing the State Back In* (Cambridge University Press, 1985), pp. 169–92.

round-trip between Lisbon and Goa.[19] On their return to Portugal, the main cargo was pepper, but also other spices like cinnamon, cloves, nutmeg and mace, all valued for their supposed medicinal as much as culinary qualities. In addition, there was an enormous range of other commodities, from rubies and diamonds to ebony, gold and ivory, cardamom, sandalwood, indigo, saffron, cotton and silks, and a range of finished goods, exotic animals and slaves.[20] Though they were armed, these ships relied primarily on their huge size for defending their precious cargoes in the Indian Ocean, a measure that was successful in relation to local fleets, but much less so later against European opponents. Apart from hostile actions, the weather inflicted a terrible toll on the carracks, with 10 or 20 per cent being lost on each round-trip, while disease cut down many passengers even on those ships that did make the journey intact. Between 1500 and 1635 at least 912 such ships left Portugal for the Indian Ocean, while from Goa and Malacca at least 550 made the return journey.[21] From 1510 to 1570 this route (and the continuation to Macau and Japan) was a crown monopoly, though thereafter there was some contracting out to private merchants.[22]

Putting this historical material in context, the Estado da Índia is important in answering two broader questions for the argument put forward in the book. One relates to how the Portuguese successfully established their maritime network across the huge expanse of the Indian Ocean. Here the discussion centres on the relative importance of the military balance between the Portuguese and local forces, as compared with the role of differing preferences and mentalities. The more immediate question, however, is whether the Estado da Índia can be classified as a state. The section below argues that, although the match is not perfect, especially considering the Portuguese use of heteronomous tributary relations, the Portuguese domain was organized on recognizably statist lines, especially relative to the other main actors considered. This claim raises the prior question of how we can distinguish a state from other kinds of polities.

[19] C. R. Boxer, *The Portuguese Seaborne Empire 1415–1825* (London: Hutchinson, 1969), pp. 205–20.

[20] Russell-Wood, *The Portuguese Empire*, p. 127.

[21] *Ibid.*, p. 30.

[22] Boxer, *Portuguese Seaborne Empire.*

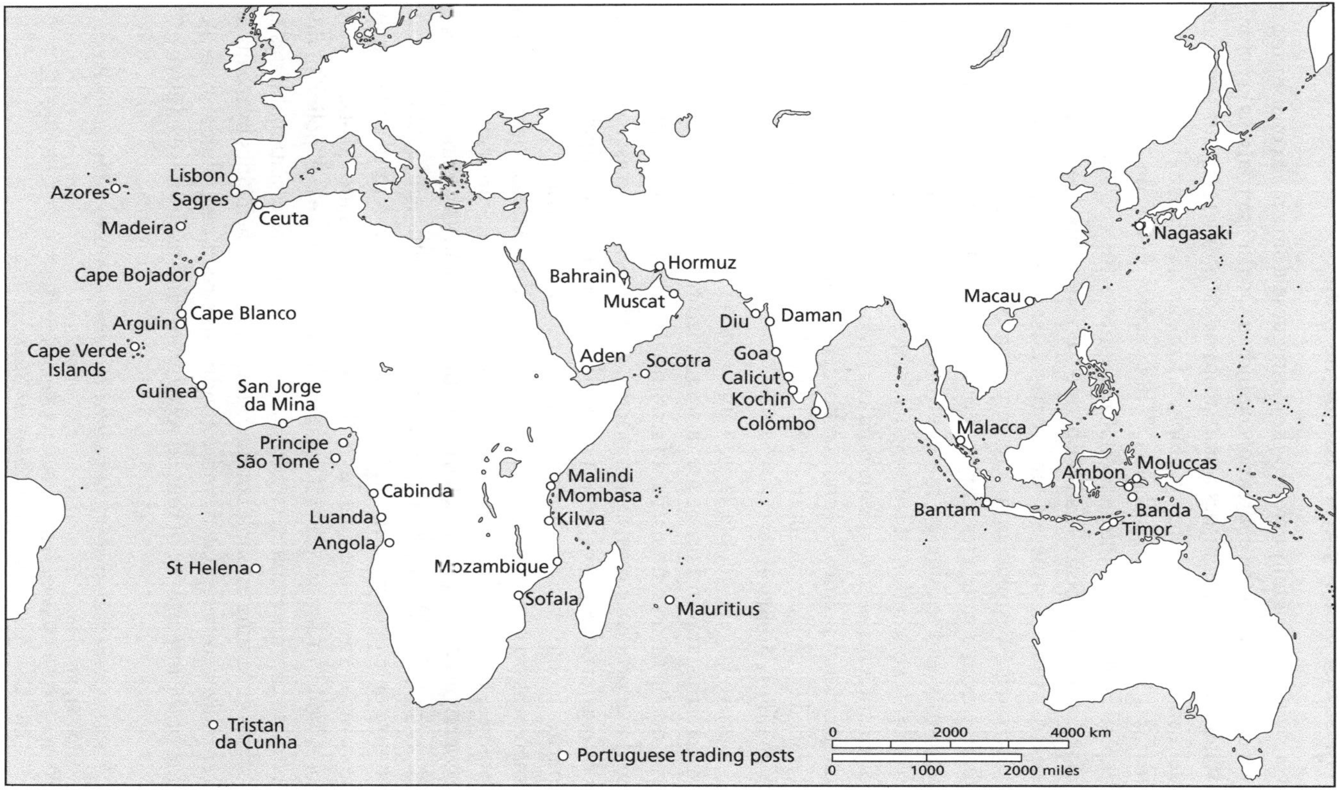

Figure 2.1 The Estado da Índia, *c.* 1600.

The statist model and the Estado da Índia

Can we meaningfully refer to the Portuguese domain as constituting a sovereign state in the context of the Indian Ocean international system? What exactly distinguishes a state from other polity forms? If states are defined by their sovereignty, Stephen Krasner has incisively laid out the features of sovereign authority. These centre firstly on the ability to extend and receive international recognition (to conclude treaties, to make war and peace, establish and receive embassies, and so on), referred to by Krasner as 'international legal sovereignty'. The second criterion is 'Westphalian sovereignty', the exclusion of outside authority claims from a state's territory.[23] Both are carefully specified in terms of authority and legitimacy, not control or practical influence. Stemming from this conception of sovereignty, states are characterized by a sharp distinction between domestic politics that occurs inside the borders, and international politics beyond the border. Domestic politics internally is typified by a hierarchical structure of public authority, something akin to a chain of command.

Spruyt largely adopts these same criteria when he maintains that sovereign states in Europe are distinguished from their medieval predecessors by their combination of territorial exclusivity, internal hierarchy and independence from external actors.[24] This is in contrast to the cross-cutting jurisdiction of non-state medieval polities, in which different parties could exercise authority over the same territory, and where there was no meaningful distinction between domestic and international politics, due to the absence of definite borders and mutually exclusive sovereignty.[25] A further characteristic often said to define states is a monopoly on the legitimate use of violence, although arguably even many contemporary states fail to meet this criterion. A third and roughly consistent view from Charles Tilly uses the term 'national state' (Tilly uses 'state' in a more general sense in the same way we use 'polity' in this book to capture empires, city-leagues, etc.). Tilly defines national states as 'states governing multiple contiguous regions and their cities by means of centralized, differentiated, and autonomous structures', while also speaking of the importance of mutual recognition and territorial exclusivity.[26]

[23] S. D. Krasner, *Sovereignty: Organized Hypocrisy* (Princeton University Press, 1999), pp. 3–4.

[24] Spruyt, *The Sovereign State and its Competitors*, p. 3.

[25] *Ibid*., p. 12.

[26] Tilly, *Coercion, Capital and European States*, p. 3.

While jibbing at the notion of a monopoly of force, Tilly does speak of national states' forces having a comparative advantage in the use of violence within their territory.[27]

Given these congruent views, how close or distant was the Portuguese domain from this template of the ideal sovereign state? Although there are important differences, it is argued here that the institutional arrangements of the Estado da Índia were fundamentally closer to this template than any of the empires, suzerainties or chartered trading companies considered in this or the next chapter. This closeness relative to these other forms is important, because in the European context the conventional view is not that ideal-typical states sprang fully formed from the womb of the medieval order, but rather that polities which bore a successively closer resemblance to the ideal were disproportionately 'selected in' and favoured by the mechanisms driving convergence. In keeping with the Darwinian and Lamarckian evolutionary analogies that underpin the realist and rationalist explanations, systemic pressures in early modern Europe are said to have progressively moved proto-states closer and closer to the sovereign state ideal. The states that Spruyt looks at in early modern Europe are thus not a perfect fit with the ideal-type. Krasner mounts a persuasive case that even many contemporary states deviate from the model of international legal and Westphalian sovereignty in some respects.[28] In this sense the category of sovereign state might be a 'family resemblance' concept. Here a category is defined by a number of characteristics, and even though there may not be any one characteristic common to every member of the category, they are all recognizably related through sharing a majority of such features.[29]

The structure of the Estado da Índia has been described as 'precociously statist'.[30] Another historian similarly speaks of 'The model of centralized power delegated by the king that was applied from the very start of the Portuguese expansion in Asia'.[31] The Portuguese favoured a centralized structure of authority and a unified chain of command that flowed directly

[27] Tilly, 'War Making and State Making as Organized Crime'.
[28] Krasner, *Organized Hypocrisy*, p. 24.
[29] D. Collier and J. E. Mahon, 'Conceptual "Stretching" Revisited: Adapting Categories in Comparative Analysis', *American Political Science Review* 87:4 (1993), pp. 845–55.
[30] Wills, 'Was There a Vasco da Gama Epoch?' p. 354.
[31] F. Bethencourt, 'Political Configurations and Local Powers', in F. Bethencourt and D. Curto (eds.), *Portuguese Oceanic Expansion, 1400–1800* (Cambridge University Press, 2007), p. 221.

down from the king to the governor of the Estado da Índia in Goa, and then to his subordinate officials throughout the region. This structure of authority extended in scope to military and commercial domains as well as to strictly administrative affairs. Senior officials were appointed by the king for three-year terms.[32] Town councils and local administrations had the same formal structure and duties as in metropolitan Portugal, replicating the state structures down to the local level.[33] These arrangements were far closer to the sovereign state ideal than either the Mughal Empire, with its heterogeneous rule through intermediaries, or the Dutch and English private–public company sovereigns (as discussed below).

Militarily, payment for garrisons and forts (often inadequate) came from central funds.[34] Like all early modern polities, the Portuguese hired mercenaries in Asia and Africa, cultivated local allies to supplement their chronically under-strength numbers, and on some occasions even used slave soldiers. Yet there was no equivalent of the completely private armed forces of the Dutch or the English East India Company, or the quasi-feudal organization of Mughal military power whereby the emperor depended on forces that owed their primary allegiance to hundreds of separate vassals. The same centralized and hierarchical organization of command went for naval forces too: 'The Portuguese ships and the guns were primarily owned by the state. This makes the Portuguese enterprise look strikingly modern.'[35]

For most of the sixteenth century trade also was a highly centralized state monopoly, with both bullion and spices being reserved for royal agents, and all goods from the Indian Ocean passing through the Casa da Índia in Lisbon.[36] Even after this point, merchants were consistently subordinated to royal interests.[37] For the Portuguese, trade was 'an extension of the state'.[38]

Unsurprisingly, the ambitions of royal and viceregal control far outstripped the ability to enforce their wishes over the vast distances and

[32] Disney, *History of Portugal*.
[33] K. N. Chaudhuri, *Trade and Civilisation in the Indian Ocean*; Bethencourt, 'Political Configurations and Local Powers'.
[34] Tracy, 'Introduction', p. 9.
[35] Jan Glete, *Warfare at Sea, 1500–1650: Maritime Conflicts and the Transformation of Europe* (London: Routledge, 2000), p. 89.
[36] Boxer, *Portuguese Seaborne Empire*, p. 60.
[37] Chaudhuri, *Trade and Civilisation in the Indian Ocean*, p. 71; Glete, *Warfare at Sea*, p. 87.
[38] Tracy, 'Introduction', p. 2.

with the available technology and scarce manpower. Public officials often shirked their duties, while merchants surreptitiously evaded the royal monopoly. But the Portuguese never gave up on their centralized, statist model. Indeed, it was only in 1752 that officials in East Africa were able to make decisions independent of Goa, though not, of course, of the king. The strict chain of command, the patterns of direct appointment from the administrative centre, and the public control of military and economic prerogatives gives the Estado da Índia a modern, statist feel.

There were, however, some aspects of layered sovereignty in the Estado da Índia which deviate from the contemporary standard, whereby states exercise uniform and complete sovereignty right up to a definite border, but no further. In particular these relate to the cultivation of tributary and vassal relations with subordinate polities. Thus for most of the Indian Ocean the Portuguese king claimed a kind of overlordship that both legitimated the Portuguese claim of a trading monopoly and specifically excluded European competitors. King Manuel grandiloquently referred to himself as 'Lord of conquest, navigation and commerce of Ethiopia, India, Arabia and Persia', in addition to his other extra-European title of 'Lord of Guinea'.[39] In practice the Portuguese captains and emissaries extended an offer of 'friendship and brotherhood' from the king, which could mean several different things. The Portuguese sought to interact with the other powerful rulers in the region on a basis of equality, a notion so offensive to the imperial Chinese, who brooked no equal, that they beheaded some of the first Portuguese delegation.[40] For most of the time the Portuguese managed an accommodation with the Muslim Mughals and Safavids on these terms, though not the Ottomans, who sporadically contested Portuguese naval domination of the region from the Red Sea to Gujarat to Sumatra in the sixteenth century.[41] Generally cordial relations were established with Buddhist Siam and the larger Hindu polities of India.

For smaller polities, however, 'friendship and brotherhood' came to mean a tributary relationship. This was particularly evident in the Swahili Coast, extending from present-day Mozambique to Somalia, as well as on the Malabar Coast of India. The Swahili port city-states were ruled by Muslim sultans, and had formed extensive economic ties

[39] Disney, *History of Portugal*, p. 127. [40] *Ibid.*, p. 142.
[41] Glete, *Warfare at Sea*, p. 82.

both with the African interior and across the 'Afrasian Sea' to India.[42] Their anti-Islamic views earned the Portuguese an initially hostile reception from most, though the sultan of Malindi welcomed an alliance against his local rivals. As these rivals were subordinated, the sultans were forced into a tributary relationship, especially after the Portuguese survived Ottoman raids in the 1580s and conquered Mombasa in 1593.

Such a relationship might involve payment in kind of foodstuffs and other goods, promises to sell goods to Portuguese settlements and ships at local prices, observing the *cartaz* system and banning trade with Portugal's enemies, and acknowledging the supremacy of the king in Lisbon.[43] As a matter of both practice and principle, however, this left the East African sultans with a good degree of autonomy to rule in their own right, which often extended to ignoring Portuguese wishes.[44] More broadly, Prestholdt argues that the Portuguese came to see the interior of Africa according to Muslim Swahili concepts and mental maps, for example referring to those living in the interior as *kaffirs* (unbelievers).[45]

With these deviations from the ideal-typical state in mind, it must be repeated that the verdict on the Estado da Índia is a relative judgement: the Portuguese domain was closer to the statist form than the other polities in the region, and thus to some extent coming to a definitive conclusion must wait until the imperial and corporate forms have been considered. Nevertheless, provisionally it is possible to say that the Estado da Índia shared important characteristics with the sovereign state model. Authority was clearly organized on strictly hierarchical lines from king to viceroy to individual officials. The Portuguese did not acknowledge any superior authority, and they were independent from outside actors. They clearly had ambitions of exclusive sovereignty, at least as much over sea as land. Military and naval forces were primarily organized by the public authorities, though they were often augmented with mercenaries. All these factors support historians' judgements

42 Pearson, *Port Cities and Intruders*; J. K. Thornton, 'The Portuguese in Africa', in Bethencourt and Curto, *Portuguese Oceanic Expansion*, pp. 138–60.

43 Pearson, *Port Cities and Intruders*, pp. 130–2; J. Prestholdt, 'Portuguese Conceptual Categories and the "Other" Encounter on the Swahili Coast', *Journal of Asian and African Studies* 36:4 (2001), pp. 395–6.

44 Pearson, *Port Cities and Intruders*, pp. 149–52.

45 Prestholdt, 'Portuguese Conceptual Categories'.

about the 'precociously statist' and 'strikingly modern' features of the Estado da Índia.

The Mughals

The Portuguese re-routed trade, but deliberately did not project power deep into the populous interiors of Asia or Africa. By contrast, as noted, the Mughal Empire was a superpower of its day, having a population five or six times greater than France or the Habsburgs in 1600, and earning twenty-five times more revenue annually than King James I of England.[46] A century later the Mughals governed something like a quarter of the world's population. The Mughals probably had more population, revenue and men under arms than the whole of Europe combined from the late sixteenth to the early eighteenth century, when they dominated an area between present-day Afghanistan and Burma. Despite this, the Mughals are almost entirely unknown to International Relations scholars. The first order of business for this section is thus to present a brief introduction on the Mughals from 1526, including the organization of their military forces.

The Mughals are of interest not just in their own right, but also as an instance of a more general type: empire, a fundamentally different form from sovereign states. Explaining these differences is important in substantiating our claims about the diversity of units with the Indian Ocean regional system. Despite the tendency to project the current dominance of states back into history, it is crucial to remember that all around the world 'The early modern period was for the most part a patchwork of competing and intertwined empires, punctuated by the odd interloper in the form of a nascent "nation-state".'[47] Distinguishing features of empires hinge on the absence of definite borders that separate domestic from international politics, and a hub-and-spoke incorporation of subordinate polities, which nevertheless have their own international identities, combining to create a layered and shared distribution of authority.

The final question to be answered is why the Mughals, with their fantastic power and wealth, so far in advance of anything the Europeans could muster, allowed the Portuguese and then subsequently

[46] Pearson, 'Merchants and States', p. 1.
[47] Subrahmanyam, 'Holding the World in Balance', p. 1359.

other Europeans to engage in their violent attempts to carve out domains in the Indian Ocean, and in South Asia especially. As we explore in greater detail in the third and fourth sections below, the answer here is very different from the materialist logic of military competition or superior economic performance. It depends in its simplest form on the idea that the Portuguese (and other Europeans) had different preferences from the Mughals. The Mughals did not, and did not need to, attach much importance to maritime affairs, and regarded the Europeans as just another minor, subordinate trading community who were sometimes marginally useful for Mughal purposes.

The word 'Mughal' itself is derived from the Persian word for 'Mongol', reflecting the Mughals' Central Asian origins and descent from the dynasties of Genghis Khan and Timur.[48] The Mughals were Muslims, and they combined Mongol, Turkic and Persian cultures, with Persian becoming the language of administration and high culture, though the historic link with Central Asia remained vital to the Mughals' identity. The beginnings of the Mughal Empire date from Babur, who began as a minor ruler of a fragment of Timur's empire in the Ferghana valley, and who campaigned to restore this realm in current-day Tajikistan, Afghanistan and Uzbekistan. In 1526–7 Babur led a successful expedition south, defeating the two dominant Muslim and Hindu rulers in northern India and capturing Delhi. However, Babur died in 1530, with his successors unable to hold the territory he had conquered. The Mughal Empire proper was a product of Babur's grandson, Akbar, who during his almost fifty-year rule (1556–1605), established Mughal control of present-day Afghanistan, Pakistan and northern India, as well as developing the Mughal system of rule (explained below). The empire went into decline from the early eighteenth century in a process that saw authority seep away from the emperor to powerful local rulers, and later the English East India Company (see Chapter 5).[49]

[48] E. Tucker, 'Seeking a World Empire: Nadir Shah in Timur's Path', in J. E. Woods (ed.), *Historiography of Post-Mongol Central Asia and the Middle East* (Wiesbaden: Harrassowitz, 2006), pp. 337–8; L. Balabanlilar, 'Lords of the Auspicious Conjunction: Turco-Mongol Imperial Identity on the Subcontinent', *Journal of World History* 18:1 (2007), pp. 2–3; R. L. Canfield, 'Introduction: The Turko-Persian Tradition', in R. L. Canfield (ed.), *Turko-Persia in Historical Perspective* (Cambridge University Press, 1991), p. 20.

[49] Richards, *The Mughal Empire*.

The historian Jos Gommans puts much of the Mughals' success down to their ability to exploit the best of two different socio-economic worlds. First, they could reap the benefits of the spectacularly rich and well-populated sedentary agricultural producers along South Asia's major river systems, providing a correspondingly bountiful source of regular tax revenue. Second, they could draw upon the massive reserves of nomadic military power, particularly horse archers, on the frontiers of their lands.[50] One military census counted that in 1595 the empire had access to a total potential of 4.4 million infantry and 342,696 cavalry.[51] Given these fiscal and military advantages, Mughal conquest was more constrained by geographic and logistic obstacles than the presence of equally matched opponents.[52] The Mughals' vast numbers, reputation for victory in battle, and (not least) their habit of buying off potential enemies meant that most other polities, including the Europeans, preferred to avoid tangling with such a formidable force.

Mughal military victories were above all won by a combination of horse archers and light mobile artillery, with infantry playing at best a secondary and supporting role. Once again, the scale of the Mughal enterprise is notable, with cavalry armies numbering in the tens of thousands, supported by three times as many horses, together with thousands of camels and elephants. Further reinforcing the verdict of studies of East Asia and elsewhere, the introduction of gunpowder weapons did not transform the conduct of warfare along the lines of Europe. Cavalry, not infantry pikemen or musketeers, remained the dominant arm, and the conduct of siege warfare changed little. This fact underlines the danger of extracting purportedly universal lessons from idiosyncratic European historical experience. Technological and material changes did not produce the political or cultural changes they 'should' have, according to the military revolution thesis.[53]

[50] Gommans, *Mughal Warfare*.

[51] Streusand, *Islamic Gunpowder Empires*, p. 263.

[52] Richards, *The Mughal Empire*, p. 56.

[53] P. A. Lorge, *The Asian Military Revolution: From Gunpowder to the Bomb* (Cambridge University Press, 2008); Streusand, *Islamic Gunpowder Empires*; Gommans, *Mughal Warfare*; J. Gommans and D. Kolff, *Warfare and Weaponry in South Asia 1000–1800* (Delhi: Oxford University Press, 2003); Richards, *The Mughal Empire*.

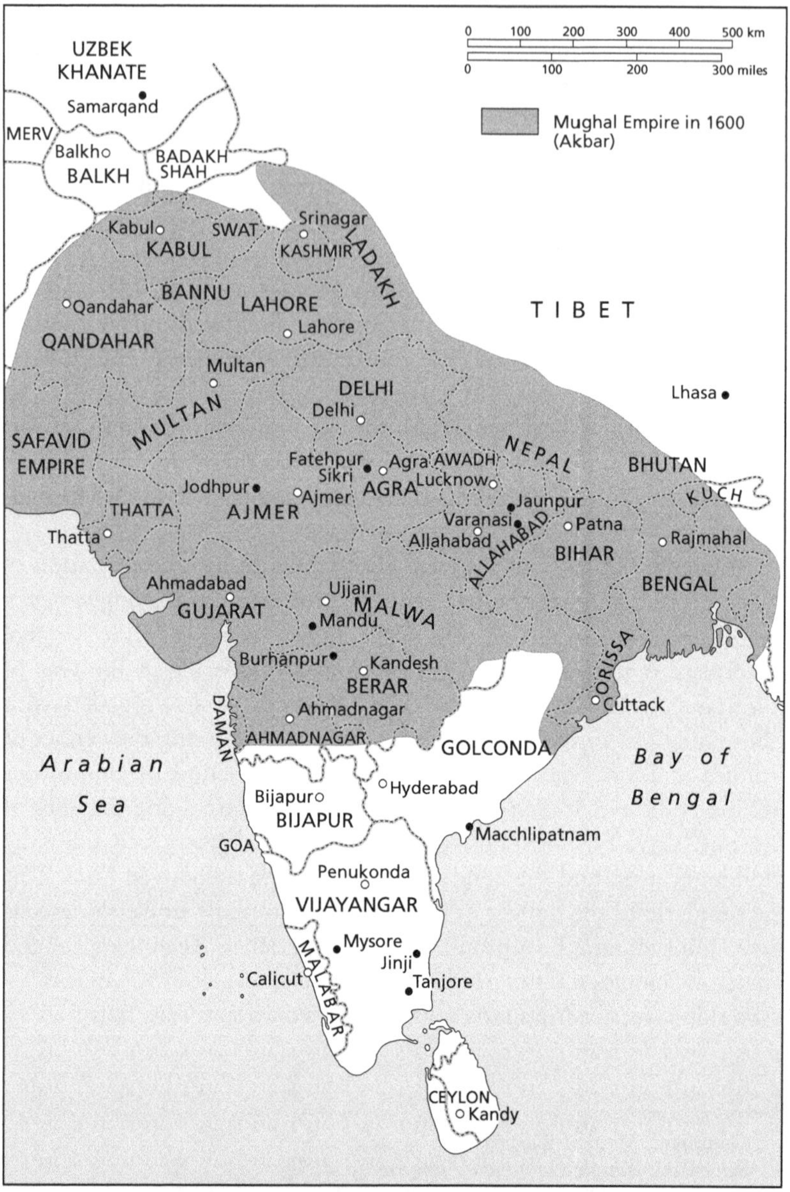

Figure 2.2 The Mughal Empire, *c.* 1600.

The Mughals as an empire

Was the Mughal realm an empire? To answer this, and therefore to help establish the diversity of the Indian Ocean system, it is necessary to answer the prior question of how an empire differs from what is now taken to be the norm in the international system, the sovereign state.

One of the clearest recent formulations on the subject holds that empires are characterized by rule through intermediaries, and by different allocations of authority between the imperial centre and the various constituent polities within the empire. According to this rendition, empires can be represented as a 'rimless hub and spoke system', with connections between the imperial metropole and the various subordinate polities, but not between the peripheral polities themselves.[54] David Lake's work on hierarchy in international politics holds that empires are defined by the high level of authority that a superior polity wields over subordinate polities (which he terms protectorates) in both security and economic affairs.[55] Working from a constructivist point of view, Reus-Smit comes up with a broadly similar definition: 'Empires are hierarchies; their defining features are the asymmetrical distribution of power between the metropolitan state and peripheral polities, and the unequal distribution of social powers between metropolitan "citizens" and colonial subjects.'[56] A further definition again brings out similar elements in speaking of 'parcellated sovereignty . . . by which we mean a polycentric polity in which a centre holds together and dominates subordinate, multi-ethnic polities with which it shares power'.[57]

Imperial relations are held together by a mix of coercion and legitimacy. International and domestic politics become blurred within

[54] Nexon and Wright, 'What's at Stake in the American Empire Debate?'

[55] Lake, *Hierarchy in International Relations*, pp. 52–3.

[56] Reus-Smit, 'Struggles for Individual Rights', p. 216; for other constructivist discussions of empire, see also J. Donnelly, 'Sovereign Inequalities and Hierarchy in Anarchy: American Power and International Society', *European Journal of International Relations* 12:2 (2006), pp. 139–70; J. Donnelly, 'Rethinking Political Structures: From "Ordering Principles" to "Vertical Differentiation" – and Beyond', *International Theory* 1:1 (2009), pp. 49–68; J. Hobson and J. C. Sharman, 'The Enduring Place of Hierarchy in World Politics: Tracing the Social Logics of Hierarchy and Political Change', *European Journal of International Relations* 11:1 (2005), pp. 63–98.

[57] L. I. Rudolph and S. H. Rudolph, 'Federalism as State Formation in India: A Theory of Shared Sovereignty', *International Political Science Review* 31:5 (2010), p. 557.

empires, as there is no clear, sharp border that separates the empire from foreign polities. Like states, empires do not acknowledge any higher authority. Unlike states, however, there is an explicit denial of the principle of sovereign equality, with empires having a hierarchical authority structure in which subordinate polities defer to imperial authority. Subordinate, vassal or suzerain territories are thus the flip-side of empire: actors within the international system that nevertheless acknowledge superior authority, rather than just being administrative or constitutional divisions of sovereign states which are confined to domestic politics. Empires may or may not extend recognition to other empires as equals. The Habsburgs, Ottomans and Chinese styled themselves as rulers of the world, or at least polities superior to any other.[58]

There is thus a rough working consensus on the features of an empire, and on how empires differ from states. These centre on the exclusion of any higher authority but receiving deference from other polities, the creation of a hierarchical structure, and the absence of a sharp division between internal and external political relations. As such, 'empire' is not just a synonym for a big and powerful state, but a qualitatively different form of unit in the international system. Empires were not only the dominant actors within the international system in the early modern period, but, as Reus-Smit points out, they were the most important form outside the North Atlantic core until after 1945.[59]

Given the characteristics of empire described above, do the Mughals fit the template? The Mughal emperor acknowledged no superiors, or even equals, and claimed to rule the world, having inherited the mantle of 'Lord of the Auspicious Conjunction' from Timur.[60] The Mughal word for foreign country was 'province' (*wilayet*).[61] The Mughals did not have a conception of definite borders. Once again, the linguistic convention is suggestive, with the word for frontier (*marz*) referring to an area rather than a dividing line.[62] The centre of authority was very much the person of the emperor himself, with the conception being that authority radiated from the emperor and petered out, though never definitely terminated, around the limits of the Mughals' logistical

[58] Richards, *The Mughal Empire*; Subrahmanyam, 'A Tale of Three Empires'.
[59] Reus-Smit, 'Struggles for Individual Rights', p. 212.
[60] M. Alam and S. Subrahmanyam, 'Introduction', in M. Alam and S. Subrahmanyam (eds.), *The Mughal State 1526–1750* (Delhi: Oxford University Press, 1998), p. 17.
[61] Gommans, *Mughal Warfare*, p. 20. [62] *Ibid.*, p. 15.

range.[63] This radial conception of authority was not static, in that the imperial court was a vast procession that maintained authority by travelling a circuit of the imperial domains. Taking on the dimensions of a city in motion, the imperial court comprised 60,000 cavalry, 100,000 infantry, 50,000 camels and 3,000 elephants, perhaps half a million people in all, supplied by the accompanying treasury that in the late 1600s held 28,000 pounds of gold and 56,000 pounds of silver.[64] The purpose of this peripatetic capital was to maintain order among subordinate polities.[65] As can be imagined, the sheer scale of the emperor's forces acted as a powerful inducement to loyalty.

In addition, the Mughal rulers cultivated an elaborate series of rituals to elevate and sustain imperial prestige, overawe their subordinates and establish their legitimacy among them. These ranged from a daily viewing of the emperor, to giving away his weight in precious metals and other rarities on his birthday.[66] The most important of the Mughals' integrative practices was the symbolic incorporation of Mughal vassals through their attendance and participation in ceremonial rituals at the imperial court. Compelling regular attendance of his lieutenants at court provided the emperor with an efficient means of maintaining surveillance over his most powerful (and thus most dangerous) clients.[67] Beyond this instrumental function, the court offered a public space in which the emperor and his vassals could ritualistically reaffirm the asymmetric relations of benevolence and obedience that bound them together. At court, imperial clients would proclaim their undying loyalty as the Emperor's 'slaves', and in return receive the 'honour robe', a garment that had been brushed against the emperor's body.[68] In this manner, 'Court rituals culminated in the symbolic incorporation of the servant into the body of his royal master.'[69] These and other elaborate practices of tributary gift exchange and court ceremonial reinforced a key aspect of court ideology – that 'Royalty [was] a light from god', the divine aura invested in the emperor capable of transcending the

[63] Richards, *The Mughal Empire*, p. 12.
[64] Gommans, *Mughal Warfare*, pp. 105–8; Richards reports smaller but still impressive figures, *The Mughal Empire*, p. 42.
[65] Tambiah, 'Profiling the Mughal Empire', p. 380.
[66] Richards, *The Mughal Empire*, pp. 47–9; Streusand, *Islamic Gunpowder Empires*, pp. 248–9.
[67] Tambiah, 'Profiling the Mughal Empire', p. 380.
[68] *Ibid.*, p. 377.
[69] Richards, *The Mughal Empire*, p. 49.

otherwise insuperable differences in creed, caste and ethnicity that divided the empire's constituent communities.[70]

Through their rituals,

> in the process of expansion in the seventeenth century, the Mughals came to be seen in all of the subcontinent as the only true source of sovereignty, the only 'sovereign idea' as it were. Even the Marathas, whose power *de facto* may have exceeded that of any Mughal military force in the eighteenth century, continued to work largely behind a Mughal facade, as indeed did the English East India Company in Bengal and Hindustan after 1765.[71]

The strength of Mughal imperial legitimacy thus lasted long after their military power had waned.[72] Importantly, and despite the fact that the Mughals themselves were Muslim, the imperial court was a highly diverse assemblage, with many of the most favoured courtiers and office-holders being Hindus. Thus in the early seventeenth century there were 126 Persian *mansabdars* (high officials, explained below), 103 Central Asians, 65 Indian Muslims, 26 Afghans as well as 90 Hindus.[73] The official religious policy of the empire was 'peace with all'. In keeping with this book's emphasis on the importance of improvised localizing practices to span cultural differences, significant elements of Mughal imperial ritual were taken from Hindu cosmology.[74]

For most of its history, the empire expanded by a process of incorporating polities, whose rulers then acknowledged Mughal supremacy, rather than through the outright destruction of enemies.[75] Even those local rulers defeated by the Mughals in battle often had the option of retaining their post, subject to paying tribute to the emperor, reading his name at Friday prayers, minting coins in his image, and attending court to participate in the rituals of obeisance. If anything, the ritual submission may have been more important to the Mughals than the tribute.[76] For example, in 1569, Emperor Akbar besieged the capital of the small Hindu domain of Bundi. After the Mughal artillery breached the walls, the ruler of Bundi opened negotiations which ended with him remaining in place, but paying taxes to and formally acknowledging

[70] Tambiah, 'Profiling the Mughal Empire', p. 377.
[71] Alam and Subrahmanyam, 'Introduction', p. 33.
[72] F. Hassan, *State and Locality in Mughal India: Power Relations in Western India c. 1572–1730* (Cambridge University Press, 2004), p. 48.
[73] Richards, *The Mughal Empire*, p. 145. [74] *Ibid.*, p. 39.
[75] Hassan, *State and Locality in Mughal India*, p. 22.
[76] Bose, *A Hundred Horizons*, p. 70.

Akbar's position as supreme authority.[77] Mughal military commanders were known to sponsor their defeated opponents' entry into the imperial court, enhancing the process of incorporation of subordinated polities, and perhaps cultivating a useful protégé for the commander in question.[78]

Speaking of the relationships with subordinates, historians like Bose have noted how 'The Mughal imperial centre, like its Ottoman and Safavid counterparts, had always aspired to be the repository of the highest level of sovereignty, leaving room for negotiating the terms of imperial unity with a plethora of local and regional governments.'[79] He continues that these empires were defined by 'looser, cascading political structures and espoused layered and shared sovereignty with lower-level leaders'.[80] A study of Mughal rule in Gujarat stresses that 'Imperial authority was established and maintained through a dynamic, ever-expanding and inclusive co-sharing of sovereignty with an increasing number of local intermediaries.'[81] Similarly, in conceptualizing the Mughal Empire as a gigantic 'galactic confederacy', anthropologist Stanley Tambiah has described a behemoth polity 'ringed on the north-west by independent tribal polities, in the south by independent kingdoms, and [with] much of its internal territory in the indirect rule of rajas, whose military capacity was indispensable to contain competitive challenges'.[82] Finally, a contemporary mid-seventeenth-century observer described how 'The empire of the Great Mogol [sic] comprehends several nations, over which he is not absolute master. Most of them still retain their own peculiar chiefs or sovereigns, who obey the Mogol or pay him tribute only by compulsion.'[83]

In particular, the empire relied on the institution of the *mansabdars* and *zamindars*. The *mansabdars*, numbering 150 when first formally established in the 1570s, later growing to over 700 by the close of seventeenth century, were allocated the revenues for a particular piece of land in return for supplying a set number of cavalrymen for the imperial army. Unlike feudal arrangements in Europe, however,

[77] Streusand, *Islamic Gunpowder Empires*, p. 257.
[78] Gommans, *Mughal Warfare*, p. 90. [79] Bose, *A Hundred Horizons*, p. 45.
[80] *Ibid.*, p. 70. [81] Hassan, *State and Locality in Mughal India*, p. 43.
[82] S. J. Tambiah, 'What did Bernier Actually Say? Profiling the Mughal Empire', *Contributions to Indian Sociology* 32:2 (1998), p. 380.
[83] Quoted in S. Subrahmanyam, 'The Mughal State: Structure or Process? Reflections on Recent Western Historiography', *Indian Economic and Social History Review* 29:3 (1992), p. 291.

mansabdars were rotated around the empire, rather than holding a permanent, heritable fief.[84] In this regard there were close similarities with the Ottoman and Safavid Empires.[85] Although their forces owed loyalty to the *mansabdar* in a personal capacity rather than to the emperor, imperial prestige, generosity and power proved sufficient to make this system work in providing the bulk of the imperial army until the eighteenth century.

Another bulwark of the system was the *zamindars*. Something akin to a local gentry stratum, the *zamindars* collected agricultural tax from one or more villages, retaining a share for themselves, but passing the majority on to imperial officials.[86] Unlike the *mansabdars*, the *zamindars* remained the masters of one area, rather than being moved around. *Zamindars* also maintained their own personal military forces, and although officially their commanders were imperial appointees, these troops were exempt from imperial call-up unless the fighting took place in the *zamindar*'s local area. As Streusand notes, 'From one perspective, then, the empire was actually a series of small *zamindar* principalities that paid tribute to the imperial centre.'[87]

It is important to note that historians disagree with each other about how to best describe the Mughal realm.[88] In trying to separate empire from state the terminology is often confusing. Thus John Richards begins his book *The Mughal Empire* with the sentence: 'The Mughal empire was one of the largest centralized states known in pre-modern world history.'[89] Two other leading historians on the subject routinely refer to the Mughals' empire, but entitle their co-authored book *The Mughal State*.[90] In his article 'The Mughals as a Patrimonial-Bureaucratic Empire', Stephen Blake interchangeably uses the term 'patrimonial-bureaucratic state'.[91] (Of course readers can see the same tendency to

84 Richards, *The Mughal Empire*, pp. 24–5, 63–8.
85 R. Murphey, *Ottoman Warfare 1500–1700* (New Brunswick, NJ: Rutgers University Press, 1999).
86 Richards, *The Mughal Empire*, pp. 79–88.
87 Streusand, *Islamic Gunpowder Empires*, p. 208.
88 Subrahmanyam, 'The Mughal State'; Hassan, *State and Locality in Mughal India*, pp. 1–3 and 32–3; Richards, *The Mughal Empire*, pp. 1–3; Streusand, *Islamic Gunpowder Empires*, pp. 205–10; Alam and Subrahmanyam, 'Introduction'.
89 Richards, *The Mughal Empire*, p. 1.
90 Alam and Subrahmanyam, *The Mughal State*.
91 S. Blake, 'The Mughals as a Patrimonial-Bureaucratic Empire', *Journal of the Royal Asiatic Society* 39:1 (1979), pp. 77–99.

use 'empire' and 'state' as synonyms in the titles of the works cited on the Estado da Índia too.) International Relations scholars have an equivalent bad habit of using the word 'state' to refer first to those polities with the particular features of the sovereign state discussed above, but second as a catch-all term for any unit in any international system. The confusion of terms that results is one of the reasons why International Relations as a field has done such a poor job of conceiving, let alone explaining, international systems apart from those comprising sovereign states under anarchy.[92] Yet despite their tendency to use empire and state as synonyms, historians nevertheless agree on the basic features of how the Mughals organized their authority, administration and military forces.

Based on the evidence above, the Mughals' realm is a close fit with the template of empire. Both those working from a rationalist and from a constructivist perspective are reasonably agreed concerning the defining features of empire, and how these set this form of polity apart from the sovereign state. The consensus among historians is that the Mughal authority was organized in a layered, cascading fashion. The Mughal armies were a combination of a small minority of troops and the artillery train under the direct control of the emperor, tribal allies from the frontiers, the *mansabdar* troops and local *zamindar* forces, with each element drawing on the massive South and Central Asian military labour markets. The contrast whereby the Portuguese forces were organized in a unified direct military chain of command is readily apparent.

Explaining European entry into the Indian Ocean region – contesting the orthodoxy of the 'military revolution'

Having established the Portuguese Estado da Índia and the Mughals as exemplars of two distinct polity forms, one approximating the sovereign state and the other very clearly an example of empire, we now proceed to an examination of how these actors interrelated as interaction between them increased. We begin by contesting the most traditionally popular explanation – the so-called 'military revolution' thesis. The thesis that the dominance of the sovereign state and European

92 D. A. Lake, 'New Sovereignty in International Relations', paper presented at the 98th American Political Science Association Conference, Boston, 29 August–1 September 2002, p. 38; Spruyt, *The Sovereign State and its Competitors*, p. 1.

expansion more generally were both primarily the result of military superiority is most succinctly put by Geoffrey Parker, the leading exponent of early modern 'military revolution' historiography: 'the key to the Westerners' success in creating the first truly global empires between 1500 and 1750 depended upon precisely those improvements in the ability to wage war which have been termed "the military revolution"'.[93] In Europe this revolution is said to have reflected complex political dynamics, rather than just advances in technology in isolation. New tactics and weapons necessitated larger armies, correspondingly larger amounts of money, and thus a more intrusive and developed administrative apparatus. The debate over the military revolution in Europe and more generally is far too extensive to be recapitulated here.[94] But nevertheless this literature does relate to vitally important questions for our study. For while the account at the heart of this book privileges the role of ideational and cultural factors in explaining the formation and stabilization of a diverse regional system jointly comprising European, African and Asian polities, the orthodoxy puts far more emphasis on material factors, especially superior European technology.[95] As noted previously, this historical view similarly underpins the default explanation in the field of International Relations for European expansion and the current dominance of the sovereign state. More specifically, it also indirectly informs implicit realist accounts for heterogeneous international systems, from which we distinguish our own argument. Realist explanations for diversity stress asymmetric military specialization as the key to polity variation. Although they could potentially be marshalled in the Indian Ocean context through an emphasis on Europeans' specialization in blue-water naval warfare, this thesis obscures the ideational underpinnings of European expansion.

Even before their period of complete domination in the nineteenth and the first half of the twentieth century, Europeans achieved notable successes in capturing and holding pivotal strong points across the

[93] Parker, *The Military Revolution*, p. 4.

[94] See C. J. Rogers (ed.), *The Military Revolution Debate: Readings on the Military Transformation of Early Modern Europe* (Boulder, CO: Westview, 1995).

[95] C. M. Cipolla, *Guns, Sails, and Empires: Technological Innovation and the Early Phases of European Expansion* (New York: Pantheon, 1965); W. H. McNeill, *The Pursuit of Power: Technology, Armed Force and Society since AD 1000* (Oxford: Blackwell, 1982).

whole of the Indian Ocean littoral, and overawing or coercing a range of small and medium-sized local powers. They did so thousands of miles from their home base, and with only tiny military forces more often numbering in the hundreds than the thousands. Illustrating this disparity, in the seventeenth century Portugal and the Netherlands had total populations of around 2 million, England around 5 million, and the Ottoman Empire 25 million, while the Mughals had a population of 100–120 million.[96] Even relatively minor polities like the sultanate of Mataram in Java might have had a similar population as the Netherlands and Portugal.[97] Unlike in the Americas, local polities were not decimated by epidemics of new diseases; in fact, in Africa the Europeans were far more susceptible to African diseases than vice versa. So how did the Europeans enjoy such success?

For Parker and many others, in sub-Saharan Africa and South-East Asia locals were unable to emulate Western technology, especially firearms (which of course are originally a prominent example of Eastern technology), together with cannon-armed sailing ships and advanced fortifications.[98] Among the Muslim great powers, which did have more or less the same technology in cannons and other gunpowder weapons, Parker sees a failure to successfully emulate Western military institutions, particularly close-order infantry drill and volley fire.[99] Even for Parker, however, such infantry tactics were first practised in India only from 1746 (by the French), so this does not explain the preceding 250 years.

Opposing Parker's account of how Western expansion was above all driven by a pronounced military superiority is a revisionist view that has been most eloquently put by Jeremy Black.[100] He critiques the work of his fellow historians in ways that parallel this book's criticisms of much International Relations scholarship:

> The central conceptual problem with military history is how to acknowledge, appreciate and analyze its diversity. This problem stems from the linked

[96] Richards, *The Mughal Empire*, p. 1; Pearson, 'Merchants and States', p. 68; Subrahmanyam, 'A Tale of Three Empires', p. 84.

[97] M. C. Ricklefs, *War, Culture and the Economy in Java, 1677–1726* (London: Allen and Unwin, 1993), p. 5.

[98] For example, Cipolla, *Guns, Sails and Empires*; McNeill, *The Pursuit of Power*; Glete, *Warfare at Sea*.

[99] Parker, *Military Revolution*, p. 136.

[100] Among many other works, see J. Black, *War and the World: Military Power and the Fate of Continents* (New Haven, CT: Yale University Press, 1998); J. Black, *Rethinking Military History* (London: Routledge, 2004).

characteristics of the presentation of the subject in western work, with its tendency first to focus largely, if not exclusively, on western developments, and secondly to consider those elsewhere in terms of western paradigms and the interaction of non-western powers with the west, these latter two factors being closely entwined.[101]

In a further important parallel with the argument presented here, Black goes on to note that a crucial factor in explaining Western expansion was the ability to reach compromises whereby locals endorsed the legitimacy of new arrangements. More generally, Black cautions that:

> Across the world, the notion of effectiveness was framed and applied in terms of dominant cultural and social patterns. The analysis latent in most military history, which assumes some mechanistic search for efficiency and a maximization of force driven by a form of Social Darwinism, does violence to the complex process by which interests in new methods interacted with powerful elements of continuity; it also overlooks the manner in which efficiency was culturally constructed, and a lack of clarity as to what defined effectiveness in force, structure, operational method or tactics.[102]

More specifically, revisionists emphasize that an 'Asian military revolution' in China had already introduced the most important purported innovations of the European variety several centuries earlier, that the technological gap between Western and local forces was essentially trivial, that Europeans were as likely to learn from locals as the other way around, and, finally, that differences in styles of warfare reflected local adaptations to geography, politics or culture, rather than indicating 'backwardness'.[103] These accounts further stress the importance of the Europeans' indigenous allies in winning wars, a testament to diplomacy over military might as such. In a caveat that once more very much applies to International Relations literature, these scholars caution against the tendency to read the supremacy of European militaries in the nineteenth century back into the previous era.

101 J. Black, 'A Wider Perspective: War Outside the West', in G. Mortimer (ed.), *Early Modern Military History1450–1815* (Houndmills: Palgrave Macmillan, 2004), p. 212.

102 J. Black, *Rethinking Military History* (Abingdon: Routledge, 2004), p. 169.

103 See Lorge, *Asian Military Revolution*; Ricklefs *War, Culture and the Economy in Java*; M. W. Charney, *Southeast Asian Warfare 1300–1900* (Leiden: Brill, 2004); J. K. Thornton, *Warfare in Atlantic Africa 1500–1800* (London: Routledge, 1999); Gommans and Kolff, *Warfare and Weaponry in South Asia 1000–1800*.

How do these competing historical visions relate to the Portuguese entry into the Indian Ocean region? Although they did score some spectacular military success in the region, like the initial capture of Hormuz and Malacca, the Portuguese also suffered important losses against local African and Asian forces, including the capture of advanced and extensive European-style *trace italienne* fortifications.[104] In addition, they carefully avoided challenging the Mughals, based on a realistic appreciation of their chances against such a formidable foe. Despite their naval strength, the Portuguese were never able to execute their programme of religious vandalism in the Arabian Peninsula, thanks to the strength of the Ottomans. The key stronghold of Hormuz was captured from the Portuguese by the Persians in 1622, though the latter enjoyed some support from the English. In Ceylon, the raja of Kandy inflicted a major defeat on the Portuguese in 1630 during one of their rare inland expeditions. The Portuguese were defeated by the Omanis when the latter captured Muscat in 1650, and again when the Omanis successfully besieged Fort Jesus in Mombasa in 1698, while around the same time the Portuguese were driven out of the Zimbabwe Plateau by local Shona warriors following another atypical inland incursion. Goa itself was only saved from a Hindu Maratha army by a Mughal intervention in 1683, while the Marathas captured several other Portuguese settlements between 1737 and 1740. Even at the height of their power in the sixteenth century, 'The Portuguese knew from many military reverses suffered in Africa, the Red Sea, India, and Indonesia that they were too weak on land to defend a determined enemy assault. It was necessary to reach an agreement with local rulers and merchants that would allow them to hold on to their early commercial and territorial gains.'[105]

Even the most dedicated revisionists, however, admit that Western naval forces were clearly superior to those of local powers, or even the Ottomans, both when it came to fighting other ships and in projecting power onto land through bombarding ports and fortifications with their ships' iron cannons.[106] And of course without innovations in

[104] J. Black, 'On Diversity and Military History', in D. A. Yerxa (ed.), *Recent Themes in Military History: Historians in Conversation* (Columbia: University of South Carolina Press, 2009).

[105] Chaudhuri, *Trade and Civilisation in the Indian Ocean*, p. 78.

[106] Cipolla, *Guns, Sails and Empires*; Andrade, *Lost Colony*; Charney, *Southeast Asian Warfare*; Black, 'War Outside the West'; A. Clulow, 'European Maritime

boat-building and navigation the Europeans would not have been able to round the Cape and enter the Indian Ocean at all. Might naval technology provide the materialist answer to European expansion, consistent with realist emphases on asymmetric military specialization as a possible explanation for polity diversity? If so, does this not make the discussion of beliefs about rightful authority and the proper ends of rulers' activities a moot point?

Here the answer relates to the cultural determinants of actors' preferences, determinants that are not easily encompassed in traditionally materialist and realist explanatory models. Asians and Africans did not 'fail' to 'arm the seas' in pursuit of control of maritime trade in the manner of the Europeans; they simply did not see this as an appropriate or even efficient course of action. The same goes for trans-oceanic expansion. For Black and for Jan Glete, writing about the 'failure' of major powers like the Mughals to develop a blue-water navy is simply an ethnocentric assumption that all powers should follow the same path trodden by Europeans. These historians explain the absence of transcontinental conquest by non-Western powers like the Mughals and others by the fact that these were culturally, economically and politically land-based powers. Certainly there was nothing that culturally prohibited Muslim or other non-Western powers from building powerful ocean-going navies. The Chinese made well-known expeditions across the length of the Indian Ocean as far as East Africa in the fifteenth century on a scale that dwarfed those of the Europeans.[107] The 'failure' of the Chinese to formally take control of maritime trade routes or set up a colonial empire on the European model clearly was not for lack of material capacity or technology. Instead it reflected a political disinclination to do so. Likewise, in the seventeenth and eighteenth centuries the Omanis built a navy sufficient to drive the Portuguese out of the north of East Africa, while the sultan of Aceh also built a powerful gun-armed navy.[108] These instances of indigenous naval innovation were highly anomalous for the region. They nevertheless illustrate that the far more common Afro-Asian disinclination to pursue this path arose from political choices filtered through cultural

Violence and Territorial States in Early Modern Asia, 1600–1650', *Itinerario* 33:3 (2009), pp. 72–94; Glete, *Warfare at Sea*, pp. 79–80.

[107] Glete, *Warfare at Sea*, pp. 76–7.

[108] Chaudhuri, *Trade and Civilisation in the Indian Ocean*, p. 66; Glete, *Warfare at Sea*, p. 82.

preferences, rather than reflecting any innate incapacity to emulate introduced European military innovations.

Local rulers in East Africa, South and South-East Asia were almost uniformly puzzled by Portuguese demands for monopolies, and for the exclusion of Muslim and other European traders. Across the region the norm was that ports were open to all merchants.[109] Bose notes that pre-colonial polities generally created certain autonomous spaces for the inhabitants of port cities.[110] Some speculate that the Portuguese enterprise in the East might in fact have been significantly more profitable had they integrated into existing local patterns of free trade, rather than seeking to impose control.[111] This speculation aside, the novelty of Portuguese thalassocratic ambitions when introduced to the traditionally open Indian Ocean region cannot be overstated. How were the Portuguese successfully integrated into the region, despite their violent and unorthodox maritime goals?

Compatible preferences and regional polity diversity after 1500

Given the overwhelming superiority of the Mughals in military force and economic resources over the Portuguese, how did the latter successfully enter the region and survive in South Asia alongside this mighty neighbour? Much the same question can be asked of the English and Dutch presence a hundred years after the Portuguese first arrived. Explaining this co-existence of the puny Europeans with the Mughal superpower relies on establishing in greater detail the Mughals' indifference to maritime affairs. Mughals and Europeans could co-exist because of the coincidence whereby each side had different but compatible preferences and goals, and thus rarely came into competition. This situation is fundamentally different from the zero-sum struggle for power between states that is assumed to describe the essence of all international systems according to realists in International Relations.

109 K. N. Chaudhuri, 'Reflections on the Organizing Principle of Pre-Modern Trade', in Tracy, *The Political Economy of Merchant Empires*, p. 439; Bose, *A Hundred Horizons*, p. 25; Chaudhuri, *Trade and Civilisation in the Indian Ocean*, p. 14.

110 Bose, *A Hundred Horizons*, p. 70.

111 Tracy, 'Introduction'; Pearson, *Port Cities and Intruders*; Pearson, *The Indian Ocean*.

The Mughals wanted for little, and raised the large majority of their taxes from the agricultural surplus of South Asia, at that time one of the most productive areas in the world.[112] Customs duties from seaborne trade provided a negligible share of Mughal revenue,[113] while the Portuguese did not cause any interruption in the supply of foreign goods desired by the Mughal aristocracy. The Mughal Empire had a structural trade surplus with the rest of the world.[114] In security terms, the Portuguese were regarded as unthreatening. Portuguese gains 'were mostly made at the expense of rulers who had had no reason so far to defend their trading ports with strong military forces ... No strong Asian power at the time, whether in India, the Middle East, or China, considered the Portuguese to be a serious threat to the existing balance of power.'[115] The Portuguese generally understood their precarious position: in 1539 the viceroy of the Estado da Índia wrote to the king that peace with the local powers in India depended on the latter understanding that the Portuguese would continue to confine themselves to a maritime domain.[116] Confirming this point of view, one sixteenth-century Mughal evaluation of the Portuguese concluded that 'They are very good at using firearms (*tufang*), and they are particularly brave on ships and in the water. But in contrast to this they are not so brave on land.'[117] Keen to avoid a confrontation, the Portuguese exempted Mughals from paying for their ship passes.

The Europeans' maritime ambitions were sometimes encouraged by local powers: 'Major rulers, such as the Mughals in India or the Safavids in Persia, usually co-operated with the Europeans who were regarded for a long time as useful partners on the maritime fringes of their essentially land-based empires.'[118] Emperor Aurangzeb referred to 'the Christian Lions of the Sea' for whom 'God has allotted that Unstable Element for their Rule'.[119] Gommans writes that the Portuguese were seen by the Mughals as a type of 'unpaid servants': 'for the Mughals, the maritime activities of the Europeans were certainly not a matter of equal

112 Richards, *The Mughal Empire*, pp. 68–76.
113 E. Tagliacozzo, 'Trade, Production and Incorporation: The Indian Ocean in Flux, 1600–1900', *Itinerario* 26:1 (2002), p. 85.
114 Gommans, *Mughal Warfare*, p. 163.
115 Chaudhuri, *Trade and Civilisation in the Indian Ocean*, pp. 78–9.
116 Subrahmanyam, 'Holding the World in Balance', p. 1373.
117 Quoted in Subrahmanyam, 'Taking Stock of the Franks', p. 87.
118 Glete, *Warfare at Sea*, p. 77.
119 Quoted in Pearson, *The Indian Ocean*, p. 116.

partnership, but rather the result of the benevolence and generosity they had shown to a subordinate community'.[120] To the extent that the Europeans served a purpose at all for the Mughals, it was primarily as 'nomads (*khana da dush*) patrolling the seas', and suppressing piracy along the Indian coast.[121] In a similar vein, Lauren Benton observes: 'To insist that Europeans collaborate to pacify the pirate-ridden Indian Ocean was, in effect, to hold these powers to their jurisdictional claims over oceanic space.'[122] Secondarily, in introducing New World crops like tobacco and maize, European maritime activities also enriched the empire and boosted revenue to the central treasury, rather than posing any economic threat.[123] The resulting coincidence of interests between the Europeans and the Mughals was too tentative and improvised to be characterized as one of institutionalized complementarity. But the presence of interests that were at least generally compatible with one another was crucial in stabilizing the expanded diversity the Portuguese and Mughals brought with their entry into the region.

Aside from trade, fiscal and military concerns, the Mughals (as well as the Safavids in Persia) were temperamentally indifferent to maritime affairs. Emperor Akbar saw the sea once a third of the way through his forty-nine-year reign after the conquest of Gujarat and, curiosity satisfied, never bothered to repeat the experience.[124] Glory and prestige were won on land, especially in battle. The oft-quoted Mughal aphorism held that 'wars by sea are merchants' affairs, and no concern to the prestige of kings'.[125] Richards again emphasizes that 'the Timurid emperors never considered or pursued expansion by sea. The culture of seafaring was completely foreign to the Mughal elite.'[126] Perhaps the only exception to Mughal indifference here was the ability to complete the Hajj pilgrimage from the port of Surat in Gujarat. On the odd occasions where there was friction with the Portuguese (and later the English and Dutch) at sea, the Mughals proved amply capable of leveraging their terrestrial supremacy to ensure that Europeans respected their oceanic interests. Thus, in 1695, when an English vessel

120 Gommans, *Mughal Warfare*, p. 164. 121 *Ibid.*
122 Benton, 'Legal Spaces of Empire', p. 715.
123 Richards, *The Mughal Empire*, pp. 190 and 202–3.
124 Pearson, *The Indian Ocean*, p. 116.
125 Quoted in Chaudhuri, *Trade and Civilisation in the Indian Ocean*, p. 79; Tagliacozzo, 'The Indian Ocean in Flux', p. 85; Bose, *A Hundred Horizons*, pp. 44–5.
126 Richards, *The Mughal Empire*, p. 283.

seized the largest ship of the Mughal merchant fleet laden with precious goods and pilgrims returning from Mecca, the Mughals not only temporarily embargoed trade from English factories, but also demanded that English and Dutch ships henceforth send armed ships in convoys to protect Mughal shipping.[127]

It is important to repeat that there was nothing essential about Asian or Muslim polities and cultures that barred them from an interest in maritime trade, or navies and naval power projection. The feats of the Chinese, Omanis and Acehnese in the Indian Ocean have already been noted. Further afield, in 1592 a Japanese army of 160,000 was ferried across the sea to invade Korea, a naval feat unequalled by Europeans until the twentieth century.[128] Seaborne trade played a much more important economic role for the small coastal polities of the region, yet, as described earlier, in East Africa, South Asia and South-East Asia rulers adopted a laissez-faire attitude to merchants.[129] In their indifference to maritime matters, the Mughals – by dint of their sheer size – are of most importance in explaining how the European thalassocracies were able to insinuate themselves into the region, hence our stress on them in the preceding analysis. But this indifference, with some minor exceptions, was pervasive throughout the Indian Ocean, and proved a crucial condition of possibility for the expanded polity diversity that arose there after 1500.

Thus, in general, 'The conclusion has to be that Portugal's relations with major states around the Indian Ocean in the sixteenth century were mostly civil enough, in part because the maritime interests of the Portuguese seldom conflicted with the major interests and activities of these land-oriented states.'[130] The existence of compatible European and local preferences was key in explaining the coincidence of expanding interaction and increasing polity diversity that defined the region in the sixteenth century. This compatibility rested on a distinction between maritime and terrestrial powers, superficially supporting realist accounts of diversity arising from asymmetric military specialization. But this specialization rested on cultural foundations. This recognition is important not merely to understanding how diversity first emerged, but also (as we will see in Chapter 5) to explaining how it was

127 Benton, 'Legal Spaces of Empire', p. 714.
128 Lorge, *Asian Military Revolution*, p. 82.
129 Steinberg, *The Social Construction of the Ocean*, p. 46.
130 Pearson, *The Indian Ocean*, p. 132.

later reconfigured once these preferences shifted in the three centuries following the Europeans' initial intrusion into the region.

Conclusion

This chapter has argued that the Portuguese Estado da Índia was generally formed on a statist model, while the Mughals formed a classic empire. This judgement is premised first on drawing up rough working definitions of state and empire, and then matching the Portuguese and Mughal domains to these contrasting templates. Key evidence includes the way each related to external actors, their internal organization of authority and the way they structured their military and (in the Portuguese case) naval forces. These two very different polities managed to co-exist in the sixteenth century, and indeed long afterwards. The idea of compatible preferences between maritime networks and land-based empires sustaining continuing diversity is once again important in the next chapter in considering the company sovereigns and their interactions with the Mughals and other powers.

The Portuguese entry and survival within the region was much less due to a material military superiority, either in the narrow sense of better technology, or in the broader sense of the purported institutional advantages provided by the sovereign state over rival forms. Although technological advances were important in allowing the Portuguese to round the Cape of Good Hope, it was the different and compatible preferences of Europeans and local polities that were crucial. The following chapter is devoted to exploring the third major polity type in the early modern Indian Ocean international system, the Dutch and English company sovereigns that entered the region at the turn of the seventeenth century.

3 *The expansion of diversity and competition under heteronomy, 1600–1650*

The preceding chapter introduced two of the early modern Indian Ocean's key players: the Portuguese Estado da Índia, spread across the maritime littoral of the whole region, and the fantastically rich and powerful Mughal Empire, concentrated in the north and centre of the Indian subcontinent. This chapter is devoted to a different kind of actor, the company sovereign, represented by the English East India Company (EIC) and the Dutch East India Company (Vereenigde Oost-Indische Compagnie, abbreviated to VOC, literally United East India Company). These companies were profit-making private concerns that pioneered the modern corporate form, but also enjoyed prerogatives now conventionally regarded as the exclusive preserve of sovereign states, like making war and peace and conducting international diplomacy. As private–public hybrids without modern equivalents, different in their corporate form from both the statist Portuguese and imperial Mughal domains, these actors further accentuated the diversity of the Indian Ocean international system when they burst upon the scene from 1600.

The two companies transformed international politics and trade in the Indian Ocean. Built as the world's first joint stock and multinational company, the VOC 'smashed to pieces' the existing trade system, savaged the Portuguese domains, and sometimes employed near-genocidal levels of violence in consolidating its hold over the spice trade.[1] By the time the company eventually went bust in 1800 it dominated swathes of the archipelago that later became present-day Indonesia. In a recent on-line controversy about the most valuable company ever, the peak value of the VOC, put at 78 million Dutch guilders in 1637, is said to be equivalent to $7.4 trillion in inflation-adjusted 2012 dollars, larger by far than the value of any other publicly traded company.[2]

[1] Tracy 'Introduction', p. 3.

[2] http://scybites.wordpress.com/2013/03/11/most-valuable-companies-in-history-adjusted-for-inflation/ (accessed 19 July 2013).

If anything the impact of the English East India Company was even greater. Though at first lagging behind their Dutch counterparts, the EIC ultimately displaced the mighty Mughal Empire (albeit after the Mughals had declined for unrelated domestic reasons) as South Asia's pre-eminent power. At one time this private company ruled around a fifth of the planet's entire population, and earned more revenue than Britain itself.[3] As a concern with governing its growing domains came to supersede its focus on trading, the EIC was gradually bound by the British government, which ultimately ruled India via the imperial Raj. But rather than trace the whole arc of these two companies' rise and decline, this chapter is confined to the early part of their emergence and ascendancy, and the pursuit of three goals within the book's broader argument.

The first of these is to establish the distinctiveness of the company sovereigns in substantiating the claim that their entry into the region enhanced diversity in the Indian Ocean international system. To this end, we explain the origins and nature of the two companies, which despite their historical importance remain comparatively underexplored within International Relations. As public–private hybrids, their unique corporate form distinguished them from the statist model of the Portuguese. Despite their sovereign powers, the companies were neither states in their own right, nor simply extensions of their Dutch and English home states. At the same time, despite their penchant for indirect rule, neither did the companies match the classically imperial structure of the Mughals. Even to their contemporaries, the companies were hard to classify. Adam Smith referred to the EIC as a 'strange absurdity', while Edmund Burke later attacked the company as 'a state in the disguise of a merchant'.[4] Because this company sovereign form was so singular, the Indian Ocean international system thus became even more diverse in the seventeenth century than it was in the sixteenth. Harking back to the scholarship discussed in Chapter 2, this is exactly the opposite result to that predicted by conventional accounts, premised on the idea of the homogenizing effects of interaction and competition.

[3] D. Ciepley, 'Beyond Public and Private: Toward a Political Theory of the Corporation', *American Political Science Review* 107:1(2013), p. 139.
[4] Stern, *The Company-State*, p. 3.

The second task is to explain the institutional bases for the success of the two company sovereigns in absolute terms, but even more so relative to the statist Portuguese model. Western European historical experience primes us to expect that the 'precociously statist' Portuguese would dominate the companies, but in fact the Estado da Índia, was eclipsed, but never eliminated, by the Dutch in particular. In explaining the companies' success, part of the answer lies in the institutional advantages conferred by their hybrid company sovereign form. The VOC and the EIC were able to deploy the means of organized violence on land and especially at sea more effectively, consistently and efficiently through their in-house navies and armies, rather than depending on public or private third parties for these services. They were also better able to control radical fluctuations in the price of key commodities in Europe than the ad hoc private merchant partnerships that had preceded them. They could generally subordinate the short-term individual interests of shareholders to the long-term collective interests of the corporate enterprise, allowing for the more efficient use of capital. The crucial advantage the company sovereigns enjoyed vis-à-vis the Portuguese was being relatively better able to align the interests of their far-flung agents with that of the corporate principals based back in Europe. In contrast, by relying on a public monopoly on force and a relatively bureaucratic chain of command that generally excluded merchant interests, the Portuguese king's efforts to control local agents often had exactly the opposite effect. Key officials faced strong incentives to make private profits directly at the expense of the state, while Portuguese merchants often evaded the tax demands of the Estado da Índia, directly undermining the latter's military effectiveness.

The final goal is to explain why this strategic competition and these institutional features cannot be understood outside the ideational contexts that help constitute actors' purposes and strategies. Thus, once again we see that a vital condition of entry for the European company sovereigns was local indifference to their maritime ambitions. Europeans fought for different purposes from locals, and this manifested itself especially in the profit-obsessed company sovereigns, who even more than the Portuguese abjured large-scale territorial conquest. When they did exert influence on land, the companies favoured different forms of indirect rule as a means of maximizing influence and profit while minimizing administrative overheads. Yet the fact that indirect rule was more economical stemmed from Europeans' unwillingness and inability to replicate the legitimacy of local rulers, and so again a functional institutional response is a product of underlying beliefs and norms.

Relations between the Europeans tended to be more antagonistic than those between Europeans and local polities precisely because the companies and the Portuguese had similar preferences and sought the same goals. Unlike the different but compatible preferences that allowed for co-existence between the Europeans and the Mughals, the Dutch and English were every bit as concerned with controlling key ports and sea lanes as the Portuguese had been since King Manuel first dreamed of recapturing Jerusalem from the East. That the same preferences sparked fierce competition between the European thalassocracies supports our central theoretical point concerning how compatible preferences otherwise fostered durable diversity.

Lastly, we demonstrate that even the market forces driving European demand for Asian spices – the motive force that lured Europeans in the first place – were culturally conditioned, being quite literally a matter of taste and superstition. Spices that were fantastically valuable in Europe were worthless in China, while luxury commodities for the Chinese (like sea slugs) were often irrelevant to Europeans, Africans and South Asians. Demand and supply ultimately reflected cultural, rather than strictly economic, values. European purposes and strategies in war, methods of exerting political influence over locals, and commercial motivations for being in the Indian Ocean in the first place all rested on ideational foundations.

The company sovereigns: neither state nor empire, public nor private

If one of the main goals of this chapter is to establish the growing diversity of the Indian Ocean international system in the seventeenth century, then discerning the nature of the company sovereigns is central to our broader argument. Our first proposition is that the Dutch and English company sovereigns were neither states in their own right, nor were they simply extensions of the United Provinces of the Netherlands or of England. Instead, the companies were defined by their private character, yet nevertheless were also hybrid actors, thanks to their ability to exercise prerogatives normally reserved for governments.[5] Both enterprises were among the first ever examples of joint stock companies, and their boards maintained a strong focus on the bottom line, rather than seeking extensive territorial expansion (though this orientation began to change after 1750). Yet both companies maintained powerful naval and military forces, and had the authority to wage war, make treaties, administer criminal justice and establish colonies. Given that the Dutch and English East India Companies were the main drivers of European expansion in the Indian Ocean in the seventeenth and eighteenth centuries, and that these were not simply states or extensions of states, European expansion in the region thus cannot be explained by the superior military, fiscal or organizational properties of sovereign states that are said to account for the dominance this form achieved in Europe.[6] These points are substantiated first with reference to the VOC, and then to the EIC.

The origins and nature of the VOC

Dutch merchants began journeying around the Cape of Good Hope and into the Indian Ocean from 1597.[7] These voyages took place in the context of the long-running war between the United Provinces of the Netherlands and the Habsburg kings who ruled Spain and (until 1640) Portugal. As detailed in the previous chapter, the latter had for a hundred years previously claimed and sought to enforce a monopoly on all seaborne trade between Europe and the Indian Ocean. In these early Dutch expeditions to the Indian Ocean, a few investors from a certain region or city would put their capital into a single expedition, with all the capital and any profit distributed once the ships returned to

[5] C. R. Boxer, *The Dutch Seaborne Empire 1600–1800* (New York: Alfred Knopf, 1965); Steensgaard, *Carracks, Caravans and Companies*; L. Blussé and F. Gaastra (eds.), *Companies and Trade: Essays on Overseas Trading Companies During the Ancien Régime* (Leiden University Press, 1981); Tracy, *The Political Economy of Merchant Empires*; J. D. Tracy (ed.), *The Rise of Merchant Empires: Long Distance Trade in the Early Modern World 1350–1750* (Cambridge University Press, 1990); K. Ward, *Networks of Empire: Forced Migration in the Dutch East India Company* (Cambridge University Press 2008); Stern, *The Company-State.*

[6] Tilly, *Coercion, Capital and European States*; Spruyt, *The Sovereign State and its Competitors.*

[7] Boxer, *The Dutch Seaborne Empire*, p. 22.

Europe (if they returned).[8] A profusion of such expeditions began to erode profit margins on the spice trade. In response, merchants joined with the States General (the ruling body of the confederation of the seven provinces that jointly comprised the Netherlands) to issue a charter to a new United East India Company, formed from a merger of existing regional companies, together with additional capital from private investors. The Vereenigde Oost-Indische Compagnie was thus founded in 1602, two years after the EIC.

The charter entitled the VOC to a monopoly of all trade east of the Cape of Good Hope right through to the shores of the Americas for an initial period of twenty-one years, an arrangement that was subsequently renewed on a rolling basis. The company was granted a special exemption on the general prohibition on the export of specie. Unusually for the time, the liability of all those investing in the company was limited to the capital they had put in. This feature marked the origins of the limited legal liability for investors that is the defining characteristic of the modern corporation. The VOC was run by a board of seventeen directors (the Heeren XVII). Eight of the directors were from Amsterdam, with the remainder from the five smaller towns of Delft, Rotterdam, Enkhuizen, Middelburg and Hoorn. The directors quickly established their dominance over the general stockholders, refusing requests for audits and the publication of financial results. While the stockholders preferred large dividends to be paid early and often, the directors preferred to hold on to capital for reinvestment. Steensgaard regards the institutional ability to subordinate the short-term, individual interests of the stockholders to the long-term, collective interest of the company as a whole as the fundamental change fostered by the innovation of the joint stock form.[9] Rather than the loose partnerships established for one voyage, the new corporate form outlasted the individual owners.[10] It also reflected the beginnings of the idea of separating ownership from management.[11] At crucial moments the States General intervened on the side of the directors to overrule

[8] F. Gaastra, 'The Shifting Balance of Trade of the Dutch East India Company', in Blussé and Gaastra, *Companies and Trade*, pp. 47–69.

[9] Steensgaard, *Carrack, Caravans and Companies.*

[10] Boxer, *Dutch Seaborne Empire*; Steensgaard, *Carracks, Caravans and Companies*; P. W. Klein, 'The Origins of Trading Companies', in Blussé and Gaastra, *Companies and Trade*, pp. 17–28; Gaastra, 'Dutch East India Company'.

[11] Chaudhuri, *Trade and Civilisation in the Indian Ocean*, p. 82.

stockholders, and thus preserve this longer-term, collective orientation. The company's capital increasingly took on an air of permanence, rather than a temporary pooling of funds from individual merchants. Hence the VOC became the world's first joint stock company with limited liability, and the first multinational corporation.

Right from the start, however, the VOC combined essentially public functions with its private, profit-driven nature. Primary among the former were such fundamental sovereign prerogatives as the right to declare war and make peace with non-European powers, and conclude treaties with foreign polities. It could further administer civil and criminal justice, and coin its own money, while it was also responsible for religious instruction.[12] There was no right of appeal to the Netherlands for any criminal cases.[13] Backing up these legal entitlements, the VOC was allowed, or encouraged, to maintain its own substantial military and naval forces, and to establish fortresses and settlements. VOC strength in Asia grew from 40 ships and 5,000 men in 1608, to 150 ships and 15,000 men in 1644, to 200 ships and 30,000 men in 1700.[14] The position of governor-general was established in 1609, being located at Batavia (present-day Jakarta) from 1619 to co-ordinate the company's strategy in Asia, assisted by a twelve-man Council of the Indies.[15] This move was necessitated by the vast distance from Europe, in that communication from Amsterdam to Batavia took eighteen months, sometimes even longer.

From very early on, the VOC moved away from a laissez-faire trading position and defensive military posture and instead 'shifted to a single-minded focus on controlling the supply of key commodities, starting with fine spices'.[16] In the Spice Islands the aim was to become a monopsonistic purchaser of spices and a monopolistic seller of rice, controlling the price of each to turn the terms of trade against the local rulers and inhabitants.[17] This involved a succession of campaigns to capture Portuguese outposts in the Spice Islands, Malacca, fortresses on the east and west coasts of India, Ceylon, and later an outpost on the Cape of Good Hope.

The company's hybrid commercial–military nature was epitomized in a report from one of the company's most combative governor-generals,

[12] Ward, *Networks of Empire*, pp. 9–10. [13] *Ibid.*, p. 12.
[14] Boxer, *Dutch Seaborne Empire*, p. 69.
[15] Ricklefs, *War, Culture and the Economy in Java*.
[16] Tracy, 'Introduction', p. 6. [17] Boxer, *Dutch Seaborne Empire*, p. 99.

Jan Pieterszoon Coen, to the Heeren XVII in 1614: 'Your Honours should know by experience that trade in Asia must be driven and maintained under the protection and favour of Your Honours' own weapons, and that the weapons must be paid for by the profits from the trade; so that we cannot carry on trade without war nor war without trade.'[18] No mere rhetoric: in 1621 Dutch and Japanese VOC troops largely exterminated the population of the Banda Islands, selling the few remaining survivors into slavery, in order to secure a monopoly on nutmeg production. Tracy notes that 'In the Eastern seas, no European enterprise was more willing to resort to war to gain its objectives than the VOC.'[19] Coen had to be reminded by the directors that 'there is no profit at all in an empty sea, empty countries, and dead people'.[20] The VOC operated a system of passes for ships along the Portuguese lines, and engaged in the same sort of piracy and maritime violence that again brings to mind Tilly's analogy between early modern state-making and a protection racket.[21] For rather than engage in war for glory or extensive conquests, the innovation of the VOC was to subordinate the use of violence for the pursuit of profit.[22] The VOC was at the peak of its power around 1650 (i.e. about fifty years before that of the Mughal Empire). At this time it maintained outposts from Taiwan and Japan through the Spice Islands and Ceylon, to the west and east coasts of India and South Africa, before later being progressively displaced by the EIC in the eighteenth century.

As a matter of both law and practicality, the VOC can by no means be regarded as an extension of the Dutch state. In 1644 the VOC directors informed the States General that 'The places and strongholds which they had captured in the East Indies should not be regarded as national conquests, but as the private property of merchants, who were entitled to sell those places to whomsoever they wished, even if it was to

[18] *Ibid.*, p. 96. [19] Tracy, 'Introduction', p. 2.

[20] Quoted in J. Adams, 'Principals and Agents, Colonials and Company Men: The Decay of Colonial Control in the Dutch East Indies', *American Sociological Review* 61:1 (1996), p. 16.

[21] Tilly, 'War Making and State Making as Organized Crime', pp. 169–92; see also Pearson, 'Merchants and States', p. 79; T. B. Duncan, 'Niels Steensgaard and the Europe–Asia Trade of the Early Seventeenth Century', *Journal of Modern History* 47:3 (1975), p. 517; Chaudhuri, *Trade and Civilisation in the Indian Ocean*, p. 86.

[22] Steensgaard, *Carracks, Caravans and Companies*; North, 'Institutions, Transaction Costs, and the Rise of Merchant Empires', pp. 22–40.

the King of Spain, or to some other enemy of the United Provinces.'[23] The VOC and the government of the Netherlands often had important foreign policy differences. Even though the interests of the Netherlands would have been best served by an alliance with Portugal against Spain after the former regained its independence in 1640, the VOC fiercely resisted this possibility, afraid as it was of losing the opportunity to capture more of the Portuguese Estado da Índia. When the States General did sign a ten-year truce with Portugal in 1642, the VOC did its best to subvert this agreement in Asia. Though the VOC was largely independent of the States General, it did assist in wars by lending money and leasing ships to help the Dutch fight the English in Europe.[24] But in an age where both domestic and foreign private agents and even foreign rulers routinely provided financing for wars and complete military and naval units, this sort of collaboration was commonplace.[25]

The origins and nature of the EIC

Despite its later spectacular success, outshining even the VOC in the eighteenth century, the English company sovereign initially came off very much second-best to its Dutch competitors in the direct military competition over the Spice Islands. A presence along the Indian coast was something of a consolation prize for the English. Despite being formed two years earlier, the EIC lagged behind its Dutch counterpart in adopting the institutional innovation of the joint stock company, and it was initially much less well capitalized.[26] Although the EIC retained the same independent public–private hybrid form as the VOC, it had to work much harder to escape the demands of the English government compared to the Heeren XVII in relation to the Estates General.

The company received its charter from Queen Elizabeth I on New Year's Eve 1600, eight years after the first English ship had rounded the Cape of Good Hope. Like the VOC's founding document, the charter

[23] Boxer, *The Dutch Seaborne Empire*, p. 45.
[24] Pearson, 'Merchants and States'.
[25] J. Thomson, *Mercenaries, Pirates and Sovereigns: State-Building and Extraterritorial Violence in Early-Modern Europe* (Princeton University Press, 1994).
[26] Subrahmanyam, *The Portuguese Empire in Asia*, p. 223.

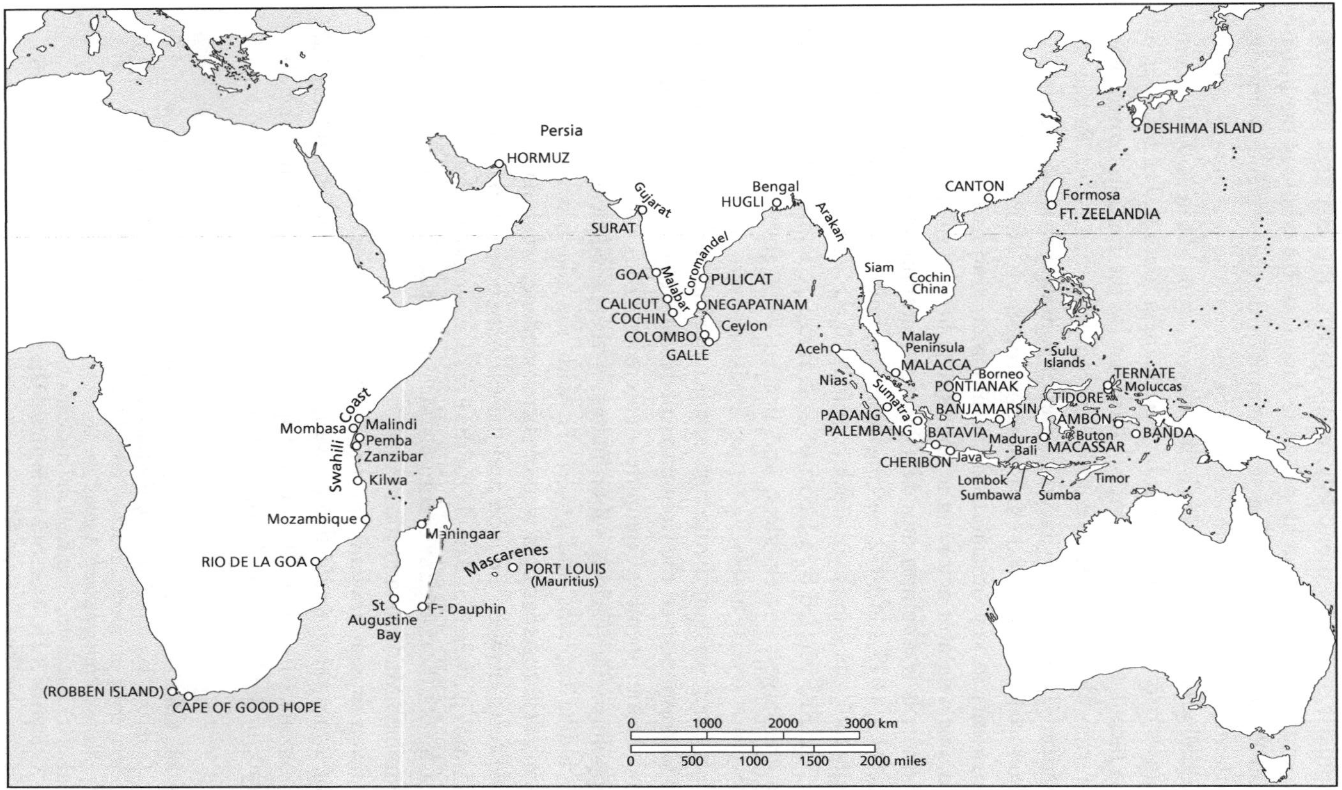

Figure 3.1 The Dutch East India Company's nodes in the Indian Ocean, *c.* 1700.

similarly granted a monopoly on all trade in the vast area extending from the Cape of Good Hope to the Americas, the whole of the Indian and Pacific Oceans. In fact the company's domain extended into the Atlantic as well, with the island of St Helena also a company colony. Initially the charter was for a fifteen-year term, but in 1607 the company's corporate life was put on a permanent footing. The EIC was by no means the first such entity chartered by the English crown, with charters also extended to companies trading in the Levant, Russia and Africa.[27] The company faced a series of political battles to maintain its monopoly position and expand its prerogatives, often involving large payments to key officials and the monarch, and as a result the EIC became a notable actor in the domestic politics of the era. The trading monopoly was compromised by the crown granting competing charters in 1604, 1617 and 1632, forcing the EIC to buy out its rivals.[28] The EIC only took the same joint stock character of the VOC in 1657.

The EIC was led by a Court of Committees, comprising twenty-four of the largest shareholders, and headed by a governor and deputy governor serving two-year terms. Decisions were taken unanimously. This group was sub-divided into smaller committees like the Committee of Correspondence, the Committee of Treasury, Committee of Shipping and the four-member Committee of Secrecy.[29] The Court of Committees appointed the various subordinates in the presidencies in the East, including captains and governors, with the administrative structure being held together by a web of correspondence wending its way back and forth between London and the various company outposts. There was no equivalent of Batavia for the EIC, one central headquarters in the East, with the company eventually maintaining separate presidencies in Bombay, Madras and Calcutta.

Even though England and the Netherlands were allies in Europe at the time, there was a fierce rivalry between the Dutch and English companies in the 1620s, as the latter tried to break into the spice trade in the Moluccas. Efforts between their respective states to impose

[27] See, for example, W. A. Pettigrew, *Freedom's Debt: The Royal African Company and the Politics of the Slave Trade 1672–1752* (Chapel Hill: University of North Carolina Press, 2013).

[28] Adams, 'Principals and Agents', p. 16.

[29] K. N. Chaudhuri, 'The English East India Company in the 17th and 18th Centuries: A Pre-Modern Multinational Organization', in Blussé and Gaastra, *Companies and Trade*, p. 38.

a settlement in the East whereby the two companies would share the spice trade while enjoying monopolies in their respective national markets often came to naught. The VOC expelled their English competitors from Pulo Run only a few years after the EIC had arrived. The concession was restored to the English, before eventually being exchanged for New Amsterdam, later New York. A more notorious incident occurred in 1623 when ten English, nine Japanese and one Portuguese employee of the EIC were convicted for treason against the Dutch company in a VOC court on the island of Ambon, after confessions were extracted by torture, and subsequently executed. The case became a source of considerable controversy back in Europe, and a recurring propaganda theme during the subsequent Anglo-Dutch wars.

An early joint military venture with the shah of Persia saw the EIC assist in driving the Portuguese from their stronghold in Hormuz in 1622, yet the company was largely excluded from the benefits of this success by Persians. To add insult to injury, both the English lord high admiral and the king asked for payment in lieu of spoils, despite the EIC maintaining that this had been a purely private venture.[30] The EIC made attempts to set up plantations in East Africa, with an unsuccessful venture in Madagascar in the late 1640s, while it also bid for trading posts on the Atlantic coast of Africa, though these were ultimately awarded to the Royal Africa Company instead.

If the EIC was chartered by the crown, can the company be said to have been merely a servant of the English state? For the purposes of our argument it is once more important to establish that the EIC was neither just an instrument of the English state nor a state itself.

From its earliest territorial holdings in Pulo Run in the Banda Islands of present-day Indonesia (from 1617), to Madras (from 1639), St Helena (1657), and Bombay (1661), the company had the untrammelled right of making civil, commercial and criminal laws, with no right of appeal to the courts in England. These rights and the corresponding duties of government could not simply be revoked by either the crown or parliament, nor did they carry responsibilities of service to either institution, the only proviso being that the company could not adopt laws that were 'repugnant' to the laws of England.[31] Thus 'From the very first, the Company's policy was dictated by its own, not by England's place

30 Pearson, 'Merchants and States', p. 91.
31 Stern, *The Company-State*, pp. 23–5.

in the international system.'[32] The company was granted not just a monopoly on trade but also jurisdiction over any English subjects in the East, whom the company could arrest and try according to its own laws. It had the right to defend its trade and outposts by force, a prerogative it backed up with rapidly expanding military and naval forces, later augmented by militias. Once again mirroring the prerogatives of the VOC, the EIC had the right to declare war and make peace with any non-European power, as well as engaging in diplomacy and signing treaties with such polities, a right the company exercised enthusiastically from its very beginnings. Treaties with the greater and lesser polities of the region, from the Mughal emperor to local rulers around Madras and in the Banda Islands, were crucial in winning trade access and for establishing factories and forts (relations with local rulers are covered below and in greater detail in the following chapter). The EIC further had the authority to establish new colonies and settlements without having to seek permission from the crown. The company began minting its own coins, often adapting or overwriting Mughal designs with its own motto, 'From God comes peace and expansion'. Previously the lack of the ability to issue currency was felt by the London headquarters to make Bombay presidency 'lame of one foot, and not an intire Soveraign State'.[33]

The EIC thus enjoyed most if not all the major sovereign prerogatives. Although it was a privately owned merchant company, it was clearly more than just a private company. As a hybrid public–private entity, it was, like the VOC, a company sovereign. Not only was the EIC a polity in its own right, but it was one that later came to earn more revenue and govern more subjects than Britain itself. Although it had a clear, hierarchical chain of command, this was not one that was anchored to the English state in the same way that orders in the Estado da Índia were passed down from the king to his viceregal officials in Goa. Nor was the relationship between the English state and the EIC equivalent to the much looser suzerain relations between the Mughal emperor and the various subordinate polities (which came to include the EIC itself).

In sum, as public–private hybrids the Dutch and English company sovereigns bore a close resemblance to each other in their corporate

[32] Steensgaard, *Carracks, Caravans and Companies*, p. 116.
[33] Quoted in Stern, *The Company-State*, p. 34.

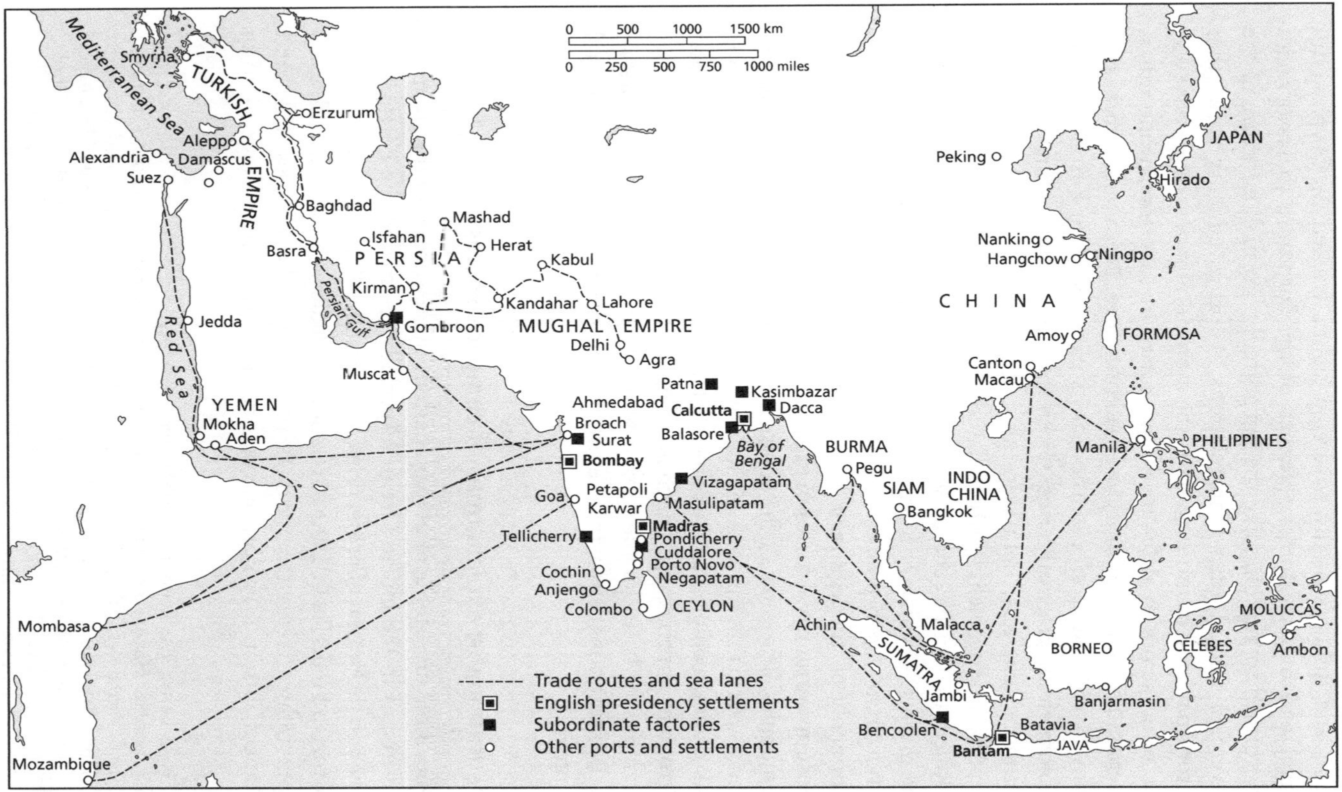

Figure 3.2 The English East India Company's settlements in the Indies, *c.* 1660–1760.

form and quintessentially sovereign rights, backed up by powerful naval and military forces. Neither of the corporate thalassocracies conformed to anything like the purportedly 'normal' structure of the sovereign state. Rather than relations of formal equality with other actors in the international system, the more dominant arrangement was for some actors to defer to the authority of superiors, while others exercised suzerain authority over subordinates. Nor could either company be reduced to an extension of its parent state in Europe in legal, diplomatic or practical terms. Given their corporate features and constitutional charters, both were also very different from the classical imperial arrangement of Mughal authority, despite their common commitment to divisible, shared sovereignty and indirect rule. Finally, given the market for military force, and the dispersal of armed force among subordinate vassal polities and protectorates, there was nothing like a monopoly on the legitimate use of force exercised by states. The two most powerful naval forces in the Indian Ocean in this era were private companies. The entry of the companies into the Indian Ocean international system thus further expanded diversity among the major powers in the region, comprising Portuguese statist, Mughal (and Safavid and Ottoman) imperial, and Dutch and English corporate forms. Below we examine the bases for the rapid rise of the companies, looking first at their institutional strengths, before putting these in a broader cultural context.

Institutionalist explanations of company success

One of the most influential explanations of the success of the company sovereigns in the Indian Ocean (especially relative to the Portuguese) relies on the notion of protection costs. First developed by the economic historian Frederick C. Lane in relation to medieval Venice, this idea has been influential in the writings of scholars like Charles Tilly and Mancur Olson.[34] Protection costs refer to 'the whole range of costs

[34] F. C. Lane, 'The Economic Consequences of Organized Violence', *Journal of Economic History* 18:4 (1958), pp. 401–17; Steensgaard, *Carracks, Caravans and Companies*; Tilly, 'War Making and State Making as Organized Crime'; Tilly, *Capital, Coercion and European States*; M. Olson, *Power and Prosperity: Outgrowing Communist and Capitalist Dictatorships* (New York: Basic Books, 2000); J. Glete, *Warfare at Sea 1500–1650: Maritime Conflicts and the Transformation of Europe* (New York: Routledge 2000).

incurred in using and controlling violence', which could range from gifts and bribes to customs officials, insurance premiums, convoy fees, arming merchant ships or even forming an army or navy.[35] Lane argued that in the period 700–1700 relative protection costs were the single greatest determinant of success in long-range trade. For example, the Venetians' success in the medieval period is ascribed to their ability to provide better protection at lower cost than their rivals.[36] Merchants had the option to pay public or private third parties for protection, whether they were pirates, mercenaries or states. Lane's work tends to erase the divide between the public and private use of violence (a distinction that has comparatively little meaning in the early modern sphere in any case), as states can extract profit from their armies and navies, while merchants may further their commercial aims by developing and deploying military force.[37] Given that violence may have been Europeans' primary export to the Indian Ocean littoral, Lane's work on the relationship between violence and profit is especially apposite for the early modern Indian Ocean, and for the VOC and the EIC in particular.[38]

From this perspective, the innovation of the company sovereigns was that these merchants successfully internalized their protection costs by developing an in-house capacity for organized violence that was subordinated to their commercial ends. According to Steensgaard, not only were protection costs lower in this manner, they also became more predictable.[39] This advantage was combined with the ability to control severe and damaging price fluctuations, thanks to the company sovereigns' monopoly or oligopolistic position, and lower transaction costs.[40] These price fluctuations had earlier prevented individual traders, who were price-takers rather than price-makers, from consistently exploiting the gains of trade from the Indian Ocean region to Europe. North similarly regards the company sovereigns as efficient

[35] Lane, 'Economic Consequences of Organized Violence', p. 409.
[36] *Ibid.*, p. 415.
[37] F. C. Lane, *Profits from Power: Readings in Protection Rents and Violence-Controlling Enterprises* (Albany, NY: State University of New York Press, 1979).
[38] S. Subrahmanyam, 'Of *Imârat* and *Tijârat*: Asian Merchants and State Power in the Western Indian Ocean, 1400–1750', *Comparative Studies in Society and History* 37:4 (1995), p. 753; Glete, *Warfare at Sea*, pp. 84–5.
[39] Steensgaard, *Carracks, Caravans and Companies.* [40] *Ibid.*

institutional solutions to external problems like piracy and contract enforcement, as well as internal principal–agent challenges.[41]

More generally, according to North, the companies were sophisticated solutions for information and governance transaction costs, and their early successes drove a self-reinforcing feedback loop of more trade, lower transaction costs, greater efficiency and higher productivity. In this sense, protection costs and transaction costs seem to be very closely linked, or perhaps even different perspectives on the same thing, with common institutional solutions for each. This work sees the company sovereigns' merging of violence and trading functions as a better organizational response to the difficult market conditions of intercontinental trade compared with an arrangement relying on the typical modern division between public institutions wielding organized violence and private bodies seeking profit. Thus Glete argues that organizational coordination will be superior to relying on markets 'if market conditions are characterized by great uncertainty, if there are few suppliers, if long-term contracts are necessary, if a high degree of "asset specificity" is involved and if there is a high risk that instructions from the buyer are interpreted in an opportunistic way'.[42]

Company over state: why did the Portuguese lose to the VOC and the EIC?

By far the most important development in the international relations of early modern Europe is said to be the ascendance of the sovereign state, which, as the story goes, out-competed its various non-state rivals in military and/or economic terms. For the reasons explored in Chapter 1, sovereign states are conventionally held to be more efficient at mustering and supporting the increasingly specialized and expensive armies necessary for geopolitical success and survival, as well as being better able to provide institutional solutions to lower transaction costs and increase growth.[43] In the early modern Indian Ocean region, however,

[41] North, 'Institutions, Transaction Costs, and the Rise of Merchant Empires'.
[42] Glete, *Warfare at Sea*, p. 71.
[43] North and Thomas, *The Rise of the Western World: A New Economic History* (Cambridge University Press, 1973); G. Parker, *The Military Revolution: Military Innovation and the Rise of the West* (Cambridge University Press, 1988); Tilly, *Coercion, Capital and European States*; J. Glete, *War and State in Early Modern Europe: Spain, the Dutch Republic and Sweden as Fiscal-Military States, 1500–1660* (London: Routledge, 2002).

we saw a completely different result: the closest equivalent to the European state was bested in fierce competition by a political actor organized along corporate lines. This strikingly different result is important not just in terms of demonstrating fundamental regional differences, but also because the implication of much of the literature derived from the European historical experience is not just that the state happened to win, but that it *had* to win, thanks to the inherent institutional advantages of the sovereign state. Looking at the Indian Ocean brings this judgement into question. In this sense, the success of the VOC and the EIC compared with the Portuguese is not just significant for the Indian Ocean. More generally, it raises doubts about what we think we know about why the international system is comprised of states, rather than companies, empires or some other kind of polity.[44]

In many respects much of the older historical literature on the Portuguese in the Indian Ocean writes of their success in the sixteenth century only as the prelude to their failure in the seventeenth. The Portuguese domain is portrayed as a fairly ramshackle affair, while the temporary success of the Estado da Índia is attributed to the absence of any serious (i.e. European) competition.[45] Thus the Portuguese system is slighted as resembling the backward, Asian redistributive tributary mode, whereas the Dutch and English represented the modern, capitalist productive model.[46] The tribute referred to here is the difference in the price charged for protection (whether genuine or in the sense of a protection racket) net of the cost of supplying it.[47] The success of the company sovereigns is put down to their ability to provide better protection at lower cost than the Portuguese. Subrahmanyam in particular sees this kind of portrayal as reflecting an ethnocentric valorization of Northern European Protestants over Southern European Catholics, who are lumped in with the non-Western non-whites.[48] He notes that

44 J. Branch, *The Cartographic State: Maps, Territory, and the Origins of Sovereignty* (Cambridge University Press, 2014).

45 Most notably J. C. van Leur, *Indonesian Trade and Society: Essays in Asian Social and Economic History* (The Hague: W. van Hoeve, 1955); Lane, *Profits from Power*; Steensgaard, *Carracks, Caravans and Companies*; but see also Pearson, *The Indian Ocean*.

46 Chaudhuri, *Trade and Civilisation in the Indian Ocean*, p. 69; Subrahmanyam, 'A Tale of Three Empires', p. 69.

47 Lane, 'Economic Consequences of Organized Violence', p. 405.

48 Subrahmanyam, *Portuguese Empire in Asia*.

contemporary judgements of the Netherlands itself were often unflattering, as in 1652 when one English traveller described the country as 'the great Bog of Europe ... and the buttock of the World'.[49] Nevertheless, the superiority of the company sovereigns, and the VOC in particular, over the Portuguese Estado da Índia is undeniable, and thus it is important to analyse the relationship between them.

In the earliest beginnings of Dutch and English trading in the 1590s, and the first few years after the companies were founded, they sought to avoid areas of Portuguese strength. This deference was rapidly replaced by a much more aggressive posture, however, with the EIC quickly coming into naval conflict with the Estado da Índia around Gujarat, and the Dutch further east in the Spice Islands (where the Dutch and English also fought each other in naval battles in the 1610s). The VOC expelled the Portuguese from Ambon in 1605, though Dutch attacks shortly afterwards on Malacca and Mozambique failed. Loss rates of the Portuguese shipping from Asia, always high, mounted even further thanks to VOC predation, reaching a third in 1630s,[50] while the number of VOC ships rounding the Cape had exceeded those of the Portuguese in the previous decades (though the Dutch ships were smaller). At this time the VOC instituted repeated blockades of Goa itself. Although the Spanish had never extended any help in defending Portuguese possessions in Asia or Brazil, the separation of the two countries in 1640 further disrupted the Portuguese trading routes that had run through Manila. After a partial truce in the 1640s, the VOC continued to apply heavy pressure to the Estado da Índia, capturing several other settlements on the Malabar and Coromandel Coasts of India, and completing the conquest of Ceylon. Only in 1669 was a lasting peace attained with the VOC (a treaty with the EIC had been concluded much earlier in 1629), leaving the Estado da Índia to lick its wounds and later stage a modest recovery around Goa and in Mozambique.

It is important not to over-generalize either from the success of the companies or the failure of the Portuguese. The struggle between the Portuguese and the Dutch West India Company in the Atlantic had a very different result from that equivalent in the Indian Ocean, with the Portuguese defeating the Dutch in Brazil, in significant part thanks to

[49] Subrahmanyam, *Portuguese Empire in Asia*, p. 154. [50] *Ibid.*, p. 172.

reinforcements from Portuguese Angola.[51] The Dutch West India Company was always much more of an instrument of the Dutch state than the VOC. In part this reflected the fact that geographical proximity allowed for greater control, but also because Europe and the Atlantic were the primary sites of military struggle with the Spanish arch-enemy.[52] As such, the tension between commercial and national strategic interests was always much more acute for the West India Company.[53] Interestingly, the VOC enjoyed very little success against the Spanish in the Philippines despite repeated attacks.[54]

The poor showing of the Portuguese in the Indian Ocean between 1600 and 1650 may have also reflected strategic priorities, whereby Lisbon chose to concentrate its resources first in Europe, then in the Atlantic and Americas, with the Indian Ocean coming last.[55] Thus the Portuguese Council of War noted: 'We should give up in Asia as much as we need to, in order to leave us free in Brazil.'[56] In this sense the institutional characteristics of the state, or the Estado da Índia's approximation thereof, become less important. Nevertheless the superior military and commercial performance of the companies relative to the Portuguese over at least a century, and the scope of the companies' success in remaking the whole Indian Ocean trading system, cry out for explanation. For it was not a case of isolated and contingent victories achieved by the VOC over the Portuguese, but a consistent record of success after success during the period 1605–63. From very early on after their arrival, the Dutch company sovereign (and to a lesser extent the EIC also) out-performed the Portuguese in the military, naval, commercial and diplomatic spheres over these decades and into the eighteenth century. Thus although there were proximate tactical and technological reasons, like the inferiority of the huge Portuguese *nao* ships relative to the smaller but better-armed Dutch and English competitors,[57] or disastrous individual Portuguese leaders,[58] there seem to have been more structural causes for this radical institutional inferiority across the region, in different spheres, for sixty years.

[51] Disney, *History of Portugal*, pp. 221–31.
[52] Boxer, *The Dutch Seaborne Empire*, p. 100.
[53] G. D. Winius, *The Fatal History of Portuguese Ceylon: Transition to Dutch Rule* (Cambridge, MA: Harvard University Press, 1971), p. 62.
[54] Boxer, *The Dutch Seaborne Empire*, p. 25.
[55] Winius, *The Fatal History of Portuguese Ceylon*, p. xiv.
[56] *Ibid.*, p. 117.
[57] Glete, *Warfare at Sea*, p. 171.
[58] Winius, *The Fatal History of Portuguese Ceylon*, p. 161.

The Estado da Índia also lost a number of key nodes in its maritime network at the hands of local polities during the first half of the seventeenth century. In some instances this seems to be a case of local polities opportunistically capitalizing on previous VOC victories over the Estado da Índia,[59] but in many other cases these conflicts were essentially unconnected with the rivalries between the Europeans in the Indian Ocean region, and were instead the product of indigenous power shifts.[60] Thus a new Burmese dynasty drove the Portuguese from their settlement of Syriam on the Irrawaddy delta in 1612, and the informal Portuguese settlement of Hugli on the Bay of Bengal was destroyed by the Mughals in 1632. Although the help of the EIC was crucial in the successful siege of Hormuz in 1622, the shah of Persia was the driving force behind this move. Local forces in Ceylon administered sharp defeats to the Portuguese in 1630 and 1638, while in alliance with the VOC they had largely expelled the Portuguese from the island by 1656. In 1639 the Portuguese were banished from Japan on pain of death; when they failed to heed this warning and tried to re-establish trading relations the following year sixty-one of seventy-four representatives were beheaded, with the remainder sent back to Macau to tell what had transpired. The lucrative Japanese trade, especially the export of Japanese silver, fell to the VOC. The Portuguese did manage to win an important defensive victory in besting an Acehnese siege of Malacca in 1629, with the city being saved thanks to a relief force sent by the sultan of Johor, though the latter's change of allegiance to the Dutch saw the city fall to the VOC in 1640 (a report to the Heeren XVII noted 'Without their help we could never have become masters of that strong place'[61]). As hostilities with the VOC eased off from the mid-seventeenth century the Portuguese faced a new challenger in the western Indian Ocean with the rise of the Omanis, who took Muscat from them in 1650. Local Indian rulers sought to pre-empt VOC moves by capturing several important Portuguese ports in the 1650s and early 1660s.

Subrahmanyam at least sees a pattern of the Dutch learning from earlier Portuguese experiences, especially in cultivating intra-Asian trade as a solution to the lack of demand for European goods in the

[59] Disney, *A History of Portugal*, p. 168.
[60] Subrahmanyam, *The Portuguese Empire in Asia*, pp. 186–9.
[61] *Ibid.*, p. 184.

Indian Ocean and the Far East. Rather than seeing any commercial superiority, he attributes Dutch success to a more systematic use of violence, and the diplomatic triumph of winning exclusive trading relations with Tokugawa Japan.[62] Yet the point concerning the use of violence necessitates further explanation: why was it that the Dutch were more successful in their use of violence than the Portuguese, who after all had no reticence in applying military force in the region in building and maintaining the Estado da Índia? Judging from contemporary sources there are 'very few portrayals of the Portuguese in South Asian materials that do not insist on their deceitful and violent side'.[63]

One recurring factor that explains the success of the corporate form relative to its statist competitor in the Indian Ocean was the relatively greater ability (and it was only relative) of the companies to align the personal interests of their agents in the field with the corporate interest, compared with the Portuguese. As Winius noted of the Estado da Índia 'nearly everybody was making money out of India except the [Portuguese] King'.[64] The strictly hierarchical Portuguese chain of command was designed in a generally futile attempt to keep local agents in line, and meant that they had to seek opportunities for private enrichment that were contrary to the general Portuguese interest in the region. Given the relatively short and fixed terms of office, generally non-renewable, many officials responded by misappropriating as much as they could within the limited time allotted to them;[65] 'there is no doubt that Portuguese officials often engaged in conduct that was highly detrimental to the interests of the Portuguese state'.[66] Relatedly, Portuguese private merchants received distinctly second-class treatment from the crown, and they returned the favour by trading illegally and evading the dues they officially owed whenever possible.[67] As a result, even while the Portuguese as a whole were enjoying healthy revenues from their Indian Ocean possessions, often very little of this money trickled up to Lisbon, and when it did might well have been devoted to European or American priorities, rather than being returned

62 *Ibid.*, pp. 223–4. 63 Subrahmanyam, 'Taking Stock of the Franks', p. 75.
64 Winius, *The Fatal History of Portuguese Ceylon*, p. 93; see also Subrahmanyam and Thomas, 'Evolution of Empire', p. 330.
65 Steensgaard, *Carracks, Caravans and Companies*, p. 67.
66 Pearson, *Port Cities and Intruders*, p. 136.
67 Chaudhuri, *Trade and Civilisation in the Indian Ocean*; Pearson, *Indian Ocean*; Disney, *A History of Portugal*; Subrahmanyam, *The Portuguese Empire in Asia*.

to Goa. Given that providing military and naval forces was in the main a public monopoly, this lack of public revenue directly and repeatedly translated into the lack of adequate warships and troops.[68]

Once again, it is important not to draw too stark a dichotomy between Dutch and English corporate success and Portuguese failure. The Portuguese outlasted both companies. If success is measured in terms of longevity, the Portuguese domain in the Indian Ocean was the most successful European colonial enterprise ever, by the most generous measure only coming to a close with the independence of East Timor in 2002.[69] Judging by the anachronistic standards of the current era, the Portuguese separation of the public state monopoly over the means of violence and the private concerns of merchants looks far more modern than the companies' take on these same issues.[70] Relating more directly to the problem of unreliable local agents, primary source documents from both companies are replete with complaints at every level from the directors down about the tendency of staff to routinely engage in every kind of corruption in an attempt to feather their own nests at the expense of company profits.[71] Speaking of the near-ubiquitous habit of 'private trading' carried out illegally by VOC staff, Boxer holds that 'everyone from Governor-General to cabin boy traded on the side and everyone knew it'. When the VOC eventually went broke, wags alleged the initials stood for 'Vergaan Onder Corruptie' (Collapsed Through Corruption).[72] The directors were tacitly complicit in this system, keeping wages at below subsistence level on the grounds that staff would steal to make up the difference anyway. The EIC was little better, with all the same practices rife. Thus a note from the director to Madras reprimands the local agent for 'perverting or misconstruing, procrastinating or neglecting our plain and direct orders to you, as if you were not a subordinate but a co-ordinate power with us'.[73] Employees of

[68] K. N. Chaudhuri, 'Reflections on the Organizing Principle of Pre-Modern Trade', in Tracy, *The Political Economy of Merchant Empires*, p. 9; Winius, *The Fatal History of Portuguese Ceylon*, p. 92.

[69] Although Lisbon initiated Portuguese Timor's decolonization in 1975, Indonesia's invasion of East Timor in 1975 (and occupation there until 1999) meant that Portuguese Timor existed officially until the country's formal independence in 2002.

[70] Stern, *The Company-State*, pp. 6–7.

[71] Ward, *Networks of Empire*, p. 31.

[72] Boxer, *The Dutch Seaborne Empire*, pp. 201 and 205.

[73] Quoted in Adams, 'Principals and Agents', p. 20.

one company sometimes used the financial conduits of their erstwhile rival to assist in their schemes and scams.[74]

Nevertheless, there was a relatively greater alignment of interests between the agents of the companies compared with the agents of the Estado da Índia. In the former case expanding trade increased the opportunity for both legal corporate and illegal individual gain. For private trade to work, the company ships had to get through, and the more company ships there were, the more room there was for private trade and hence private gain. Given that the merchants provided their own protection, rather than depending on the state, private corporate gain translated directly into the stock of resources that underpinned naval and military power. There was not the same buck-passing that occurred between the Portuguese royal authorities and merchants, as the VOC and the EIC knew that they could expect no help from their respective home states (though the reverse sometime obtained, with the companies expected to assist in the military ventures of the Dutch and English states with loans and ships). Something between a fifth and a third of the VOC's budget was spent on military expenses.[75] In contrast, Portuguese merchants often reasoned that any help they rendered to the crown was unlikely to be recompensed or secure an advantage for them, and that they might do just as well commercially by their own efforts as they would in the often stifling embrace of the Estado da Índia.[76]

Given the rationalist tone of much of this chapter, and the institutional success of the companies relative to the Portuguese statist model, one obvious question presents itself: why did the Portuguese not copy this corporate form? Even allowing for the difficulties of reasoned emulation discussed in Chapter 1, surely a litany of defeats across half a century in the military, naval, commercial and diplomatic arenas would have provided fairly conclusive proof of the need for institutional change and the model that could deliver success?

In fact the Portuguese did try to create an equivalent East India Company on several occasions. The fatal flaw in each case, however, was that the crown was consistently unwilling to relinquish enough

[74] Boxer, *The Dutch Seaborne Empire*; Adams, 'Principals and Agents'; Ward, *Networks of Empire*; Stern, *The Company-State*.

[75] T. Mostert, 'Chain of Command: The Military System of the Dutch East India Company 1655–1663', master's thesis, Department of History, University of Leiden, 2007, p. 11.

[76] Pearson, 'Merchants and States', p. 84.

control to the merchants to entice them to capitalize such a company.[77] Even the threat of religious persecution of New Christians (i.e. forcibly converted Jews) was not sufficient to extract funds for such a venture. The merchants feared, accurately, that the Portuguese state simply sought additional private funding to pursue the king's aims, with little priority accorded to profit, or even maintaining the initial capital stock.

The company formula was tried often throughout the various arenas of European colonial expansion, from the Hudson Bay, to Siberia, to Guinea, to Borneo, to Mississippi, but almost always failed.[78] While the Danish Guinea, West and East India Companies (the latter founded in 1616) enjoyed some success, they remained relatively weak and, unlike their Dutch and English counterparts, depended on the Danish crown for their capital, rather than private merchants. The French also attempted to copy this form, but could never attract significant private capital, again because the French king was only interested in the company serving as an instrument of his primarily non-commercial goals in the East. As a result, 'French companies always lost money.'[79] In this respect, the VOC and the EIC were very much the exception rather than the rule in being genuinely independent entities. Judging on the basis of this very mixed record, one of the great proponents of the corporate institutional form allows that:

> To create a company was to imitate a form, that in a few spectacular cases had proved eminently profitable. Just as the illiterate in the old anecdote believed that he would be able to read if only he could borrow the vicar's spectacles, the European bureaucrat of the 17th century might imagine that all the treasures of the world would be within reach if only that form of organization was applied which had brought such rich benefits to London and the Netherlands.[80]

Rational emulation, like military competition and cultural conformity, consistently failed to produce convergence in the early modern Indian Ocean littoral.

These economic functionalist accounts have been attacked by others as 'an exercise in Institutional Darwinism, wherein the organizational

[77] Disney, *A History of Portugal*, pp. 307–8; Subrahmanyam, *The Portuguese Empire in Asia*, pp. 169–71.

[78] Klein, 'The Origins of Trading Companies'.

[79] Pearson, 'Merchants and States', p. 96.

[80] N. Steensgaard, 'Companies as a Specific Institution in the History of European Expansion', in Blussé and Gaastra, *Companies and Trade*, p. 260.

superiority of the East India companies may be inferred from the very fact of their "triumph"'.[81] Subrahmanyam critiques the anachronistic tendency to put polities like the Ottomans and Mughals into the 'loser' category compared to the Northern Europeans when writing about the early modern period, given that over the period 1500–1700 these empires were expanding, and were far more powerful than any European polity, including either of the two company sovereigns. He goes on to attribute this tendency to 'the pressing momentum of Whig historiography, the desire to read the nineteenth century back into the seventeenth, and the great teleologies of Marxist and Weberian social-scientific reasoning'.[82] Without detracting from their undoubtedly important insights, it is thus important to temper this purely rationalist institutionalist account of the company sovereigns' success by situating them within the deeper cultural context that enabled them to operate so profitably and for so long.

Cultural context and corporate triumph

The company sovereigns had important institutional advantages in their pursuit of closely entwined commercial, political and military goals. As we have noted, prominent among these was the ability to internalize protection costs, to shape important markets to reduce price volatility, and to pool capital and impose long time horizons thanks to the disenfranchisement of stockholders relative to managers. Yet, as noted, it is important to qualify the rationalist and institutionalist perspectives of scholars like Steensgaard and North by setting the company sovereigns' success in their proper cultural context.

The enduring importance of compatible preferences as passive enablers of European expansion

Among their contemporaries the VOC had a reputation as arch-pragmatists whose sole yardstick was profit and loss, even (or particularly) in their wars.[83] Oliver Cromwell sourly observed that the Dutch

[81] Subrahmanyam and Thomaz, 'Evolution of Empire', pp. 298–331.
[82] Subrahmanyam, 'A Tale of Three Empires', p. 71.
[83] L. Blussé and F. Gaastra, 'Companies and Trade: Some Reflections on a Workshop and a Concept', in Blussé and Gaastra, *Companies and Trade.*

company preferred 'gain to godliness', while one Dutch merchant publicly stated he would trade with hell if there were profit in it.[84] Yet even a hard-nosed operation like the VOC was a product of its milieu, like the EIC, even when it came to war.

The company sovereigns, their Portuguese antagonists and local polities were all pre-industrial entities, whose armies tended to be at technologically similar levels.[85] Like the Portuguese before them, the Dutch and the English enjoyed a pronounced naval superiority on the open ocean. But, to reiterate, an important foundation of this advantage lay in the contrasting but compatible preferences distinguishing European thalassocracies from the Indian Ocean's most powerful host polities. These polities – especially the Mughals, but also the Ottomans, Safavids and (further afield) Qing China and the Tokugawa shogunate – were land-based empires that had little interest in building maritime trading empires or establishing far-flung colonies. Conversely, the company sovereigns, again like the Portuguese before them, had little or no interest in building territorial empires, as opposed to networks of entrepôts.[86] In this sense, the historiographical consensus is that during the seventeenth century the VOC and the EIC were 'reluctant imperialists'.[87] This aversion to territorial conquest was perhaps most pithily expressed by Sir Thomas Roe, England's first ambassador to the Mughal court, who admonished EIC employees thus: 'lett this bee recieued as a rule that if you will Profitt, seeke it at Sea, and in quiet

[84] Boxer, *The Dutch Seaborne Empire*, p. 113.

[85] Ricklefs, *War, Culture and the Economy in Java*; Lorge, *Asian Military Revolution*; G. V. Scammell, *The World Encompassed: The First European Maritime Empires, c. 800–1650* (Berkeley: University of California Press, 1981); P. J. Marshall, 'Western Arms in Maritime Asia in the Early Phases of Expansion', *Modern Asian Studies* 14:1 (1980), pp. 13–28; M. W. Charney, *Southeast Asian Warfare 1300–1900* (Leiden: Brill, 2004); J. Gommans, *Mughal Warfare: Indian Frontiers and the High Road to Empire 1500–1700* (London: Routledge, 2002).

[86] Ricklefs, *War, Culture and the Economy in Java*; K. H. Kian, 'How Strangers Became Kings: Javanese–Dutch Relations in Java 1600–1800', *Indonesia and the Malay World* 36:105 (2008), pp. 293–307; Lauren Benton, *A Search for Sovereignty: Law and Geography in European Empires, 1400–1900* (Cambridge University Press, 2010).

[87] A. Clulow, 'European Maritime Violence and Territorial States in Early Modern Asia, 1600–1650', *Itinerario* 33:1 (2009), pp. 72–94; Kian, 'How Strangers Became Kings'; E. Locher-Scholten, 'Dutch Expansion in the Indonesia Archipelago around 1900 and the Imperialism Debate', *Journal of Southeast Asian Studies* 25:1 (1994), pp. 91–111; Stern, *The Company-State*.

trade; for without controuersy it is an effort to affect Garrisons and land warrs in India'.[88] Moreover, even if they had been inclined, the company sovereigns were not in a position to militarily challenge any of the major local powers beyond the range of their ships' guns. Though both the VOC and the EIC did come into conflict with the Mughals or Mughal vassals at various points (1612, 1623, 1648, 1686–90), these clashes were generally minor and fleeting.[89] As discussed in the previous chapter, thanks to their wealth, and in keeping with their standard strategy for co-opting local opponents, the Mughals generally found it easier to pay off the company sovereigns or to conscript them for anti-piracy patrols rather than contesting their mastery of the sea. Moreover, when Europeans did clash with their imperial hosts, they frequently ended the encounter the worse for wear. Thus, the most significant clash in 1686–90 in the Anglo-Mughal War saw the EIC take a heavy defeat.[90] Likewise, the Dutch were later driven from their positions in south-west India by the raja of Travancore, after having been expelled from Taiwan by Chinese forces in 1662.

Thus, because of their compatible preferences, the Europeans concentrating on trade and control of the sea, the local major powers seeking glory on land, the pattern of company sovereign expansion remained heavily conditioned by ideational factors. This similarity in enabling conditions remained constant for the company sovereigns as it had for their Portuguese predecessors, and forms an important commonality in their experience, notwithstanding the aforementioned institutional differences distinguishing the company sovereigns from the Estado da Índia. In a field that takes the concept of zero-sum security competition as a constant, the notion that European expansion did not entail Asian diminution is hard to grasp. Yet this was largely the situation between the company sovereigns and the Estado da Índia on the one side, and the great empires of the region on the other, from 1600 to 1750.

88 Sir Thomas Roe, quoted in R. Sapra, 'A Peaceable Kingdom in the East: Favourable Early Seventeenth Century Representations of the Moghul Empire', *Renaissance and Reformation* 27:3 (2003), p. 11.

89 Clulow, 'European Maritime Violence'.

90 J. Israel and K. N. Chaudhuri, 'The English and Dutch East India Companies and the Glorious Revolution of 1688–9', in J. Israel (ed.), *The Anglo-Dutch Moment: Essays on the Glorious Revolution and its World Impact* (Cambridge University Press, 1991), pp. 407–38; Chaudhuri, 'The English East India Company', p. 87.

What makes this balance of compatible preferences especially noteworthy is its remarkable durability over time. The Portuguese undeniably enjoyed a 'first mover' advantage when they first inflicted their maritime ambitions on a region previously immune from large-scale naval predation in the 1500s. Equally, however, one might reasonably expect local powers to have marshalled a response to European naval aggression by the time the company sovereigns blasted their way into the region over a century later. That the Mughals and others failed to do so can be explained in part – but only in part – by the low direct threat to their interests that the Europeans 'scurrying and worrying at their [maritime] edges' seemed to pose.[91] This remarkable constancy in preferences – and the opening it left for the company sovereigns to compete alongside the Estado da Índia – provided a crucial enabling possibility for the continuing expansion of polity diversity into the seventeenth century.

Cultural commodities, canons of taste and the company sovereigns' ascendancy from 1600

If culturally conditioned preferences shaped the military balance between European maritime and indigenous terrestrial powers, so too did they pervade the company sovereigns' commercial strategies. In one of its relatively few early efforts to assert direct rule over Afro-Asian territories, the VOC captured the fabled Spice Islands, annihilated the local inhabitants and established monopolistic control over the production of precious spices there. At the time, the so-called 'holy trinity' of spices – cloves, nutmeg and mace – could only be grown in the Spice Islands, and were literally worth more than their weight in gold. The VOC's success in establishing monopolistic control over these spices, and its somewhat more incomplete assertion of control over cinnamon and pepper production, were key to assuring its long-term financial success. Especially during the 1600s, the bulk of the VOC's revenues were derived from the spices that had first lured Europeans to the Indian Ocean: pepper, nutmeg, mace, cloves and cinnamon.

The demand for these commodities was the primary commercial motor driving the company sovereigns onwards in the 1600s. And the VOC's success in seizing even a modicum of monopolistic control

[91] Fernández-Armesto, *Pathfinders*, p. 181.

over the supply of these spices both distinguished it from the Estado da Índia (which had typically sought only to monopolize onward supply to Europe), and was pivotal to assuring its long-term profitability. Thus, for example, the major initial problem faced by Europeans looking to trade with Asian powers was that the former had nothing that the latter regarded as valuable, except for gold and silver. It was to stop the drain of specie that the company sovereigns, in part following the lead of the Portuguese, developed a system of intra-Asian trade to generate a sufficient surplus to buy Asian goods for export to Europe.[92] Capturing a portion of the spice trade and mediating the subsequent sale of spices throughout Asia proved one remedy to this challenge.

The imperative behind the VOC's demand for spices was emphatically commercial. But this demand was quite literally a matter of taste, the spices' value deriving from arbitrary cultural judgements concerning their gastronomic, medicinal and aphrodisiac qualities (in Europe nutmeg, for example, was erroneously held to ward off the plague, going some way to explain the fantastic prices paid). More generally, throughout the early modern Old World, regionally particular 'cultures and economic patterns created subtly different patterns of exotic consumption and deportment'.[93] Everywhere, these patterns stressed the prestige and power of exotic commodities from distant lands.[94] The varying content of religious and medicinal beliefs, and diverse canons of taste in different regions, helped to constitute the markets in which profit-seekers operated.

Thus, for example, in South Asia and parts of South-East Asia, Brahminical food restrictions meant that high cuisine followed the mainly rice-based food offerings Hindus rendered to deities during daily worship at Hindu temples.[95] Once European traders introduced chillies to local palates, demand for the new commodity soared, providing Europeans with another commodity apart from bullion to trade for Indian textiles.[96] Conversely, edible birds' nests and sea slugs were fantastically valuable to the Chinese, and played a particularly significant role in the diets of the Confucian scholar gentry, but were

[92] Steensgaard, *Carracks, Caravans and Companies*.
[93] C. A. Bayly, '"Archaic" and "Modern" Globalization in the Eurasian and African Arena, c. 1750–1850', in Hopkins, *Globalization in World History*, p. 51.
[94] *Ibid*., p. 52. [95] *Ibid*., p. 70. [96] *Ibid*.

generally worthless elsewhere.[97] Gastronomic traditions throughout Persia, the Arab world, India and Europe all prized the Spice Island trinity of cloves, mace and nutmeg as 'indispensable to aristocratic tables and festive occasions'.[98] However, Chaudhuri argues that the finer spices 'did not move eastwards in the direction of China', at least in the early modern period.[99]

In the Indian Ocean world and well beyond, then, culture simultaneously constituted markets for exotic consumption goods while fragmenting them into regionally diverse expressions. Within this culturally conditioned and regionally variegated context, the supply of exotic commodities such as spices was often inelastic, and price variations were therefore more strongly driven by variations in demand.[100] But these variations in demand and accompanying price shifts were themselves the product of evolving and regionally diverse gastronomic tastes, religious customs and beliefs. Thus the company sovereigns' commercial strategies, much like their military ones, were shaped by ideational factors. These factors – be it local indifference to open seas warfare or a hunger for spices that stretched from Lombok to London – set the terms in which both intra-European competition and European-local interaction took place. They were also evident in European attitudes to rule.

Culture, economy and indirect rule

The EIC and the VOC had three broad modes of relating to the local political economies.[101] The first and most common arrangement was to compete commercially with Asian traders on a basis of nominal equality. This often happened when trading in the emporia of major powers, although politically it meant that the company sovereigns frequently had to assume a role as formal vassals of their host, as with the Mughals. The second, and rarest, was to conquer and occupy territory.

97 *Ibid.*, p. 54. See also Chaudhuri, *Trade and Civilisation in the Indian Ocean*, p. 21.

98 Chaudhuri, *Trade and Civilisation in the Indian Ocean*, p. 21. 99 *Ibid.*

100 *Ibid.*, p. 222. In the case of the spices, the problem of supply inelasticity was compounded by Europeans' erroneous belief that trees and plants could only grow in places where they were discovered naturally, a belief that persisted down to the mid-eighteenth century. See C. Corn, *The Scents of Eden: A History of the Spice Trade* (New York: Kodansha, 1999), p. 218.

101 Boxer, *The Dutch Seaborne Empire*; Pearson, 'Merchants and States'.

As noted, this was generally a strategy employed only in a few small, crucial Spice Islands, and later also in coastal entrepôts in India. The last approach was to apply political, economic and military pressure on the rulers of smaller coastal or island domains in pursuit of monopolistic and monopsonistic trading privileges, with the effect of subordinating these polities as company protectorates or vassals. Apart from matters of trade, such arrangements would allow the EIC or the VOC to station military forces, entitle employees to extraterritoriality, and give the company the right to adjudicate local disputes. This last privilege became especially important in local succession disputes, where one side appealed to the company for military support in besting a rival claimant.

For example, in Mataram in Java the VOC went from a vassal of the ruler to overlord from 1677, thanks to just such an intervention, as discussed in the following chapter. The result was very much a suzerain arrangement, however, rather than the kind of direct rule the Dutch state authorities began to impose on Java from the 1820s (after the demise of the VOC itself). Local rulers were obliged to pay tribute to the company in cash and kind, cede important trading privileges, send their first ministers to Batavia to pay homage when a new governor-general was installed, and in some cases refer to the governor-general as 'father' or 'grandfather' to acknowledge their status as vassals. Yet these same local rulers remained free to govern their own dominions as they saw fit, maintain armies, and conduct diplomacy with other non-European powers.[102] Rather than being exclusive to Java or the East Indies, the Dutch employed similar suzerain solutions in their Indian possessions also. Thus, after ousting the Portuguese from Cochin on India's Malabar Coast in 1663, the company arranged the coronation of a new raja with a golden crown conspicuously stamped with the VOC design.[103] In Ceylon, terms with the raja of Kandy once again included toll-free trade for the Dutch, the exclusion of all other European traders, local payment for the company troops, delivering set quantities of cinnamon and elephants at a fixed price, and a strict ban on any Catholic priests.[104]

[102] M. C. Ricklefs, *Jogjakarta under Sultan Mangkubumi, 1749–1792: A History of the Division of Java* (London: Oxford University Press, 1974); Ricklefs, *War, Culture and the Economy in Java*; Kian, 'How Strangers Became Kings'.

[103] Mostert, 'Chain of Command', p. 121.

[104] G. D. Winius, *The Fatal History of Portuguese Ceylon: Transition to Dutch Rule* (Cambridge MA: Harvard University Press, 1971), p. 38.

The EIC often went through a parallel process of beginning as vassal and ending up as master. Thus in 1639 the company first obtained authorization to build a settlement and fort in what later became Madras from a local noble of the declining Hindu Vijayanagara Empire. In return, the company had to agree to pay an annual tribute of half the customs revenue paid. In 1645 the company was able to renegotiate a more favourable deal. They gained more land around the settlement, and the formal rights to govern and administer justice in the territory. By 1658 the EIC had converted the payment from a half-share to a smaller, fixed annual payment and induced the local ruler to renounce any and all rights over Madras.[105]

At one level, the companies' preference for suzerain or vassal arrangements of indirect reign rather than direct rule was a simple matter of economic logic: wherever they were suzerains, the companies could often obtain the trading and legal privileges they wanted without the expense of having to subordinate and then administer substantial territories and populations, expenses that were consistently the main worry of the respective governing bodies in London and Amsterdam. Yet there is a vital prior question: *why* was this solution of indirect rule through continued heteronomy cheaper? No doubt the number of Europeans east of the Cape of Good Hope was tiny relative to the local population. Yet this ratio did not radically change in the British Raj or the Dutch East Indies in the early twentieth century, at which time the colonists' reach penetrated far deeper in Asian societies.

The suzerain character of rule over even those petty kingdoms that the Europeans could dominate militarily was primarily driven by cultural factors. Direct rule by the VOC and the EIC, unmediated by local intermediaries, would have been so much more expensive because it could not replicate the legitimacy enjoyed by indigenous rulers. Tracy relates:

> Perhaps the single most significant historiographical development in recent decades has been the emergence of an understanding that early Southeast Asian states made extensive use of ritual as a means of attracting and maintaining support. The king manifested his power by sponsoring rituals that reenacted a great cosmological drama, and satellite regions participated in the prosperity and glory that was seen as flowing from the ruler's power by providing tribute, in order to support the activities of the great temples at the

[105] Stern, *The Company-State*, pp. 19–20.

centre of the realm ... In this view of the monarchy, a ruler had trouble making himself accepted unless he came from a house perceived as having sacred power.[106]

Europeans had great difficulty and in any case little inclination to engage in these rituals. For this reason, in Java VOC military forces were very much a double-edged sword for local contestants in succession disputes. While the company's soldiers might prove useful or even decisive in fighting rivals, being perceived as puppets of the European infidels tended to encourage further dissent and rebellion.[107] The Javanese saw the Dutch as treacherous and untrustworthy.[108] In the west of the Indian Ocean region also 'The [Europeans] are seen, especially in the Persian and Arabic chronicles, as a violent lot, who are also given to devious acts of chicanery in order to advance their interests.'[109]

In most of South Asia, the material power of the Mughals checked any thoughts the Europeans may have had about direct rule, but even when it came to more minor local rulers in the waning days of the empire it is striking to notice the extent to which the EIC still depended on the aura of the Mughal 'sovereign idea' described in the previous chapter to legitimize instances of de facto European overlordship.[110] In the absence of the local legitimacy that indigenous intermediaries possessed, direct rule generally became prohibitively expensive, and thus suzerain, vassal or protectorate solutions were preferred. The economic calculation of the way the companies built their domains thus reflected deeper cultural determinants. As we will see in greater detail in the next chapter, a common commitment to heteronomous authority arrangements, and a shared willingness to engage in two-way practices of localization to support these arrangements, were key to stabilizing Europeans' enmeshment with local polities in the longer term. That this 'light touch' strategy happened to fit the company sovereigns' existing desire to keep administrative overheads to a minimum was no coincidence. For the enhanced legitimacy hybrid arrangements could bring naturally mitigated the local resistance that more intrusive strategies would have carried in their wake.

106 Tracy, 'Introduction', p. 16.
107 Ricklefs, *War, Culture and the Economy in Java*; Kian, 'How Strangers Became Kings'.
108 Ricklefs, *War, Culture and the Economy in Java*, p. 45.
109 Subrahmanyam, 'Taking Stock of the Franks', p. 73.
110 Alam and Subrahmanyam 'Introduction', p. 33.

Conclusion

Given their hybrid form of private companies imbued with quintessentially sovereign prerogatives, the entry of the Dutch and English companies from 1600 further expanded diversity in the Indian Ocean international system. Rather than just holding their own, the VOC especially decisively eclipsed the Portuguese in the first half of the seventeenth century, despite the Estado da Índia most closely approximating what IR conventionally regards as being the best-adapted unit, the sovereign state. They came into conflict precisely because they shared the same preferences for maritime networks, creating a zero-sum competitive dynamic. The companies enjoyed important institutional advantages over the Portuguese, relating to their lower and more consistent protection costs, market power and particularly their better management of the daunting principal–agent problems inherent in managing a vast political–military multinational enterprise spread over half the planet with early modern technology. These functional advantages and the specific shape of the military, political and commercial interactions with local polities were often underpinned by the contrasting preferences, equivalent institutions and improvised practices that stabilized relations between European interlopers and local polities. Explaining these institutions and practices is the subject of the next chapter.

4 *The stabilization of diversity, 1600–1750*

Europeans were first able to enter the Indian Ocean international system in large part because their maritime goals did not threaten powerful, land-based Asian empires. Subsequent competition between different European polity forms – the state-like Estado da Índia and English and Dutch company sovereigns – saw the sovereign state lose out to company sovereigns. The latter emerged as the West's most militarily and commercially successful polity form east of the Cape of Good Hope. How did the resulting international system work? This chapter explains how European and local actors learned to mediate their diplomatic and commercial relations with one another, and thus perpetuate regional polity diversity.

That Europeans proved so successful in insinuating themselves into the Indian Ocean international system is surprising. As we have already established, Europeans did not enjoy any overwhelming military preponderance over local actors, notwithstanding a niche advantage in naval warfare that the most powerful Asian polities were unwilling to copy. On land, Europeans were always vastly outnumbered and in most instances remained sorely dependent on the goodwill of locals to secure trading privileges. Likewise, while Europeans were drawn to the region by the promise of spices and textiles, they had little to offer locals in exchange for these products, aside from American silver and gold. Access to this silver and gold quickened monetization and state-building throughout the Indian Ocean littoral.[1] This strengthened local incentives to make space for European entrants into the region. But Europeans could not count on any commercial indispensability to win them access to indigenous rulers and markets. Lastly, having had little direct contact with locals prior to the sixteenth century, the Europeans

[1] O. Prakash, 'The Dutch East Indian Company in Bengal: Trade Privileges and Problems, 1632–1712', *Indian Economic Social History Review* 9:3 (1972), pp. 273–4.

shared few if any cultural affinities with prospective diplomatic and trading partners to ease their entry into the region. On the contrary, European religious bigotry and a reciprocal cultural chauvinism between Europeans and locals augured ill for the development of cooperative relations.

When locals were confronted by boatloads of quarrelsome, bigoted, gun-toting foreign merchants, why did they not simply push the Europeans back into the sea? This is the mystery we unravel in this chapter. Up to now, we have stressed the centrality of *differences* in European and local preferences in initially generating polity diversity. In this chapter, we foreground the crucial importance of *similarities* in European and local conceptions of heteronomy, along with two-way practices of localization that together served to stabilize and reproduce diversity over time. The chapter is divided most broadly into two sections, the first theoretical and the second empirical. The theoretical portion combines attention to first structure and then agency, while supporting historical evidence is taken from East Africa, North and South India, and South-East Asia.

We start in the first section by examining the structural conditions that facilitated a reproduction of polity diversity in the Indian Ocean international system. Notwithstanding their divergent preferences, Europeans and indigenous powers often shared a commitment to heteronomous modes of governance, understood as the simultaneous co-existence of multiple, layered and overlapping authority structures. An example was the commercial extra-territoriality granted to resident trading diasporas in Europe, Asia and Africa, which enabled Europeans' entry into the Indian Ocean commercial order after 1500.

But while these structural similarities provide the potential to stabilize a diverse regional system, agents needed to work to establish makeshift institutions to facilitate exchange and collaboration. Going beyond the structural concerns above, just as important for the theoretical explanation are the efforts European and indigenous actors invested in the hybrid arrangements to mediate their relations. Foreign and local actors participated in processes of symbolic legitimation and strategic material bargaining, encompassed under the overall rubric of localization.

Historical evidence to flesh out these contentions is presented in the second section, and taken from four distinct contexts: the Portuguese Estado da Índia's enmeshment within local polities in the East African

Zambezi river valley from 1570, the EIC's diplomatic and commercial interactions with Mughal-ruled northern India in the early 1600s, the EIC's negotiations with local rulers along the Coromandel Coast (a south-eastern Indian region beyond the Mughals' reach) in 1640, and finally the VOC's establishment of suzerainty over the most powerful sultanates in Java in the mid-eighteenth century. These four different settings capture major variations in the European–local power balance, sub-regional setting and temporal context, and yet they reveal common empirical patterns consistent with our theoretical claims.

Explaining structural and agentic bases of durable diversity in the Indian Ocean international system

The structural foundations of durable diversity: heteronomy, legal pluralism and trading diasporas

In analysing how Europeans infiltrated the Indian Ocean international system, we confront an important paradox. On the one hand, the region's polities differed radically from one another in their internal constitution. On the other hand, however, rulers throughout the early modern world confronted similar limits to their ability to control subject populations. These shared constraints yielded generic structures of political authority. To be sure, differences between European and local conceptions and practices of governance remained profound. But there were enough points of equivalence for European and indigenous polities to interrelate, and eventually to partially intermesh. These included a heteronomous configuration of social power and common subscription to practices of legal pluralism, such as customs of commercial extra-territoriality.

Heteronomy refers to a situation in which multiple actors routinely exercise overlapping authority claims over a single territory.[2] It is conventionally contrasted against the combination of domestic jurisdictional supremacy and territorial exclusivity that defines the modern sovereign state.[3] As discussed in Chapter 1, far from being confined to Western Europe, as International Relations scholars too often assume, heteronomy was the rule rather than the exception in the early modern

[2] Ruggie, 'Territoriality and Beyond', p. 150. [3] *Ibid.*, pp. 150–1.

period. The company sovereigns, and the Mughal, Safavid and Ottoman Empires certainly were heteronomous polities (as discussed in Chapter 2), while even the generally statist Portuguese had some elements of this form. The point here is not to collapse the differences that separated the various European and indigenous polities in the Indian Ocean international system, but to appreciate the congruence that allowed for the interweaving of these polities.

The common commitment to heteronomy extended to the institutionalization of authority through practices of legal pluralism. Writing of European maritime expansion in the Atlantic world, the international legal historian Lauren Benton has observed: 'Structural similarities of different regional systems of law before the expansion of long-distance maritime trade made this expansion possible.'[4] Benton furthermore speaks of the layered and lumpy quality of political space in the early modern period of European expansion, which saw sovereign prerogatives alternately split and recombined in ways that reflected not only ideational factors, but also the geography of mountains, rivers, islands and sea lanes.[5] We follow Benton and others who have subsequently extended these insights to investigate the dynamics of European maritime expansion in the Indian Ocean, arguing that commensurable regimes of legal pluralism provided a key institutional commonality necessary to mediate European integration into local political systems.[6]

Where heteronomy represents an overarching organizing principle for allocating political authority centring on the idea of territorially non-exclusive rule, legal pluralism refers in this study to the specific jurisdictional practices through which heteronomous orders are realized. Specifically, legal pluralism refers to the notion that multiple forms of law might simultaneously operate within the same territory, being distinguishable through their application to specific persons or

[4] L. Benton, 'The Legal Regime of the South Atlantic World, 1400–1750: Jurisdictional Complexity as Institutional Order', *Journal of World History* 11:1 (2000), p. 28.

[5] L. Benton, *A Search for Sovereignty: Law and Geography in European Empires 1400–1900* (Cambridge University Press, 2010).

[6] For a recent account of how legal pluralism functioned to aid commercial integration throughout maritime Asia, see G. D. S. Sood, 'Sovereign Justice in Precolonial Maritime Asia: The Case of the Mayor's Court in Bombay, 1726–1798', *Itinerario* 37:2 (2013), pp. 46–72.

spheres of social life.[7] In the West, the writ of the Church, which for centuries administered a body of canon law that operated alongside a growing body of state law, helped reproduce legal pluralism in medieval and early modern Europe.[8] Elsewhere, the formation of modern European colonial empires from the late eighteenth century saw a transformation of regimes of legal pluralism, away from a flatter, more fluid and more polycentric form, and towards a more hierarchical form where indigenous legal codes were partially subsumed to colonial authority without being completely effaced.[9]

Heteronomy is distinguishable from legal pluralism in that while all heteronomous orders are instantiated through regimes of legal pluralism, not all polities that embrace legal pluralism are heteronomous. Modern multi-faith nation-states such as Malaysia, for example, subscribe to the sovereign state template of domestic jurisdictional supremacy and territorially exclusive rule, while still permitting people of different religions to govern matters of faith and family law through appeals to their religious laws, in effect presiding over a state-centred (and state-subordinated) regime of legal pluralism.[10] By contrast, the congruences that linked major European and indigenous polities in the Indian Ocean world encompassed common commitments to heteronomy and legal pluralism. Rule was seen as both layered and territorially non-exclusive (i.e. heteronomous), and this principle was practically realized through sharing jurisdictional powers among many local and indigenous actors (legal pluralism).

[7] John Griffiths' classic definition of legal pluralism highlights the inherent indeterminacy that systems of legal pluralism frequently exemplify: 'a situation of legal pluralism . . . is one in which law and legal institutions are not all subsumable within one "system" but have their sources in the self-regulatory activities of all the multifarious social fields present, activities which may support, complement, ignore or frustrate one another'. See J. Griffiths, 'What is Legal Pluralism?' *Journal of Legal Pluralism and Unofficial Law* 18:24 (1986), p. 39.

[8] H. Berman, *Law and Revolution: The Formation of the Western Legal Tradition* (Cambridge, MA: Harvard University Press, 1983), p. 199.

[9] L. Benton, 'Colonial Law and Cultural Difference: Jurisdictional Politics and the Formation of the Colonial State', *Comparative Studies in Society and History* 41:3 (1999), p. 563.

[10] On the hybrid and legally plural character of the Malaysian legal system, see, for example, S. S. Faruqi, 'The Malaysian Constitution, the Islamic State and Hudud Laws', in K. S. Nathan and N, H. Kamali (eds.), *Islam in Southeast Asia: Political, Social and Strategic Challenges for the 21st Century* (Singapore: ISEAS, 2005), pp. 256–77.

For both the Estado da Índia and the company sovereigns, heteronomy and legal pluralism in the Mughal, East African, Hindu South Indian and Javanese polities provided a congenial context for Europeans to entrench themselves as yet another node of authority in an already crowded institutional environment. An example of these plural authority claims helping to stabilize durable diversity was a shared toleration of self-governing resident trading diasporas. Up to at least the sixteenth century, resident trading diasporas provided the main means of mediating long-distance trade throughout the Old World.[11] Diasporas proved relatively effective in managing the vast informational asymmetries separating merchants from their local interlocutors. They also served to address the intrinsic insecurities foreign traders confronted in operating in politically, legally and culturally unfamiliar environments, and the inevitable principal–agent problems home-based merchants faced when managing locally embedded agents across vast distances.[12]

Minimizing the uncertainties and risks associated with unfamiliar political, legal and cultural environments posed a major challenge for late medieval and early modern long-distance merchants. Across the Old World, trading diasporas generally addressed this challenge by taking advantage of customs allowing for a degree of self-government for foreign merchant communities.[13] Interested in reaping the increased customs revenues greater trade would bring, and disinclined to adjudicate merchants' internal disputes, rulers generally accommodated merchants' desires for self-government through customs of commercial extra-territoriality.[14] Rulers qualified this revocable privilege in many ways. Foreign merchants were generally sequestered in tightly delimited enclaves within port cities, exercised jurisdiction only within their own communities, and remained subject to the ruler's overarching suzerainty.[15] Nevertheless, rulers' authority was pockmarked by self-governing foreign trading communities, which were themselves enmeshed within webs of kinship and commercial exchange.[16]

[11] On this point, see, generally, Curtin, *Cross-Cultural Trade in World History.*
[12] C. Tilly, *Trust and Rule* (Cambridge University Press, 2005), pp. 65–6.
[13] Fisch, 'Law as a Means and as an End', p. 23. [14] *Ibid.* [15] *Ibid.*
[16] Sood, 'Sovereign Justice in Precolonial Maritime Asia', pp. 46–7.

Agency in the stabilization of diversity: the centrality of localization

Having considered the structural conditions of heteronomy and legal pluralism that permitted durable diversity, we now turn to the crucial role agency-centred processes of localization played in stabilizing diversity. These include both symbolic legitimation and more pragmatic compromises grounded in mutual material gains. It was these processes of localization that instantiated distinct but potentially compatible beliefs about the proper organization of political authority held by Africans, Asians and Europeans, and that thereby enabled the stabilization of polity diversity.

European polities worked to be accepted into local political systems through two-way processes of localization premised in part on symbolic legitimation. Within a trading world as cosmopolitan as that of the Indian Ocean system, and among communities long familiar with resident merchant trading diasporas, the Europeans' mere foreignness did not disqualify them from integrating into indigenous political and commercial networks.[17] But the Europeans' early belligerence, and the identification of the Portuguese vanguard as Franks – 'the forsworn enemies of the Muslims' – unsurprisingly won neither the Portuguese nor their English and Dutch successors many friends.[18] For Europeans to win acceptance as legitimate political and commercial interlocutors (rather than being seen and treated as merely a piratical nuisance) they had to adapt themselves to local conceptions and practices of political legitimacy.

As we will see, English and Dutch company agents faced radically different challenges in accomplishing this task in the Mughal Empire as compared with European relations with the smaller polities of the Zambezi river valley, the Coromandel Coast and Java. Portuguese estate-holders in East Africa rendered tribute to African kings, while the EIC and the VOC both formally assumed roles as vassals to the Mughal emperor, a symbolic submission to imperial authority that they would faithfully observe long after the Mughals had slipped into

17 See C. de Silva, 'Beyond the Cape: The Portuguese Encounter with the Peoples of South Asia', in S. B. Schwartz (ed.), *Implicit Understandings: Observing, Reporting, and Reflecting on the Encounters Between Europeans and Other Peoples in the Early Modern Era* (Cambridge University Press, 1995), p. 296.

18 *Ibid.*

decline. By contrast, in maritime South-East Asia Europeans also faced pressures to conform to local political idioms, but this time, counter-intuitively, as overlords rather than subordinates. Thus, the Dutch found themselves fortuitously placed to exploit indigenous 'stranger king' traditions that legitimized foreign rule as a means of containing local antagonisms. Although far from ubiquitous, the presence of this tradition provided the Dutch East India Company with powerful normative traction as it attempted to extend its networked authority across the Indonesian archipelago.

Working from equivalent foundations of heteronomy, securing symbolic legitimation was crucial for Europeans seeking to entrench themselves in indigenous political and economic systems. But legitimation through symbolic practices alone was not enough to cement Europeans' presence within local orders. Cross-cultural alliances of convenience were also vital, enabled by congruent norms but even more so by tentative and often transient alignments of local material interests. To win local actors' consent to the establishment of a permanent European presence, Europeans frequently needed to cultivate indigenous patrons by providing either opportunities for profit, or by acting as guns for hire.

For example, as discussed at length below, the EIC's early efforts to legitimize the company's establishment of a commercial presence in Gujarat entailed not merely a submission to the Mughal emperor, but also the provision of generous 'gifts' – in the form of both cash and commodities – to the emperor and his local agents in Gujarat.[19] Portuguese office-holders also had to make regular payments to the kings of the Zimbabwe Plateau. The VOC's expansion in Java entailed the construction of cross-cultural alliances of convenience as a means of complementing the company's attempts to conform to local forms of symbolic legitimation. Here the VOC depended on its ability to win allies through the selective provision of military power to competing local factions. Looking at the other side of the equation, local powers from the king of Ethiopia to the sultans of Java keenly exploited the Europeans' penchant for violence in settling scores with domestic rivals and historic enemies.

[19] J. Flores, 'The Sea and the World of the *Mutasaddi*: A Profile of Port Officials from Mughal Gujarat (c. 1600–1650)', *Journal of the Royal Asiatic Society* (3rd series), 21:1 (2011), pp. 55–71.

The process of stabilizing relations between the Indian Ocean's diverse unlike units varied considerably across time and place. These diverse accommodations reinforced the durable diversity of polity forms in the region in the Indian Ocean international system. Structural commonalities enabled diversity to stabilize through the mutual enmeshment of European with indigenous polities. But the agency of both Europeans and locals played an equally important role in legitimizing and so stabilizing these arrangements.

Stabilizing polity diversity in practice from East Africa to South-East Asia

The Portuguese Estado da Índia and the Zambezi river valley from 1570

As discussed in Chapter 2, compared to the empires, galactic polities and company sovereigns, the Portuguese Estado da Índia most closely resembled the sovereign state form. Yet in the frontier zone of their East African possessions there were also significant elements of heteronomy, as Portuguese laws came to overlay and hybridize with existing African practices. In line with the theoretical discussion above, the Portuguese presence, which endured across five centuries, was crucially shaped by existing heteronomous authority arrangements and legal pluralism, mediated by practices of localization centred on symbolic legitimation and strategic bargaining.[20]

From the outset, the Portuguese presence along the East African coastline was important as a way-station for traffic passing between Europe and Asia, but also in its own right as a market and source of commodities, especially gold brought from the Zimbabwe Plateau. After an alliance with the sultan of Malindi in 1498, the Portuguese captured the rival port sultanate of Kilwa and fortified it from 1505, later taking control of other port bases up and down the Swahili Coast.

[20] This section draws on A. Isaacman and B. Isaacman, '*Prazeros* as Transfrontiersmen: A Study in Social and Cultural Change', *International Journal of African Historical Studies* 8:1 (1975), pp. 1–39; Thornton, 'The Portuguese in Africa'; Disney, *History of Portugal*, pp. 198–200 and 350–3; Subrahmanyam, *The Portuguese Empire in Asia*, pp. 206–11; Pearson, *Port Cities and Intruders*, pp. 63–100; and Boxer, *The Portuguese Seaborne Empire*, pp. 139–43.

From such coastal outposts they forced their way into existing trade networks, reaching a rough modus vivendi with local Muslim Swahili traders, while fending off occasional Ottoman raids. In the 1540s a Portuguese expedition fought for the Ethiopian king against his local Muslim and Ottoman opponents, before assimilating into the local nobility. After decades of being largely content with their littoral presence, in the early 1570s the Portuguese made a rare and uncharacteristic attempt at land conquest by advancing from their base on the coast of present-day Mozambique up the Zambezi river valley. They were in search of the biblical gold mines of Sheba, which represented a kind of El Dorado in the Portuguese imagination.[21] The expedition was ravaged by malaria and sleeping sickness, and hindered by stiff military resistance, and so turned back. Portuguese Jesuits blamed their failure on local inland Muslim communities, who were massacred as a result (though this violence was the exception to more typically harmonious relations with the Muslims of the coast).[22]

Having failed in their attempts at conquest, with sporadic later efforts at colonization from metropolitan Portugal also proving abortive, the Portuguese instead took the Muslim lands around the Zambezi and allocated them as estates (*prazos*) of the king, creating the class of *prazo*-holders, whose direct descendants still populate the region today. The Portuguese were lucky in their timing. The more powerful African kingdoms which might otherwise have disputed this land-grab were preoccupied with civil wars, and later regarded the Zambezi river valley as an unimportant frontier zone.

Like much else in the Estado da Índia, from a formal point of view these estates were subordinated in a strict, centralized chain of command. *Prazos* or, to give them their full title, *prazos da coroa* (crown estates), were held by right of a grant from the king for a set period of time, though during that time they were inheritable only via the female line. Later in the seventeenth century these estates became permanent and fully inheritable, though *prazo*-holders were still formally royal officials subordinated to the Estado da Índia. This suggests the classically modern authority structure of a defined hierarchy of command flowing down from a central government via intermediating

[21] Isaacman and Isaacman, '*Prazeros* as Transfrontiersmen'.
[22] Prestholdt, 'Portuguese Conceptual Categories', pp. 383, 403.

subordinate officials, with definite borders for each estate, as well as between the Portuguese crown possessions and foreign polities. In fact, however, matters were much more complicated, and the *prazos* were part of a strongly heteronomous political environment.

For as well as owing allegiance to the Portuguese crown, *prazo*-holders also themselves paid and received tribute from superior and subordinate African polities. Thus, as well as swearing fealty to the king in Lisbon, the *prazo*-holders pledged loyalty and paid tribute to powerful inland African rulers of the Zimbabwe Plateau, and received traditional payments of tribute and taxes in kind from local village chiefs.[23] So like the galactic polities of South-East Asia, *prazo*-holders had more than one suzerain overlord. In this practice, the Portuguese were conforming to pre-existing local authority arrangements. For as Subrahmanyam explains:

> the Zambezi River in the early seventeenth century had a fluid political system, in which outsiders could insert themselves without great difficulty, and seek suitable vertical and horizontal links to legitimize their positions. The grant by the Portuguese King of a *prazo* was merely one way of legitimizing a political alliance and tribute system that already functioned on the ground.[24]

This dual subordination to both Portuguese and African suzerain authority did not preclude the *prazo*-holders from wielding extensive de jure and de facto powers themselves, however. These potentates, numbering over eighty by 1637,[25] ruled their estates in line with local African customs, raised slave armies which might number in the thousands, fought private wars against each other and their nominal subordinates, and mounted various expeditions further into the interior.[26] The main goal of these activities was to increase the flow of tribute by subordinating other local groups, in particular to increase their stocks of cattle, ivory and gold. A contemporary described the powers of the *prazo*-holders as follows: 'the holders of these lands have the same power and jurisdiction as the Kaffir *fumos* [chiefs] from whom they were conquered . . . and therefore they are like the potentates of Germany, and can pronounce sentence in all cases, put to death, declare

23 Isaacman and Isaacman, '*Prazeros* as Transfrontiersmen', pp. 5–6.
24 Subrahmanyam, *Portuguese Empire in Asia*, p. 207.
25 Disney, *History of Portugal*, p. 199.
26 Russell-Wood, *The Portuguese Empire*, p. 104.

war, and impose tribute'.[27] In practice, the Portuguese officials on the coast had almost no control over the *prazo*-holders. Boxer refers to them as 'virtually private principalities ruled by individuals of the "robber baron" type'.[28] Indeed, it was only from the 1890s that the Portuguese in their coastal settlements exercised effective control of the interior of what became Mozambique.[29]

The early Portuguese impressions of the peoples of the interior were not positive. One sixteenth-century Portuguese observer wrote:

> The Moors of this place [Malindi] have as their inland neighbours some Kaffirs who are utterly different from those in the entire coast . . . They are very warlike and the report goes that in their fights they are wont to cut off the foreskins and swallow them, and that when they appear before the king they do cast them out again from their mouths so he may make them knights. They wear animal skins and have sundry other barbaric customs.[30]

In contrast, the *prazo*-holders – who were actually compelled to deal with the peoples of the interior – did not hold and in any case could not afford to have such negative views. Instead, they became highly assimilated, often by marrying local heiresses. Europeans were a minority among the estate-holders, as many of those ruling estates were indigenous Christians that had come from Portuguese possessions in India. Other *prazo*-holders not hailing from India may have had some European ancestry but much more by way of local African populations. In fact, this community represented an even broader range of diversity. Thus in 1633 a Portuguese school in the interior taught children of Chinese, Javanese, Malabar and Sinhalese extraction, as well as Africans and a few Europeans.[31] Rather than a one-way process of Europeans adopting African mores, there was a mingling of European, African, Arab and South and East Asian cultures. As well as being Catholics they consulted local spirit mediums, and while fluent in Portuguese the household language was Shona, Bantu or another African tongue. Yet there were limits to this mingling of cultures; when the powerful inland king of Monomotapa converted to Catholicism, he quickly lost legitimacy among his nobles and other followers.

[27] Quoted in Boxer, *Portuguese Seaborne Empire*, p. 139.
[28] Boxer, *Portuguese Seaborne Empire*, p. 140.
[29] A. Isaacman, *Mozambique: The Africanization of a European Institution: The Zambezi Prazos, 1750–1902* (Madison: University of Wisconsin Press, 1972).
[30] Quoted in Pearson, *Port Cities and Intruders*, p. 71. [31] *Ibid.*, p. 150.

In sum, despite the statist character of the Estado da Índia in general, Portuguese arrangements in the Zambezi interior conformed much more closely to heteronomy than state sovereignty. *Prazo*-holders paid tribute to African kings as well as the one in Lisbon, and the imprimatur of the former was probably more important than that of the latter. They received tribute from chiefs who also sometimes acknowledged several suzerains. These Afro-Portuguese rulers had extensive legal autonomy and in practical terms were most often independent of the coastal Portuguese officials. *Prazo*-holders had to symbolically legitimate themselves according to local customs, and were to a large extent physically and culturally assimilated into these populations, marking a particularly clear example of practices of localization in action. Normative factors to one side, the Portuguese were forced into such accommodations after the failure of efforts at direct conquest and colonization. Goa simply lacked the manpower to impose its will, especially given Europeans' susceptibility to disease in the African interior. Local Arabs and Africans were generally able to strike mutually advantageous bargains with the agents of the Estado da Índia that were crucial in sustaining the Portuguese presence in East Africa, even long after the reverses in South and South-East Asia at the hands of the VOC in the seventeenth century.

The East India Company and the Mughal Empire, 1600–1619

In examining the opening of relations between the EIC and the Mughals at the start of the seventeenth century, two concerns are central: first, the EIC needed to get formal authorization to trade from the emperor, but then they also needed to win practical recognition of these privileges from the local sub-rulers. In the early 1600s, the Mughal maritime province of Gujarat was the Arabian Sea's central entrepôt and one of the Indian Ocean's most critical commercial nodes. Conquered by the Mughals only in 1573, Gujarat constituted, along with Bengal, one of the Mughal Empire's two principal gateways to the Indian Ocean trading world.[32] For the infant East India Company in the early 1600s, securing a foothold in cosmopolitan Gujarat was

[32] On the Mughals' conquest of the subcontinent's two most important maritime states of Gujarat (in 1572–3) and Bengal (in 1574–6), and the transformative impact of these conquests on the Indian Ocean trading world, see Flores, 'The Sea World and the *Mutasaddi*', pp. 55–6.

essential to achieving its broader ambitions of establishing a direct and permanent presence in the lucrative trade between Europe and Asia. In particular, the EIC sought a presence in Surat. One official celebrated the town as 'the most famed Emporium of the Indian Empire'.[33] The port was both close to the caravan routes crossing the fertile Gujarat plains, and a catchment point for goods coming down the western Indian coast for shipment overseas.[34] If the company could carve out a position in Surat, it would possess an ideal springboard for commercial expansion into Asia. But winning the right to establish a factory in Gujarat required the EIC to first secure an indulgence from the province's paramount ruler, the Mughal emperor, Jahangir. To appreciate the difficulties this endeavour entailed, we must revisit the nature of the Mughal polity and its distinctive mode of diplomatic intercourse.

Alongside the emperor's generous patronage of the empire's diverse religious establishments, court ceremonial provided a potent mechanism that symbolically strengthened the principal patron–client ties around which the Mughal Empire cohered. For the EIC, the Mughal court's cosmopolitan and ecumenical character provided company agents with an important opportunity. Specifically, if the EIC could secure recognition as a 'slave' to the emperor, they would win numerous advantages, not least an imperial *farman* granting them their sought-after privilege to trade in Mughal territory.[35]

At the same time, however, the centrality of rituals of symbolic incorporation to Mughal practices of rule nevertheless complicated this process in important ways. At the most basic level, the social practices mediating Mughal relations with other polities – centred on ceremonial submission and tributary gift exchange – contrasted dramatically with European diplomatic practice. Recognizing no distinction between the domestic and the international, the Mughals were unfamiliar with the nascent system of resident ambassadorial diplomacy then taking shape in Europe. In contrast to the routine

33 EIC official quoted in K. Chaudhuri, *The Trading World of Asia and the English East India Company: 1660–1760* (Cambridge University Press, 1978), p. 49. See also R. J. Barendse, 'Trade and State in the Arabian Seas: A Survey from the Fifteenth to the Eighteenth Century', *Journal of World History* 11:2 (2000), p. 216.

34 Chaudhuri, *The Trading World of Asia and the English East India Company*, p. 49.

35 R. Barbour, 'Power and Distant Display: Early English "Ambassadors" in Mughal India', *Huntington Library Quarterly* 61:3/4 (1998), p. 361.

acceptance of the practice of *commercial* extra-territoriality governing resident trading diasporas, *diplomatic* extra-territoriality – manifest in Europeans' experiments in maintaining networks of permanent resident ambassadors to regulate their relations with one another – remained then unknown elsewhere. Instead, consistent with most contemporary Asian and African polities, Mughal diplomacy entailed the emperor's episodic reception of 'embassies' in the form of visiting foreign delegations soliciting imperial favours in exchange for their continuing submission.[36]

This disjuncture between European and Mughal diplomatic practice did not by itself frustrate the EIC's ambitions. In the early seventeenth century European diplomatic practices were themselves far from settled. EIC representatives undoubtedly chafed at the requirement of ritual submission to the emperor, and found the ceremonies this entailed both unfamiliar and humiliating,[37] but English discomfort at Mughal condescension did not derail commercial negotiations, as it would do almost two centuries later with the infamous McCartney mission to Peking.

More problematic for the English than the formal requirements of submission to the Mughal emperor was the Mughals' own understandable confusion concerning the nature of the East India Company. In particular, the EIC's hybrid status as both traders and company sovereigns invested with governing powers by an English royal charter confounded Mughal categorizations, which relied on a sharp delineation between rulers and merchants.[38] For the Mughal emperor, the court was a place for receiving submission from two sets of actors – direct clients of the emperor from within the empire itself, and the visiting ambassadors of client rulers from the *wilayets* (provinces), that is, those territories beyond the Empire's fuzzy frontiers. The EIC did not fit clearly into either category.[39] The English certainly originated from the provinces, but their interests ostensibly appeared entirely commercial in character. For this reason, the Mughals were initially unreceptive to the EIC's entreaties for trading privileges,

[36] *Ibid.* [37] *Ibid.*, pp. 365–6. [38] *Ibid.*, p. 364.

[39] To further confuse matters, while Sir Thomas Roe represented King James I, he was the company's nominee, and the costs of the embassy were completely underwritten by the company rather than by the crown. See Sapra, 'A Peaceable Kingdom in the East', pp. 13–14.

perceiving them as 'mere merchants' unworthy of the emperor's consideration, rather than empowered delegates of the English crown.[40]

Mughal misperceptions of the EIC's purely commercial status were entirely understandable. This is because some of the first embassies seeking privileges from the imperial court *were* undertaken by a succession of private English adventurers who, taking advantage of the EIC's newly minted charter, sought to exact trading concessions supposedly on behalf of the company, but primarily to enhance their own prestige and wealth.[41] Complicating matters further, Portuguese Jesuits – by now well ensconced at the Mughal court – deliberately fostered Mughal misperceptions by attempting to reinforce the impression that EIC company factors represented purely commercial interests.[42]

Ironically, given the chartered companies' pronounced military and economic superiority over their quasi-statist Portuguese rivals, the Estado da Índia's more statist character actually favoured them in their initial dealings with the Mughals. Portuguese efforts to establish 'friendship' and 'brotherhood' between the Portuguese king and the Mughal emperor were certainly complicated by both parties' universalistic ambitions.[43] But the Estado da Índia's attempts to forge a direct relationship between the Portuguese and Mughal sovereigns gave it greater traction at the court in Agra than the petitions of the EIC.[44] Ultimately, the EIC's early diplomatic failures necessitated the dispatch of an official ambassador, Sir Thomas Roe, from England in 1615 to establish a direct relationship with the Emperor Jahangir. Roe's embassy to Jahangir's court was fraught with challenges, as he sought to undo the damage prior unofficial 'embassies' and Portuguese acts of sabotage had inflicted on the English reputation. It was nevertheless a critical circuit-breaker, yielding the indispensable *farman* necessary to secure the EIC's liberty to trade in Surat.[45]

The Mughals' eventual grant of a *farman* to the company was crucial in confirming the latter's status as a legitimate commercial presence in Mughal India. The pre-existing tradition of commercial extraterritoriality, coupled with an English willingness to familiarize themselves with and submit to the ritual imperatives of Mughal diplomacy,

[40] M. K. Jha, 'The Mughals, Merchants and the European Companies in 17th Century Surat', *Asia Europe Journal* 3:2 (2005), p. 274.
[41] Barbour, 'Power and Distant Display', pp. 353–5. [42] *Ibid.*, p. 357.
[43] Sapra, 'A Peaceable Kingdom in the East', pp. 7–8.
[44] Barbour, 'Power and Distant Display', p. 356. [45] *Ibid.*

was key in enabling this process. Likewise, the Mughals' willingness to symbolically incorporate the EIC as vassals into the empire was equally important in cementing their presence on the Indian subcontinent. Nevertheless, in order for the EIC to practically enjoy the privileges the *farman* had theoretically conferred, they needed not merely to adapt to local norms, but also to forge durable commercial and political alliances with indigenous partners.

The company's ability to maintain its toehold in Surat – let alone draw a profit – proved immensely difficult in the first decades following their establishment of a factory there. This was partially due to the EIC's precarious security situation. The emperor had not granted a right to establish any armed or fortified settlement. Instead, responsibility for security in Surat lay with the Mughal-appointed fort commander who, along with the provincial governor, responsible for revenue collection and general administration, constituted the dominant power in the city.[46]

In theory, the Mughals' retention of exclusive military power in Surat harmonized perfectly with the company's desire to avoid the overhead costs of fortifying its factories whenever possible. The direct financial costs of building fortifications and then maintaining them with properly trained and equipped troops were formidable. The political risks that militarizing the company's trading posts would antagonize the Mughals and aggravate the company's security dilemma with its European rivals further strengthened company preferences to remain 'newtors ... endevouring to doe our business, with a great deal of submission and not much charge'.[47]

Both frugality and prudence therefore counselled against the company following the example of militarized trade set by both the Estado da Índia and the VOC. The company's aversion to force as an instrument of commercial diplomacy was confirmed early on in the history of the Surat factory in 1623–4, when an attempt to extort more favourable arrangements from the local authorities through a company naval blockade against Surat spectacularly backfired. Given that company factors eventually had to return ashore to resume their trade – therefore

[46] G. A. Nadri, *Eighteenth Century Gujarat: The Dynamics of its Political Economy, 1750–1800* (Leiden: Brill, 2009), p. 11.

[47] Company official, cited in D. K. Bassett, 'Early English Trade and Settlement in Asia, 1602–1690', in P. Tuck (ed.), *The East India Company: 1600–1858*, vol. IV: *Trade, Finance and Power* (Routledge: London, 1998), p. 10.

opening themselves up to the inevitable reprisals and punishment from local Mughal authorities that followed – resort to naval coercion was rapidly abandoned as an instrument of company diplomacy.[48]

The company's commitment to a pacifist posture in Surat did not allow it to enjoy its profits unmolested, however. The most important Mughal office-holders in Surat were also wealthy merchants who had purchased their offices from the emperor at vast expense, and as such were often fierce commercial competitors to the EIC.[49] Consequently, the English were routinely frustrated by arbitrary taxation from local Mughal-endorsed agents.

In the case of the emperor, the EIC and their European rivals periodically sent gift-laden embassies to the Mughal court, where they would submit a petition to the emperor to try to win reconfirmation of their trading privileges and an enforcement of their claims against local officialdom.[50] Such embassies were rarely successful in achieving their ostensible aim. This is because the entire Mughal polity was built on 'co-sharing sovereignty' with indigenous social elites.[51] Through its reliance on extensive practices of office- and revenue-farming, the Mughal state was enmeshed within the society that it governed. An office-holder like those in Surat was consequently 'quite incapable of serving as an earnest instrument of the imposition of imperial will on local customs and practices'.[52]

This did not, however, render the EIC's dispatch of embassies to the imperial court futile. Within an imperial system in which government was conceived not primarily in rational-bureaucratic terms, but rather as 'an incorporative process of dialogue between ruler and a range of local authorities',[53] the provision of gifts affirmed the EIC's incorporation as legitimate (if subordinate) actors within the Mughal social

48 *Ibid.*, p. 12.
49 Flores, 'The Sea World and the *Mutasaddi*, p. 57. Hasan notes additionally that the Mughals farmed out the position of *mutàsaddi* to the highest bidder down to the 1640s, and that this therefore strengthened office-holders' incentives to recoup their initial costs by over-taxing merchants – including the EIC – whenever possible. See F. Hasan, 'The Mughal Fiscal System in Surat and the English East India Company', *Modern Asian Studies* 27:4 (1993), p. 715.
50 M. Siddiqi, *The British Historical Context and Petitioning in India* (New Delhi: Aakar Books, 2005), p. 10.
51 *Ibid.*, p. 34. 52 *Ibid.*, p. 39.
53 J. E. Wilson, 'Early Colonial India Beyond Empire', *Historical Journal* 50:4 (2007), p. 956.

order. For the Mughals, both the *farman* granting trading privileges to the EIC and the sale of offices to local elites were comparable in key respects. Both were seen as revocable 'gifts' that incorporated otherwise disparate actors into the imperial order as the Emperor's loyal 'slaves'.[54] In periodically sending gifts and petitioning for imperial favours, the EIC thus confirmed its legitimate position within the Mughal order, placing a real if uncertain upper limit on the exactions the emperor's servants could inflict upon the company.

While Europeans constantly complained about official harassment, their relationships with local office-holders were in fact characterized by a complex mixture of cooperation and conflict. Mughal officials aimed to maximize the rents they extracted from European traders, but they also benefited from the increased commercial activities (and therefore customs revenues) that the European presence generated.[55] European traders were critically dependent on local money-lenders for short-term credit, while linguistic and cultural obstacles likewise necessitated that the EIC retain indigenous brokers to mediate many of its most important deals.[56] At the same time, European superiority in shipping and naval warfare ensured that many indigenous merchants preferred to lease space on European ships when conveying their cargo over long distances, perversely vindicating European efforts to set up a protection racket on Indian Ocean maritime commerce.[57] The existence of multiple ports in Gujarat and elsewhere along the Indian western coast provided merchants (both European and local) with credible exit options if the exactions of officials at any one port threatened to become too onerous.[58] For this reason, as the European commercial presence in Mughal India matured over the course of the seventeenth and early eighteenth centuries, their relationship with local officialdom evolved to one of distrustful symbiosis, a 'nebulous' and 'ill-defined' alliance

[54] Hasan, *State and Locality in Mughal India*, p. 37. The gift status of the *farmans* granting the EIC trading privileges was illustrated by the fact that each *farman* signified a direct relationship between the company and the emperor, and thus needed personal reconfirmation whenever a new emperor took power. See F. Hasan, 'Conflict and Cooperation in Anglo-Mughal Trade Relations During the Reign of Aurungzeb', *Journal of the Economic and Social History of the Orient* 34:4 (1991), p. 354.

[55] *Ibid.*, p. 82.

[56] R. Maloni, 'Europeans in Seventeenth Century Gujarat: Presence and Response', *Social Scientist* 36:3/4 (2008), pp. 77–80.

[57] *Ibid.*, pp. 84–6. [58] Hasan, *State and Locality in Mughal India*, pp. 34–5.

between the company and local officials and merchants, further entrenching the company within the empire.[59]

India's Coromandel Coast, obsolescing bargains and the EIC's first fortified settlement

The company's experiences in Surat reveal the critical importance of localization – both ideational and material – in easing European entry into the Indian Ocean international system. But focusing solely on the company's interactions with the Mughals threatens to distort our understanding of the complex and varied character of localization in the Indian Ocean. Prior to Britain's confrontation with Qing China in the nineteenth century, the Mughal Empire comprised the most populous and powerful non-European polity Westerners had ever encountered. Far exceeding the wealth and power of the Ottoman caliphs, the Mughals could dictate the terms of their engagement with European actors from a position of unchallengeable material superiority. Mughal willingness to legitimate the European presence within locally dominant idioms and practices of power (e.g. the granting of *farmans*) was key to integrating the EIC into the Indian Ocean world.

More frequently, however, the power asymmetries between Europeans and local actors were far less pronounced than in the Mughal case, and the dynamics of localization were correspondingly more balanced. In the south of the subcontinent, beyond the reach of Mughal power, Europeans encountered a far more fragmented political landscape. On the Coromandel Coast in south-eastern India in particular, political power was shared among chieftains locked in a competition to attract revenues from maritime trade linking south-east India with maritime South-East Asia.[60]

Unlike the Mughal Empire, which extracted the bulk of its revenues from taxes on land and peasants even after its conquest of Gujarat and Bengal, the Coromandel Coast rulers were far more oriented towards skimming off the rents that could be extracted from Indian Ocean commerce.[61] Consistent with Mughal practice, however, they engaged in extensive revenue- and office-farming, and were of course familiar with Old World customs of commercial extra-territoriality. For these

[59] Hasan, 'Conflict and Cooperation in Anglo-Mughal Trade Relations', p. 360.
[60] Pearson, 'Merchants and States', p. 109. [61] *Ibid.*

chieftains, attracting commercial activity to the territories over which they ruled promised to raise their revenues and thus strengthen their wealth and power.[62] Equally, for Europeans – and for the English in particular – establishing factories along the Coromandel Coast offered a means of accessing the region's valuable textiles, in turn equipping them with the tradable goods needed to purchase spices from South-East Asia.[63]

The story of the EIC's establishment in Madras in 1639 is even in its barest details strongly counter-intuitive. It powerfully illustrates the dynamics of localization that shaped the company sovereigns as they configured themselves around indigenous political and economic systems. Unlike the Mughals, the local rulers of the Coromandel Coast had no objections to the Europeans establishing fortifications to protect their trading outposts.[64] On the contrary, local rulers regarded fortifications as essential commercial infrastructure, the additional security they offered to both foreign and indigenous merchants, making them a magnet for attracting taxable commerce.[65] Fortifications nevertheless constituted a formidable expense that the rulers preferred to pass on to the merchants themselves if possible.

In the 1620s and 1630s, the EIC – while keen to acquire a permanent commercial foothold on the Coromandel Coast – remained leery of the costs associated with establishing fortified trading settlements. In the Spice Islands, the company had earlier agreed to share with the VOC the costs of maintaining fortified factories that the two companies briefly maintained together.[66] The immense burdens associated with upholding their share of these costs nevertheless significantly drained EIC coffers, hastening their eventual withdrawal from the archipelago.[67] The initial

62 *Ibid.*

63 Prakash, 'Europeans, India and the Indian Ocean in the Early Modern Period', *South Asia: Journal of South Asian Studies* 19, supplement 1 (1996), pp. 18–19.

64 Pearson, 'Merchants and States', p. 109.

65 D. Vigneswaran, 'A Corrupt International Society: How Britain was Duped into its First Indian Conquest', in S. Suzuki, Y. Zhang and J. Quirk (eds.), *International Orders in the Early Modern World: Before the Rise of the West* (London: Routledge, 2013), p. 184. The following account draws heavily on Vigneswaran's pioneering historical analysis of this case.

66 V. C. Loth, 'Armed Incidents and Unpaid Bills: Anglo-Dutch Rivalry in the Banda Islands in the Seventeenth Century', *Modern Asian Studies* 29:4 (1995), p. 722.

67 *Ibid.*, pp. 738–9.

establishment of a small fort at Armagon north of Madraspatam in 1625 had likewise proved a costly failure.[68] Accustomed to entrusting the security of their factories to local authorities, as in Mughal Surat, the EIC's directors were initially emphatic in instructing their factors to refrain from any undertakings to local rulers that imposed an obligation to secure new trading settlements through the establishment of fortifications.[69]

Despite receiving explicit instructions not to establish a fortified settlement, company employees ultimately contracted with the local ruler Damarla Venkatadri to found a fortified factory in the vicinity of Madraspatam on a strip of coastal land that had been alienated to the company.[70] The contracting EIC agent, Francis Day, initially justified the deal to his superiors on the basis that Venkatadri had agreed to pay the costs for the fort's establishment, which would attract commerce while simultaneously strengthening his own security.[71] Day furthermore justified the need for a fortified self-governing settlement as being in the company's interests, given that the Dutch had already established one at Pulicat, and could threaten English trade unless and until the company emulated the VOC's example.[72] However, when company factors returned to Madraspatam to commence work on the fort, the original bargain obsolesced, Venkatadri now claiming that he had been misunderstood and had in fact offered no such undertaking to defray the fort's establishment costs.[73]

Prolonged recriminations and an internal inquiry within the company followed. But the momentum for establishing a fortified trading settlement in Madras eventually proved impossible to resist, with Fort St George being completed in 1644. In time, as one of the company's three presidencies in the subcontinent (alongside Bombay and

[68] Vigneswaran, 'A Corrupt International Society', p. 193.

[69] The directors' reticence to countenance the immense costs entailed in building fortifications was hardly exclusive to the EIC, for the VOC directors repeatedly evinced similar reservations with respect to the VOC's defence overheads in the Indonesian archipelago. See Loth, 'Armed Incidents and Unpaid Bills', p. 736.

[70] Vigneswaran, 'A Corrupt International Society', pp. 109–11.

[71] *Ibid.*, p. 110. [72] *Ibid.*

[73] *Ibid.*, p. 111. An alternative (possibly apocryphal) account has it that the local ruler had initially agreed to build the fort himself in return for a payment of Persian horses, but that when Day found 'to his horror' that the intended fort was to be made of palmyra leaves, he took it upon himself to build it of sturdier materials. See T. Roy, *The East India Company: The World's Most Powerful Corporation* (New Delhi: Penguin, 2012), p. 72.

Calcutta), Madras would form one of the nuclei of the British Raj, as well as carrying the unenviable distinction of being the first city in modern history to have an officially designated urban colour line.[74] Especially when contrasted against the company's demilitarized presence in Mughal Surat, what we see in the Coromandel Coast is the decisive influence of local norms and interests in shoving and shaping the very form that the company assumed as a polity.

As with the Portuguese estate-holders around the Zambezi, in both Mughal Gujarat and the Coromandel Coast, then, processes of localization were at work. The EIC's incorporation into indigenous commerce was facilitated because its presence at least temporarily served the ideational and/or material interests of local actors. The varying dynamics of localization in Mughal Gujarat and the Coromandel Coast's maritime states compounded regional diversity and heterogeneity, consistent with our central argument. The EIC's varying institutional presence – as a quiescent if self-governing mercantile community in Surat, and as founders and rulers of a fortified city-colony in Madras – testifies to the varying impact of local norms and alliance opportunities in conditioning the shape of the company. The result was that the company developed as varying networks of military, commercial and legal authority, woven into local power structures while being linked back to the company directors in London. To demonstrate the generalizability of our argument, we turn now to the VOC, the most tenacious and aggressive European competitor of the Estado da Índia and the EIC, and its establishment of hegemony in what would eventually become the Dutch East Indies.

The VOC, the 'stranger king' tradition and the creeping conquest of eighteenth-century Java

In contrast to the EIC – 'duped' into its first imperial conquest in Madras[75] – the VOC proved much more predatory from the very beginning of its expansion into the Indian Ocean international system. It was better armed and better capitalized than either the Portuguese or the EIC, and it evinced remarkably few moral inhibitions in its pursuit of power and profit.

[74] C. H. Nightingale, 'Before Race Mattered: Geographies of the Early Modern Color Line in Early Colonial Madras and New York', *American Historical Review* 113:1 (2008), p. 50.

[75] Vigneswaran, 'A Corrupt International Society', p. 94.

A velociraptor in an already ferociously competitive environment, the VOC's political ambitions remained subordinate to its commercial goals for most of its existence. The adage 'What the lord spends, the merchant has to pay' reflected an acute recognition within the VOC that the goals of profit maximization and power maximization were rarely in harmony, and most often in direct conflict with one another.[76] Like the EIC, the VOC's dominant concern was the bottom line, especially after the United Provinces' independence from the Habsburgs was confirmed in 1648. The VOC minimized its overheads wherever and whenever it could, and this extended to efforts to swear off the commercially unrewarding responsibilities of rule.[77]

Within Java in particular in the seventeenth century, the company repeatedly refused to entertain indigenous requests that it assume suzerainty over local regencies of the Mataram sultanate, fearful that such obligations might bring with them diplomatic and financial costs.[78] But by the time the VOC went bankrupt in 1800, it was on the cusp of completing the conquest of Java, the Indonesian archipelago's most populous island. A brief investigation of how the VOC as 'reluctant imperialists' came to conquer central and eastern Java illustrates the influence that localizing dynamics played in shaping polity interaction and reproducing regional diversity.[79]

To understand the processes that drove the VOC's emergence as Java's sovereign power, we must first briefly consider the local political and economic context. Two features of the Javanese landscape demand particular attention: its intensely fragmented and competitive character, and its historical permeability (alongside the rest of maritime South-East Asia) to outside influence. Eighteenth-century Java was divided between the VOC (dominant in an enclave of western Java centred around its port capital of Batavia) and the sultanate of Mataram, the paramount power in central and eastern Java. Like most of early modern South-East Asian

[76] The adage 'What the lord spends, the merchant has to pay' is generally attributed to VOC governor-general Jacob Mossel. See W. Remmelink, 'Expansion Without Design: The Snare of Javanese Politics', *Itinerario* 12:1 (1988), p. 111.

[77] Loth, 'Armed Incidents and Unpaid Bills', p. 736.

[78] Kian, 'How Strangers Became Kings', p. 297.

[79] On the VOC as 'reluctant imperialists', see *ibid.*, p. 301. The 'reluctance' here of course denotes a reluctance only to assume the costs and responsibilities of direct rule over local populations, not a reluctance to use any means – including violence – to maximize the VOC's profits and political influence.

polities, Mataram was a 'galactic polity'. Spiritual cum political power was concentrated in the body of the sultan and his palace, and radiated outwards in circles of steadily diminishing influence to encompass the sultan's vassals in gradated degrees of subjection.[80] Unlike the Mughals, however, Javanese rulers did not enjoy access to a large, taxable and reliably sedentary peasantry. While populous in relative terms for South-East Asia even in the early modern period, Java's population remained sparse in absolute terms relative to the island's territory.[81] For this reason, '"Territoriality" . . . was defined more by population than by physical area.'[82] Indigenous power-maximizing elites consequently were less interested in conquering territory per se. Instead, power was to be had through asserting control over a large subject population, securing the fealty and submission of neighbouring rulers, and by attracting and retaining as many local and foreign merchants as possible.[83]

While Mataram was the pre-eminent polity in eighteenth-century Java, basic power realities meant that Mataram's sultan struggled to convert nominal suzerainty into practical dominance. Given existing land–labour ratios, peasants could always 'vote with their feet' and flee oppressive rule. This situation left Java's elites locked in a constant tug of war for mobile subjects, and dramatically inhibited efforts to consolidate and institutionalize sovereign power.[84] Political power was tenuous and continually contested.

Adding a further layer of complexity, Java lay at the centre of a region that attracted merchants and missionaries from throughout East Asia and the Indian Ocean littoral. In Java – and indeed throughout most of South-East Asia – this continuous exposure to cosmopolitan influences had bred a distinctive receptivity to alien rule. Dubbed the 'stranger king' phenomenon by anthropologists, the tradition of adopting foreigners into indigenous structures of rule was widespread throughout early modern Asia.[85] In some instances, as in Siamese Ayutthaya's appointment of a Greek prime minister (Constantine Phaulkon) in the late seventeenth century, this receptivity was confined to elevating individual

[80] *Ibid*., pp. 295–6. See also, more generally, Tambiah, 'The Galactic Polity', pp. 69–97.

[81] Kian, 'How Strangers Became Kings', p. 295. [82] *Ibid.* [83] *Ibid.*

[84] *Ibid.*

[85] For an outstanding survey of this phenomenon, see F. Fernández-Armesto, 'The Stranger Effect in Early Modern Asia', *Itinerario* 24:2 (2000), pp. 80–103.

foreigners to positions of high office within local courts.[86] In other cases, however, the 'stranger king' tradition proved sufficiently elastic to accommodate the wholesale surrender of sovereign power to foreign rulers.[87] Anthropologists remain divided in their efforts to account for the phenomenon of 'stranger kings'.[88] But these traditions proved critically influential in helping to suck the VOC into an unwanted position of predominance by the century's end.[89]

By the early nineteenth century, the VOC was bankrupt and Java's indigenous polities were on the cusp of complete subjection to European rule. How was this quintessentially lose–lose outcome possible? The answer to this puzzle can be found in the conjunction of equivalent European and indigenous beliefs in heteronomy and the divisibility of sovereign prerogatives, combined with the unintended consequences of European and indigenous actors' efforts to localize the VOC's presence through practices of symbolic legitimation and opportunistic alliance formation.

The VOC embodied the heteronomous principle that classically sovereign prerogatives could be unbundled and delegated to multiple actors.[90] Likewise, the Javanese system of interacting and overlapping 'galactic polities' reflected the principle that political power was fluid, emanated from multiple centres, and was territorially non-exclusive.[91] Potent 'stranger king' traditions also facilitated the spread of Dutch influence throughout Java, as locals legitimized the Dutch by imagining them as 'senior' relatives to Javanese kings.[92] Consistent with the dual stress on material strategic bargaining as well as symbolic legitimation, it was nevertheless the short-term instrumental value that local actors attached to Dutch military powers that cemented the VOC's rise to hegemony.

86 *Ibid.*, p. 89.

87 See, for example, D. Henley, 'Conflict, Justice and the Stranger-King Roots of Colonial Rule in Indonesia and Elsewhere', *Modern Asian Studies* 38:1 (2004), pp. 85–144.

88 On the broad contours of this theoretical division, see I. Caldwell and D. Henley, 'Introduction: The Stranger Who Would be King – Magic, Logic and Polemic', *Indonesia and the Malay World* 26:105 (2008), p. 170.

89 M. C. Ricklefs, *A History of Modern Indonesia since c. 1300* (Stanford University Press, 1993), p. 110.

90 V. Lieberman, *Strange Parallels: Southeast Asia in Global Context, c. 800–1830* (Cambridge University Press, 2009), pp. 861–2.

91 Kian, 'How Strangers Became Kings', p. 296.

92 Lieberman, *Strange Parallels*, p. 862.

Dutch military power, combined with the VOC's early aversion to directly asserting rule over local populations, made the VOC an attractive ally to Java's feuding actors. Central and eastern Java were rent by two main axes of struggle in the eighteenth century. The first separated the inland power of Mataram from coastal district chiefs, while the second centred on the internecine struggles within the Mataram court itself.[93] Within this febrile context, the VOC's military power as 'mafia-like enforcers' – too small to immediately threaten actors' independence, but large enough to tip the balance in local feuds – made them attractive as potential partners.[94] Thus, whereas in Mughal India and the Coromandel Coast it was the enhanced customs receipts that European commerce would bring that helped win them local acceptance, in Java it was rather the VOC's potency as useful (if dangerous) mercenaries that proved most crucial in helping them to spread their influence beyond Batavia and a handful of other commercial enclaves.[95]

Javanese actors were wary that they were 'riding a tiger' in soliciting VOC military support, and were alive to the dangers that such entangling alliances could bring with them.[96] That the VOC ultimately came to dominate Java can be attributed to the unintended consequences of its growing involvement in Javanese politics as the island's internal ructions worsened over the course of the eighteenth century. Java was exceptionally important within the VOC's sprawling empire, hosting its Asian capital (Batavia) as well as serving as both its rice-basket and timber-yard.[97] In light of this importance, the company simply could not afford to ignore escalating conflict among Java's political elite, which threatened to destroy the civil order necessary for the VOC's trade to flourish.[98] As both the sultan of Mataram and his rivals were furthermore prepared to pay for VOC military assistance through a combination of land sales, commercial tribute and the sale of regional monopolies, the scope for profiting directly from what appeared to be limited and discrete interventions also could not be ignored.[99]

Unfortunately for all concerned, the very prospect of VOC intervention fomented continuing instability. The VOC's availability as

93 Kian, 'How Strangers Became Kings', p. 297.
94 Lieberman, *Strange Parallels*, p. 865. 95 *Ibid.*
96 Kian, 'How Strangers Became Kings', p. 299.
97 Remmelink, 'Expansion Without Design', p. 111. 98 *Ibid.*, p. 112.
99 Lieberman, *Strange Parallels*, p. 866.

mercenary actors emboldened the sultan's enemies towards rebellion, thus fuelling the very disorder that jeopardized the VOC's commercial interests.[100] At the same time, the sultan's piecemeal awarding of commercial privileges and cash payments to the VOC in exchange for its help in suppressing rebels hollowed out the Mataramese polity, perversely worsening political instability.[101] The resulting cycle of instability, VOC intervention, piecemeal alienation of commercial privileges and institutional decay fatally corroded indigenous political authority in the long run. The consequence was a spiral that saw the mutual ruin of Mataram as an independent polity, and eventually also the end of the VOC as a viable commercial enterprise.

Conclusion

While the preceding chapters dealt with the origins of disparate polity forms, this chapter has been devoted to explaining the stabilization and reproduction of polity diversity from the sixteenth to the eighteenth century. European and indigenous actors negotiated diverse bargains with one another that partially integrated the former into local political structures, either as vassals, equal partners or nominal (and later, actual) suzerains. A combination of structural similarities across polity forms and processes of localization were jointly responsible for reproducing polity diversity in the Indian Ocean international system. The most important of these structural similarities was an adherence to a heteronomous configuration of social power, instantiated in practices of legal pluralism. The existence of these structural similarities allowed for otherwise unlike European and local political units to stabilize their relations with one another. But Europeans and their host communities had to creatively leverage these structural similarities. They did so through localization and European adaptation to indigenous idioms of legitimacy, as well as instrumental collaborative ventures for mutual advantage.

Both material and ideational structures shaped political processes in the Indian Ocean international system[102] and the bargains that European and indigenous actors struck. At a systemic level, the impact of continuously growing interaction compounded existing polity

[100] *Ibid.*, p. 860. [101] *Ibid.*, pp. 867–8.
[102] Waltz, *Theory of International Politics*, p. 82.

diversity rather than reducing it.[103] Despite extensive cultural creolization and intermarriage between Europeans and locals in the sixteenth to the eighteenth century, Europeans were not simply absorbed into local polities. Both the Estado da Índia and the chartered company sovereigns remained durably distinct polity forms throughout the early modern period. Equally, local polities were only rarely either entirely eliminated or comprehensively subsumed under direct European rule. Instead, statist, imperial, corporate and galactic polities continued to uneasily co-exist. Localization spawned a plethora of different arrangements through the division and recombination of sovereign prerogatives among local power-holders and European interlopers.

The footholds Europeans secured along the littoral placed them in a prime position to dominate the Indian Ocean international system. This was especially the case once local powers such as the Mughals flagged from the 1700s. But as we will see in the next chapter, the rise of the West in the Indian Ocean region was anything but premeditated. Instead, Western domination emerged as the largely unintended by-product of two processes: the globalization of European (particularly Anglo-French) rivalries from the 1740s, followed by a global crisis of political authority in the late eighteenth and early nineteenth centuries. The first of these processes injected significantly more potent European armed forces into the region, augmenting Western capacities for imperial conquest. The second entailed a global intensification of military–fiscal pressures, combined with a de-legitimation of hybrid sovereign forms among European political thinkers and statesmen. The importance of this second process lay in providing European governments with opportunities and imperatives to assert control over a wave of Western territorial conquests in Asia that was already well under way. These processes ostensibly heralded a rationalization and standardization of regional polity forms. But when Westerners abandoned localization for standardization as their preferred means of dealing with locals in the context of colonial empire formation, they confronted powerful indigenous resistance. This led to a partial reversion to heteronomy which would perpetuate regional polity diversity well into the twentieth century.

[103] B. Buzan and R. Little, 'The Idea of "International System": Theory Meets History', *International Political Science Review* 15:3 (1994), p. 248.

5 *Reconfiguring diversity in the age of empire, 1750–1900*

Durable diversity in the early modern Indian Ocean rested on three factors: contrasting but compatible preferences between Europeans and local polities, distinct but equivalent beliefs concerning heteronomous authority, and improvised practices of localization. As much as this argument stands alone, it is important to establish that after 1750 we do not see the unfolding of a familiar conventional story of interaction driving convergence on the sovereign state model, thus replicating the European experience, albeit with a 250-year lag. Instead, this chapter advances two crucial interlinked points that illustrate the Indian Ocean's continuing distinctiveness, and the danger of basing International Relations theory on the presumed universality of the European experience. First, rather than being abolished, the region's existing diversity of suzerain, galactic and vassal arrangements was incorporated within new, Western-dominated hybrid imperial frameworks after 1750. Second, whereas in Europe the international system evolved from heteronomy towards an anarchical system of sovereign states, in the Indian Ocean right down to the post-World War II era, the progression was from heteronomy to imperial hierarchy. Globally, the European sovereign state system therefore remained the exception rather than the rule right down to the second half of the twentieth century.

By 1849, despite lacking any decisive technological military advantages over its local rivals, the English East India Company had conquered a population of over 150 million people on the Indian subcontinent.[1] Beyond India, the company had also wrested control of the Cape Colony, Ceylon and Dutch settlements in the Indonesian archipelago from the Batavian Republic (the VOC having by then gone bankrupt) and had also subjected central Java's feuding sultanates to

[1] L. James, *Raj: The Making and Unmaking of British India* (London: St Martin's Griffin, 2000), p. 119.

direct European rule for the first time.[2] While London transferred the sovereignty of Dutch possessions in Indonesia to the newly formed United Kingdom of the Netherlands after 1815, the British Raj thereafter spread throughout the Indian Ocean, a web of suzerain linkages tying polities in East Africa, the Persian Gulf and South-East Asia to the empire's subcontinental core.[3] Elsewhere, for the first time Portugal extended its rule inland from the Swahili Coast and the Zambezi river, as did the newly arrived Germans from the 1880s in their East African possession.[4] Yet it was the British Empire, centred on its South Asian heartland, that dominated the Indian Ocean region as no power had ever done before or since, and which thus forms this chapter's main focus.

Might the rise of the British Raj vindicate the presumption that increased interaction will eventually breed convergence within international systems? Before the mid-eighteenth century, the region's historic diversity had rested on an equilibrium of contrasting but compatible preferences, distinct but congruent beliefs and practices supporting heteronomy, and a common commitment to practices of localization. After 1750, this equilibrium collapsed. Without abandoning their earlier maritime ambitions, Europeans increasingly pursued territorial conquest throughout Afro-Asia. This propelled them into a head-on conflict with indigenous powers. Coincident with this shift, European beliefs in heteronomy were meanwhile yielding to a new Western consensus favouring direct sovereignty and territorially exclusive forms of rule. This overturned the earlier congruence in European and local commitments to heteronomy that had previously sustained regional diversity. Finally, as Europeans expanded throughout the region, they increasingly swapped localization for European-imposed standardization as their preferred strategy for relating to local authorities.

From the mid-eighteenth century, then, a European military and ideological onslaught seemed to herald a wholesale homogenization

[2] On the British conquest of Java and its long-term consequences for the Indonesian archipelago, see, generally, T. Hannigan, *Raffles and the British Invasion of Java* (Singapore: Monsoon Books, 2013).

[3] Bose, *A Hundred Horizons*, p. 71.

[4] See, generally, L. Vail, 'Mozambique's Chartered Companies: The Rule of the Feeble', *Journal of African History* 17:3 (1976), pp. 389–416; and H. P. Merritt, 'Bismarck and the German Interest in East Africa, 1884–1885', *Historical Journal* 28:1 (1978), pp. 97–116.

of the region's political units. Amplified by the Seven Years War and the revolutionary and Napoleonic wars, military competition and ideological clashes consolidated the sovereign state's eventual triumph in West-Central Europe. But by 1900 the Indian Ocean region retained its historic diversity, albeit reorganized in a more hierarchical form. The task here is to explain how diversity persisted in the face of this massive redistribution of power from East to West.

The durability of diversity in the Indian Ocean stemmed from a combination of two factors – the collaborative dynamics underpinning Western imperial conquests, and the fierce local resistance to European strategies of standardization. Unable to conquer local societies without first harnessing local resources, Europeans struck political and commercial bargains with a variety of indigenous actors to build their empires. These bargains locked them into patterns of interdependence, which proved highly resistant to change. Later, once Europeans attempted to modernize their empires via strategies of standardization, they confronted immense resistance from local intermediaries. This forced them to largely abandon standardization for a modified unilateral variant of localization (which we dub top-down localization) that preserved regional diversity, albeit in a more unequal form than before. For the British and the Dutch in particular, top-down localization succeeded standardization as their preferred means of governing empires grounded in a bundle of suzerain arrangements. Coupled with the late revival of chartered companies as agents of imperialism towards the end of the nineteenth century, this further entrenched diversity and heterogeneity as hallmarks of the Indian Ocean system well into the twentieth century.

This chapter proceeds in four sections. The first section details the breakdown of the region's earlier equilibrium, and the intensification of material and normative pressures favouring unit convergence in the Indian Ocean international system from the mid-eighteenth century. The second section then outlines the collaborative dynamics of European conquest that built on the region's heterogeneity, and that simultaneously locked the Europeans into patterns of dependency with local collaborators. In the third section, we then concentrate on the downstream consequences of this collaboration, illustrating its constraining impact on European attempts to impose standardized forms of direct rule on subject societies in the early to mid-nineteenth century. Specifically, we examine the Java War (1824–30) and the

Indian 'Mutiny' of 1857 as instances of indigenous rebellion that forced Europeans to abandon standardization for top-down localization as their preferred method of imperial governance. The fourth section finally assesses the institutional and ideological consequences of the European retreat from standardization down to 1900. In particular, we demonstrate polity diversity as a defining feature of the age of empire, which both enabled the geographical expansion of Western power and simultaneously curtailed its practical reach. This divergence with the Western European experience, where the nineteenth century saw the consolidation of the sovereign state, again underlines the necessity of looking beyond Europe for a more comprehensive understanding of the evolution of international systems.

The breakdown of heteronomy and accelerating pressures towards unit convergence, 1740–1800

Geopolitical competition and the European shift towards territorial conquest

During the eighteenth century, accelerating commercialization and geopolitical competition dramatically reshaped regional systems across the world. The results of this competition varied markedly. In Europe, but only in Europe, major coalition wars coincided with the emergence of a competitive sovereign state system, with rival rulers balancing one another with increasing coordination and self-consciousness.[5] In China, by contrast, the Qing Dynasty continued a triumphant series of conquests, destroying or absorbing rival politics, doubling the empire's territory by the century's end, and dominating East Asia.[6] On the subcontinent, meanwhile, local rulers disproportionately benefited at the expense of the Mughal centre from quickening commercialization. After the empire's disastrous overreach into the south in the late seventeenth century, Mughal power began an increasingly steep decline. The ensuing 'post-imperial melee' saw powerful regional successor polities consolidate under the increasingly hollow shell of titular Mughal

[5] See, generally, J. Black, *The Rise of the European Powers, 1679–1793* (London: Routledge, 1990).

[6] See, generally, P. Perdue, *China Marches West: The Qing Conquest of Central Asia* (Cambridge, MA: Harvard University Press, 2005).

supremacy.[7] These polities benefited from the extensive networks of credit that had earlier developed under the Mughals. They also developed sophisticated extractive mechanisms, engaging in a frenzy of self-strengthening aimed at maximizing their power and survival.[8]

Indigenous political consolidation on the subcontinent came not only at the Mughals' expense, but also to the detriment of European players. The Estado da Índia and the VOC in particular suffered at the hands of resurgent local actors. Thus from 1737 to 1739, the Marathas inflicted a series of stinging defeats on the Portuguese, capturing Estado da Índia strongholds in Chaul and Bassein and thereafter forcing an annual payment of tribute from the Portuguese viceroy. Likewise, the raja of Travancore defeated VOC forces in 1741 and again in 1756, further weakening the company's already tenuous position in India. More broadly, across the Indian Ocean region, buoyant global trade generally worked against monopoly-seeking polities like the Estado da Índia and the European company sovereigns, in many instances reviving indigenous galactic coastal polities.[9] To cite but one example, the sultanate of Oman extended its political and commercial influence throughout East Africa, the Persian Gulf and into South Asia's western fringes. The sultan retained suzerainty over parts of what are now Kenya and Pakistan well into the twentieth century. These vignettes offer a salutary reminder that trends towards geopolitical consolidation were prevalent throughout the Indian Ocean region, but also that these processes did not always favour Europeans over local powers.

Qing China excepted, commercialization and geopolitical competition initially seemed to favour more compact, centralized and territorially bounded (that is, more identifiably state-like) polities in the early to mid-eighteenth century. The globalization of interstate European rivalries at first reinforced this trend. In particular, the spread of Anglo-French rivalry into the Indian Ocean accelerated geopolitical competition there. It also introduced to the region a disruptive new level of direct European state interest and involvement. Previously, company sovereigns had generally competed largely independently of the

[7] W. R. Thompson, 'The Military Superiority Thesis and the Ascendancy of Western Eurasia in the World System', *Journal of World History* 10:1 (1999), p. 170.

[8] D. M. Peers, 'Gunpowder Empires and the Garrison State: Modernity, Hybridity and the Political Economy of Colonial India, circa 1750–1860', *Comparative Studies of South Asia, Africa and the Middle East* 27:2 (2007), p. 253.

[9] Lieberman, *Strange Parallels*, pp. 870–2.

involvement of their distant patrons back in Europe. But, from the 1740s, London and Paris especially saw the contest for commercial advantage in Asia through the lens of a global struggle for power.[10] The resulting deployment of European state militaries into the region overlaid the older contest between the company sovereigns.[11]

By mid-century, the Anglo-French rivalry and the struggle between the Mughal successor polities formed the region's main motors of geopolitical competition. A latecomer to the Indian Ocean, the French Compagnie des Indes (established in 1719, and unlike its English and Dutch counterparts very much a creature of the French state) was under-capitalized relative to the EIC and the VOC, and struggled to carve out a viable trading presence in the face of more established European and indigenous competitors. To offset these weaknesses, from the 1740s the Compagnie committed to a policy of territorial conquest within India itself, aiming to extract wealth and power by taxing the local peasantry.[12]

Unlike the Portuguese, Dutch or English, France had historically always been a classically 'amphibious' power committed to aggrandizement on both land and sea. That the French would depart from Europeans' traditional maritime orientation in Asia is therefore unsurprising. The larger importance of French hunger for territorial conquest was that it proved contagious, infecting the EIC and thus bringing it into conflict with major indigenous polities.[13] This European tilt towards territorial conquest destroyed the earlier balance of compatible preferences between Europeans and locals that had until then helped underpin stable regional heteronomy. Thus began the disintegration of the old order and the contested shift towards a more hierarchical but still diverse regional system.

From congruence to confrontation – the European retreat from heteronomy

The Europeans' newfound hunger for territorial conquest demolished one pillar of the old equilibrium sustaining regional polity diversity. Their embrace of more statist visions of political authority meanwhile undermined the second, namely the distinct but congruent European

[10] P. J. Marshall, 'British Expansion in India in the Eighteenth Century: A Historical Revision', *History* 60:198 (1975), p. 36.
[11] *Ibid.* [12] James, *Raj: The Making and Unmaking of the British Raj*, p. 17.
[13] *Ibid.*

and indigenous beliefs and practices in heteronomy that had underpinned the old order. From as far back as the Habsburgs' defeat in the Thirty Years War, more centralized state-like polities had increasingly overshadowed divided sovereigns such as the United Provinces and the Holy Roman Empire in Europe.[14] This trend intensified significantly from the mid-eighteenth century. The Seven Years War and especially the revolutionary and Napoleonic wars radically winnowed the number and range of European polities.[15] These geopolitical pressures reinforced an ideational shift throughout Europe favouring sovereign statist forms of rule against earlier heteronomous arrangements. Supercharged by the military and ideological struggles of the revolutionary era, both rational state-building and the rise of ideologies of progress would eventually combine with industrialization to produce the world's first global international system after 1800.[16] But even before this time, European opinion was already turning against the hybrid sovereign forms – most notably the company sovereigns – that had spearheaded Western expansion into the Indian Ocean region.

Within Britain itself, the EIC's conquest of Bengal proved an especially powerful catalyst in de-legitimizing the company sovereigns. The Mughals' most agriculturally productive province, and (alongside Gujarat) their main window into Indian Ocean maritime trade, Bengal by the 1750s enjoyed de facto independence from Delhi.[17] Ruled by an ambitious Mughal governor (*nawab*) and besieged by predatory neighbours, Bengal also hosted the EIC's most important settlement, the Calcutta presidency. In 1756, resenting the EIC's generous trading privileges and tax exemptions inherited from the Mughal era, and with a prescient fear of its subversive potential, the *nawab* had expelled the company from Calcutta.[18] Local company agents

[14] On the protracted process through which European polities were reduced in number and size, see Tilly, *Coercion, Capital and European States*, pp. 43–6.

[15] *Ibid.*

[16] See, generally, B. Buzan and G. Lawson, 'The Global Transformation: The Nineteenth Century and the Making of Modern International Relations', *International Studies Quarterly* 57:3 (2013), pp. 620–34.

[17] T. Roy, 'Rethinking the Origins of British India: State Formation and Military-Fiscal Undertakings in an Eighteenth Century World Region', *Modern Asian Studies* 47:4 (2013), pp. 1130–1.

[18] P. J. Marshall, 'The British in Asia: Trade to Dominion, 1700–1765', in P. J. Marshall and A. Low (eds.), *The Oxford History of the British Empire*, vol. II: *The Eighteenth Century* (Oxford University Press, 1998), p. 492.

responded swiftly, defeating the *nawab*'s army and conspiring with disaffected courtiers and local bankers to install a supposedly more pliant *nawab* on the throne.[19] Soon disappointed by the new incumbent, the company's agents seized de facto control of Bengal in 1765, claiming the right to collect the Bengal land tax revenues as nominal vassals of a distant and ineffectual Mughal emperor.[20]

The company's conquest of Bengal – which had unfolded at the initiative of local agents and without the company directors' approval – created a moral problem unprecedented in scale for Britain. Historically, the company had of course exercised sovereign powers over its employees ever since its initial charter, and over Indians since at least the founding of Madras. But the sheer enormity of the Bengali conquest (Bengal's population of 10 million was then double that of Britain) represented an expansion of power of an entirely different magnitude. In Britain it spurred a major shift in thinking regarding the nature and legitimate scope of company sovereigns' power. For most twenty-first-century observers, the incongruity of a profit-making company with sovereign powers is obvious. But for British opinion in the late eighteenth century, the now taken-for-granted distinction between the public and private spheres was only just emerging. The rapacity and opportunism of company agents; the EIC's wanton failure to mitigate a devastating Bengal-wide famine in 1769–70; even the potential threat to British liberty at home posed by returned English 'nabobs' engorged with wealth from their Asian exploits – all cumulatively spurred new arrangements that increasingly subjected the EIC to more direct parliamentary scrutiny and control.[21]

Writing of the European shift from heteronomy to sovereign anarchy, John Ruggie has argued: 'The chief characteristic of the modern system of territorial rule is the consolidation of all parcelized and personalized authority into one public realm. This consolidation entailed two fundamental spatial demarcations: between public and private realms and between internal and external realms.'[22] Ruggie dates this dual transition in Europe from the late medieval period. But corporate sovereigns like the EIC – which embodied territorially non-exclusive forms of rule as well as blurring the public–private

19 *Ibid.* 20 *Ibid.*

21 See, generally, N. B. Dirks, *The Scandal of Empire: India and the Creation of Imperial Britain* (Cambridge, MA: Harvard University Press, 2009).

22 Ruggie, 'Territoriality and Beyond', p. 151.

distinction – in fact spearheaded European expansion overseas throughout early modernity, well beyond Ruggie's celebrated benchmark for the medieval-to-modern transition. Indeed, in Britain, it was arguably only with the 'scandal of empire'[23] attending Bengal's conquest that parliament closely scrutinized the legitimacy of the company sovereign. While the EIC would retain suzerainty over an increasingly expansive empire down to 1858, growing segments of British (and increasingly also European) opinion would see the company sovereign form as 'dangerous precisely because it was old, a vestigial form of hybrid sovereignty that was rapidly going the way of pirates, mercenaries, composite sovereigns and other alternatives to the nation-state'.[24]

It would be wrong to simplify the late eighteenth century as some sort of mass extinction event for hybrid sovereign forms, not least because of the company sovereigns' partial revival in the late nineteenth century. But the reality remains that this period saw Europeans substantially abandon earlier commitments to heteronomy in favour of more sovereign statist forms of political organization. This transition was partial, contested, regionally uneven and incomplete, to be sure. Yet it still contrasted with the earlier congruence between European and local heteronomous ideas and practices that had sustained diversity in the Indian Ocean. Once married to a European commitment to strategies of standardization over localization, this shift would destroy the region's earlier equilibrium. It left an equally diverse but distinctly more hierarchical order in its place. Before examining Europeans' abortive embrace of standardization and the local backlash it induced, however, we must first examine the collaborative dynamics of colonial empire formation, which locked in polity diversity while recasting it on hierarchical lines.

The collusive dynamics of European imperialism in Asia after 1750

From the mid-eighteenth century, intensifying geopolitical and ideational pressures appeared to push towards greater unit homogeneity throughout the world. These pressures accelerated after 1800. In

[23] Dirks, *The Scandal of Empire*, p. 9.

[24] P. Stern, '"A Politie of Civil and Military Power": Political Thought and the Late Seventeenth-Century Foundations of the East India Company-State', *Journal of British Studies* 47:2 (2008), p. 283.

particular, turmoil in Spanish Mexico from 1806 – then the world's greatest silver producer – sparked a prolonged global shortage of specie currency down to 1830.[25] The resulting intersection of escalating military costs with a systemic crisis of liquidity induced a wave of crises and wars of expansion. C. A. Bayly argues that these crises had a transformative global impact:

> Imperialism – territorial expansion within and outside Europe – was centrally driven by the scissors effect which rising military expenditure and stagnant or falling cash revenues put on all the larger regimes, European and non-European. Imperatives of military finance had driven states to strengthen internal control and to projects of external conquest throughout history. But these forces now worked with a global reach and they were reinforced by ways of deploying men, knowledge, and control over physical resources. This speeding up of quantitative changes became, in the later eighteenth century, the forcing house of qualitative change.[26]

Bayly's argument seems at first glance to vindicate realists' faith in the homogenizing effects of military competition. But a closer examination of the EIC's conquest of India, the central geopolitical drama playing out within the Indian Ocean world at this time, contradicts this line. The collusive processes that shaped the company conquests created institutions that locked in a reconfigured system of hierarchical diversity. The continued dynamism of some local polities also limited the impact of Western colonialism. In the resulting order Western power was lumpy, territorially uneven and pervasively shot through with heterogeneity.

The collaborative foundations of the emerging Western colonial order in India and beyond

Against traditional tropes of Western military dominance, contemporary historiography on the rise of the Raj confirms that 'there was no British blitzkrieg' in early modern South Asia.[27] Battles between the company and local forces from the late eighteenth century were generally closely fought. Arthur Wellesley, the future Duke of Wellington,

[25] C. A. Bayly, 'The First Age of Global Imperialism, c. 1760–1830', *Journal of Imperial and Commonwealth History* 26:2 (1998), p. 30.
[26] *Ibid.*
[27] K. Roy, 'Military Synthesis in South Asia: Armies, Warfare and Indian Society, c.1740–1849', *Journal of Military History* 69:3 (2005), p. 657.

thus described the 1803 battle of Assaye against the Marathas as the hardest fought of his career.[28] Likewise, technological and organizational disparities between company and local forces were rarely decisive in and of themselves. Cautioning against anachronistic readings of the company's rise, military historian Douglas Peers warns:

> We must not extrapolate backward, that is, assign timelessness to the kinds of technological differentials so obvious in the late nineteenth and twentieth centuries. By then, the discrepancies between highly industrialized and recently conquered peoples in Asia and Africa had become unmistakably clear. Quick-firing artillery, breech-loading rifles with smokeless powder, machine-guns, telegraphs, steam-powered vessels, and other innovations, which collectively comprise the kinds of weapons associated with modern industrial warfare, did not enter widespread service until the late nineteenth century.[29]

If technological advantages alone cannot account for the company's rise, how then can we explain its ascendancy? Western advantages in military hardware and organization mattered less in securing company hegemony in India than did the EIC's ability to synthesize mainly financial advantages with Asian resources.[30] The resulting 'hybrid military establishment' eventually beat out its local adversaries.[31] But the company's ultimate triumph is less relevant than the hybrid character of its military machine and its reliance on local collaborators. The company drew extensively on indigenous soldiers, credit and logistical and intelligence networks to transform itself into India's greatest military power. Equally important was its ability to ally with local rulers while preventing the formation of balancing coalitions against it. The resulting pattern of hybrid and haphazard expansion generated a web of interdependencies with local actors, which constrained the shape of the emerging Raj in ways that promoted diversity.

The EIC's dependence on local resources is best illustrated in its reliance on Indian soldiers. In the mid-eighteenth century, on the eve of company expansion, the EIC had a mere 300 and 700 soldiers stationed at Madras and Calcutta respectively.[32] European soldiers

[28] Peers, 'Gunpowder Empires and the Garrison State', p. 249.
[29] Peers, 'Revolution, Evolution or Devolution?', p. 92.
[30] On the centrality of Eastern resources in enabling the 'rise of the West' more generally, see Hobson, *The Eastern Origins of Western Civilization*, p. 162.
[31] K. Roy, 'The Hybrid Military Establishment of the East India Company in South Asia: 1750–1849', *Journal of Global History*, 6:2 (2011), p. 195.
[32] Lawson, *The East India Company: A History*, p. 66.

were expensive to send to Asia. Their horrifyingly high mortality rates through disease, both en route and in theatre, further conspired against their deployment in significant numbers.[33] Had the EIC been forced to rely only on European soldiers, the company's conquest of India would have been impossible. Instead, what enabled the EIC's success was its ability to recruit from India's vast military labour market. Dating back to the Mughals, the Indian military labour market had swollen further in the eighteenth century, tracking the processes of commercialization, war and polity formation that had followed the Mughals' decline. The fact that the company possessed superior credit to its adversaries eventually earned it a place as Indian mercenaries' preferred employer. The company's unique capacity to guarantee its soldiers employment during times of peace (rather than simply for the duration of a given campaign) ensured that its army had a coherence and permanence its less creditworthy enemies could rarely match.[34] Equally importantly, the company's superior credit enabled it to soak up surplus military labour, denying it to adversaries. In this way, it was the company's superior 'incorporating capacity' as much as its battlefield performance that accounted for its eventual dominance.[35]

The company's financial muscle helped it in many ways besides the advantages it afforded in infantry recruitment. Offsetting Europeans' marginal superiority in infantry-based warfare (which local rivals often effectively mimicked), cavalry remained a key instrument of decision on the Indian battlefield. European and European-trained company infantry could often defeat locals in pitched battle. But company deficiencies in irregular cavalry initially prevented them from pursuing and destroying defeated foes.[36] This initially inhibited their ability to translate battlefield victories into enduring political success.[37] The company's financial

[33] On European soldiers' death rates in India, see P. D. Curtin, *Death by Migration: Europe's Encounter with the Tropical World in the Nineteenth Century* (Cambridge University Press, 1989), pp. 17–25. Curtin's figures are from 1800 onwards, but there is no reason to believe that mortality costs (euphemistically referred to as 'relocation costs') were lower prior to 1800 than they were afterwards.

[34] D. M. Peers, 'War and Public Finance in Early Nineteenth Century British India: The First Burma War', *International History Review* 11:4 (1989), p. 613.

[35] J. Gommans and D. Kolff, 'Introduction', in Gommans and Kolff, *Warfare and Weaponry in South Asia*, p. 41.

[36] G. J. Bryant, 'Asymmetric Warfare: The British Experience in Eighteenth Century India', *Journal of Military History* 68:2 (2004), p. 448.

[37] *Ibid.*

resources nevertheless helped it to overcome these difficulties. In the short run, the company attracted and retained mounted Indian mercenaries by promising to indemnify them against the costs of losing their mounts in battle.[38] This led to the company emerging as Indian cavalrymen's employer of choice, and encouraged greater battlefield boldness on the part of the company's irregular cavalry.[39] In the longer run, the company moreover acquired monopsonistic dominance over northern India's major horse markets.[40] This consolidated its control over another militarily vital asset, further aiding its rise.

Beyond buying up vital battlefield assets, the company's financial muscle proved fungible in other ways, too. Bribery had been a mainstay of South Asian warfare for centuries.[41] But the company proved especially agile in encouraging key political and military personnel to defect from opposing coalitions, often on the eve of battle. Money likewise enabled the company to develop far-reaching networks of local spies. These networks reached into the heart of local courts, giving the company crucial intelligence on the intentions, capabilities and vulnerabilities of potential allies and rivals.[42] Less glamorously, the company's deep pockets finally bought access to a ready supply of bullocks, fortifying the logistical underpinnings of the company's campaigns.[43]

Money bought the company access to the soldiers, spies, horses and bullocks it needed to conquer India. *And by far the bulk of this money – roughly 90 per cent – came from Indian creditors.*[44] Thus, in Surat, Indian merchants bankrolled the 1759 'castle revolution' that saw the company wrest the office of fort commander from the Mughal incumbent, and thereafter assume military supremacy over the city.[45] The Jagat Seth banking house in Bengal proved similarly

38 Roy, 'Hybrid Military Establishment', p. 207. 39 *Ibid.*

40 S. Alavi, 'The Makings of Company Power: James Skinner in the Ceded and Conquered Territories, 1802–1840', in Gommans and Kolff, *Warfare and Weaponry in South Asia*, pp. 275–310.

41 Roy, 'Rethinking the Origins of British India', p. 1130.

42 C. A. Bayly, 'Knowing the Country: Empire and Information in India', *Modern Asian Studies* 27:1 (1993), p. 25.

43 Roy, 'Military Synthesis in South Asia', p. 687.

44 Roy, 'Rethinking the Origins of British India', p. 1139.

45 L. Subramanian, 'Banias and the British: The Role of Indigenous Credit in Processes of Imperial Expansion in Western India in the Second Half of the Eighteenth Century', *Modern Asian Studies* 21:3 (1987), pp. 473–510.

critical in engineering the company-led coup that overthrew the local ruler in 1757.[46] Beyond these early critical instances of collaboration, Indian creditors proved crucial to the company's success throughout the ensuing decades of conquest.

The company undoubtedly possessed certain intrinsic institutional advantages – most clearly and notably its ability to mobilize local credit – that helped explain its eventual dominance.[47] But it is important to stress that the company's supremacy took form within a thick web of relationships with local collaborators. These collaborative arrangements produced a powerful hybrid military machine. By the 1800s, the company's army complemented Britain's established maritime supremacy, the two working as hammer and anvil to pulverize the company's adversaries.[48] Beginning with the ousting of Bengal's *nawab* in 1757, the company army began a series of conquests in India, annexing or subordinating previously powerful polities including Mysore, Hyderabad, the Maratha confederacy and the Punjab.[49] As competition accelerated in India, the company furthermore ousted some European rivals (the Dutch being expelled from India following the Anglo-Dutch War of 1780–4), or confined them to limited enclaves (like the French in Pondicherry). The revolutionary and Napoleonic wars in Europe finally saw the company deploy its Indian army beyond India (for example, in the conquest of Java in 1811–15), again to devastating effect.[50] Thereafter, Britain's Indian army would form the mainstay of imperial power in India and beyond down to the Raj's dissolution in 1947.[51] Crucially, however, it was a collaborative and composite creation, and this would come to

[46] Peers, 'Gunpowder Empires and the Garrison State', p. 252.

[47] Roy notes, for example, that the company departed from traditional feudal systems of revenue-farming to local magnates, instead codifying, rationalizing and enforcing these relationships in a more formal contractual manner. This enabled the company to root out corrupt landlords and reward their more scrupulous counterparts over time through the establishment of a more uniform property law regime that stabilized landlords' revenue-raising responsibilities. This in turn maximized the company's land revenue take in the long term, providing the fiscal foundation against which to borrow the money from local creditors needed to finance further territorial expansion. See Roy, 'Rethinking the Origins of British India', p. 1151.

[48] P. Barua, 'Maritime Trade, Seapower, and the Anglo-Mysore Wars, 1767–1799', *The Historian* 73:1 (2011), p. 34.

[49] Bayly, 'The First Age of Global Imperialism', p. 34.

[50] See, generally, Hannigan, *Raffles and the British Invasion of Java*.

[51] Barua, 'Maritime Trade, Seapower, and the Anglo-Mysore Wars', p. 39.

radically circumscribe British ambitions to modernize India through strategies of standardization.

Before moving on from the collaborative dynamics of the Raj's emergence, we must turn lastly to the company's territorial expansion. In some instances the company simply annexed defeated polities outright, subjecting them to direct rule.[52] But in others, expansion was more indirect. As an increasingly substantial military power, the company attracted local allies from the late eighteenth century. Anxious to secure company protection, many Indian polities agreed to 'subsidiary alliances' with the company.[53] These alliances were so named because they entailed the payment of subsidies to the company in exchange for its stationing of garrisons within the territories of protected clients.[54] Prompt payment of these subsidies secured client polities' protection in the short term.[55] But as the company consolidated power, it frequently forced clients to lend money to finance further conquests unrelated to their security needs. Clients who failed to oblige were typically ousted in favour of more pliable candidates, without, however, erasing the fiction of local sovereignty.[56]

In ensnaring local polities in a 'gossamer network of subsidiary alliances and military dependency',[57] the company built upon long-standing traditions of Indian alliance diplomacy. What differed from before was the company's commitment to an increasingly rigid and exclusive idea of sovereignty. This contrasted with the earlier, heteronomous and territorially non-exclusive conceptions of political power that still informed most Indian polities. The clash between

[52] D. Washbrook, 'India, 1818–1860: The Two Faces of Colonialism', in A. Porter (ed.), *The Oxford History of the British Empire*, vol. II: *The Nineteenth Century* (Oxford University Press, 2001), pp. 400–2.

[53] C. A Bayly, 'The British Military-Fiscal State and Indigenous Resistance: India 1750–1820', in *The C.A. Bayly Omnibus* (Oxford University Press, 2009), p. 263.

[54] L. Benton, 'From International Law to Imperial Constitutions: The Problem of Quasi-Sovereignty, 1870–1900', *Law and History Review* 26:3 (2008), p. 597.

[55] Peers, 'Gunpowder Empires and the Garrison State', p. 256.

[56] It is nevertheless worth acknowledging that company strategies for dealing with indebted subsidiary allies varied with local contexts, with annexation sometimes preferred over replacing one client ruler with another. See C. A. Bayly, *Indian Society and the Making of the British Empire* (Cambridge University Press, 1991), p. 90. On the variability of contracts with client states, see, generally, R. Jeffrey, 'The Politics of Indirect Rule: Types of Relationships among Rulers, Ministers and Residents in a "Native State"', *Journal of Commonwealth and Comparative Politics* 13:3 (1975), pp. 261–81.

[57] Bayly, 'The British Military-Fiscal State', p. 263.

British sovereign exclusivity and local heteronomy enabled the EIC to ring-fence territories under direct company rule, while still exploiting expedients like the subsidiary alliance system to penetrate and eventually suborn dependent allies.[58] Embracing novel ideas of sovereign-territorial exclusivity for its own possessions, the EIC simultaneously exploited local traditions of heteronomy that left its permeable Indian neighbours dangerously vulnerable to EIC influence. At the same time, the fact that some indigenous powers became protectorates with substantial political and military capacities compounded the nascent Raj's heterogeneity even as it expanded. Drawn into the Raj through a process of incorporation rather than elimination, these polities retained important residual privileges and nominal rights of self-government, and as such were 'engulfed in the advancing tide [of EIC expansion], remaining embedded like stumps of trees in an avalanche, or left with their heads above water like islands in a flood'.[59] This lent the expanding Raj a provisional, territorially uneven and heterogeneous character. It also imposed powerful practical limits on later efforts to curtail indigenous rulers' privileges and standardize practices of colonial administration – limits that the British, and also the Dutch, would ultimately transgress at their peril.

The backlash against standardization and the consolidation of hierarchical diversity

By the Congress of Vienna, decades of war and conquest had transformed the Indian Ocean region. The identity, nature and purposes of the dominant actors in South and South-East Asia in particular had seen fundamental change. From an earlier position of relative insignificance, the EIC was by 1815 South Asia's paramount territorial power. During this time, the company had also contained the French challenge and driven the VOC to bankruptcy. Previously largely confined to its city-colonies in Bombay, Madras and Calcutta, by the end of the Napoleonic wars the company had conquered swathes of northern and southern India. In South-East Asia it had also occupied Padang, Malacca, Ambon and Java. Even further afield, the company had dislodged France from its

[58] *Ibid.*
[59] Lord Curzon, viceroy of India, quoted in J. Onley, *The Arabian Frontier of the British Raj: Merchants, Rulers and the British in the Nineteenth Century Gulf* (Oxford University Press, 2008), p. vii.

maritime stronghold in Mauritius. While the EIC had yet to project a meaningful presence into East Africa and the Middle East, the Indian Ocean system was already well on its way to becoming a 'British lake'.[60]

Changes in the nature of the region's dominant actors further marked the era as one of transition. Stung by repeated parliamentary attacks on its venality, the EIC had by now submitted to more direct supervision from Westminster. Tellingly, this included the surrender of its commercial monopoly on Britain's Asian trade in 1813, a sign that rule was replacing trade as the company's primary object.[61] The VOC, the Indian Ocean's other great company sovereign, had meanwhile expired. Already widely excoriated for its corruption, and stripped by the EIC of most of its territories after the Anglo-Dutch War, the VOC subsequently fell victim in the Netherlands to the rationalizing impulses of the French-installed Batavian Republic.[62] Across Europe, the Enlightenment, the French Revolution and the Napoleonic conquests cumulatively served, in Marx's words, as a 'gigantic broom' that 'swept away all manner of medieval rubbish, seigneurial rights, local privileges, municipal and guild monopolies and provincial constitutions' to pave the way for more classically sovereign statist forms of direct territorial rule.[63] The Asian echo of this process was the de-legitimation of hybrid forms of company sovereignty, pushing the VOC to extinction and subordinating the EIC directly (though not completely) to state control.

Lastly, and most importantly, Europe's ideological ructions were by 1815 changing Europeans' political goals in the Indian Ocean. These changes threatened to destabilize relations with local societies. A common subscription to heteronomy and legal pluralism had earlier been critical in enabling Europeans to infiltrate the Indian Ocean system. By the early nineteenth century, a new European passion for direct sovereignty and legal monism was destroying this earlier congruence. In India, the EIC increasingly sought to monopolize powers over revenue, law and war-making, which local actors had formerly shared, consistent with long-established traditions of heteronomy.[64] The company's

[60] Bose, *A Hundred Horizons*, p. 274.
[61] Lawson, *The East India Company: A History*, p. 143.
[62] Ricklefs, *A History of Modern Indonesia*, p. 110.
[63] K. Marx, V. I. Lenin *et al.*, *The Civil War in France: The Paris Commune* (New York: International Publishers, 1988), pp. 54–5.
[64] Bayly, 'The British Military-Fiscal State', p. 263.

inflexible insistence on collecting fixed tax revenues – irrespective of seasonal fluctuations in peasants' capacity to pay – marked a further departure from established practice.[65] Similarly, attempts by both Dutch and English rulers (during the latter's brief rule there in 1811–16) to impose direct rule on sultanates in central and eastern Java likewise stirred up local animosity.

This European passion for direct sovereignty and administrative standardization reflected in part broader shifts in Western understandings of the moral purpose of government. Within the Atlantic world, Enlightenment theorists increasingly conceived rulers' primary purpose as sustaining the temporal wellbeing of the ruled. Ideals of popular eudemonism increasingly informed the policies of absolutist despots and popular republicans alike, and became only more institutionalized following the tumult of the American and French Revolutions. Paralleling this development, English and Scottish Enlightenment thinkers increasingly invested their faith in the transformative power of free markets to promote the moral and material improvement of humanity.

In the context of European expansion in Asia, these ideological transformations found expression in a new faith in Europeans' capacity and responsibility to elevate the moral and material condition of their colonial subjects. P. J. Marshall notes that this metamorphosis was particularly evident in Britain. Public opinion had only decades before deplored the company's expansion in Asia as a despotic and corrupt abomination that would likely threaten British liberty at home. But by the early nineteenth century, in the wake of a rash of further territorial conquests, Britons regarded their role as Asian conquerors far more positively. The conviction that 'Instead of Asia bringing corruption to Britain, Britain was taking improvement to Asia' was increasingly taking hold in the British imagination, prefiguring the Victorian vision of imperial purpose that would later inform the British Empire at its zenith.[66] As a corollary to this more interventionist outlook, British colonial administrators now disdained earlier accommodations with indigenous elites through strategies of localization. Instead, they came to regard them as unnecessary and destructive concessions to 'feudalism', and as impediments to progress.[67] These views were hardly

[65] *Ibid.*
[66] P. J. Marshall, 'British Assessments of the Dutch in Asia in the Age of Raffles', *Itinerario* 12:1 (1988), p. 11.
[67] *Ibid.*

idiosyncratic to Britons. Instead, they reflected a more general European hostility to a compromised old order built on foundations of heteronomy and legal pluralism. The flipside of this hostility was an increased desire to replace the old order with a system of direct sovereignty and administrative and cultural standardization that would emancipate local societies from the shackles of tradition, and enhance the prosperity of locals and Europeans alike. On a much more modest scale, meanwhile, even the Portuguese expanded their area of direct rule around Goa, and further afield unsuccessfully tried to press the Chinese emperor for full sovereign authority over Macau.

The crucial point here is that the early nineteenth century witnessed an apparent watershed, as Europeans embraced liberal and utilitarian ideals favouring more interventionist and reformist mode of government, and older and hybrid forms of corporate sovereignty yielded to more unitary and stereotypically statist forms. The result was a dangerous dissonance between Europeans' newfound enthusiasm for direct sovereignty and legal monism, and indigenous elites' continuing subscription to an earlier model of heteronomy and legal pluralism, which they had until recently shared with European company sovereigns.

This tension had already been evident in the EIC's expansion throughout India from the conquest of Bengal onwards. But it became even more acute from the early 1800s, as Europeans abandoned their earlier commitment to localization. This overreach marked the collapse of the third and final pillar on which the region's earlier diversity had rested. The resulting friction ultimately sparked wide-scale indigenous rebellions against European rule in both the Dutch East Indies and the British Raj. This backlash in turn forced a partial European retreat, producing hybrid colonial regimes that mixed elements of direct and indirect rule, and built upon rather than effaced an earlier diversity. We now consider two illustrative cases – the Java War (1825–30) and the 1857 Indian 'Mutiny' – to corroborate this claim.

The Dutch East Indies, the Java War and the reconfiguration of hierarchical diversity

The collision between European reformist zeal and local conservatism found early and decisive expression in the Java War of 1825–30. The conflict's root causes were diverse.[68] They nevertheless centred on the aggressive efforts of Dutch (and briefly British) administrators to transform their relationship with local rulers from one of loose suzerainty and informal partnership to hierarchical subordination through direct rule. As late as the 1790s, the VOC were merely one polity among several in Java, dominant only in the west and the territories on the northern coast. Central Java was conversely the preserve of two powerful successors to Mataram, the sultanates of Surakarta and Yogyakarta. Both had significantly strengthened their authority since their establishment with the 1755 Treaty of Giyanti.[69] Both were also benefiting from demographic and economic growth in the late eighteenth century, with Yogyakarta shaping up as potentially the island's most powerful polity.[70] Technically, central Java's sultanates were the VOC's vassals.[71] But Yogyakarta's growing military strength and the VOC's increasing military and financial weakness made the VOC's suzerainty more symbolic than real. That the Dutch paid the sultans an annual rent for the VOC's presence on the north coast (in recognition of the sultans' erstwhile sovereignty over this territory) further underscored the negotiated nature of the VOC's relationship with its nominal vassals.[72]

By contrast, the 1800s saw a radical transformation in Europeans' understanding and management of their relations with the key Javanese sultanates. Following the VOC's wind-up and the assignment of its Indonesian possessions to the Kingdom of the Netherlands, the regime of Louis Napoleon Bonaparte appointed a new governor-general – Marshall Herman Willem Daendels – to Batavia to consolidate and extend Dutch power in Java.[73] Daendels took to his task with great vigour but minimal tact. Since the 1750s, the VOC had maintained a Resident at court in Surakarta and Yogyakarta. One of Daendels' first initiatives was to rename these Residents as ministers, and to insist on changes of protocol that affirmed these ministers as enjoying equal status to their nominal royal hosts.[74] This represented nothing less than a Dutch claim to sovereignty over all of Java, which the sultans

[68] A comprehensive overview of the conflict's multiple causes can be found in P. Carey, 'The Origins of the Java War (1825–1830)', *English Historical Review* 91:358 (1976), pp. 52–78.
[69] Ricklefs, *A History of Modern Indonesia*, p. 109. [70] *Ibid.*
[71] *Ibid.*, p. 111. [72] Carey, 'The Origins of the Java War', p. 56.
[73] Ricklefs, *A History of Modern Indonesia*, p. 111.
[74] Carey, 'The Origins of the Java War', p. 55.

found repugnant.[75] Daendels' termination of the rents the Dutch previously paid to the sultans also rankled, as did the imposition of new treaties through which Batavia annexed extensive territories from the sultans.[76]

Worse came with the British interregnum of 1811–16. While initially committed to a more conciliatory approach, the British under Stamford Raffles soon drifted into war with Yogyakarta. Disdainful of the Yogyakarta sultan's pride and threatened by his still potent armed forces, Raffles opted in June 1812 for a pre-emptive attack that saw the royal palace stormed and sacked, the treasury ransacked and the sultan and his courtiers humiliated.[77] Equipped with detachments from the EIC's formidable army, the British inflicted a decisive defeat on the sultan, reducing both Yogyakarta and Surakarta to the status of client polities.[78] Following the sack of the Yogyakarta palace – Java's spiritual inner sanctum as well as its most powerful court – the British whittled away at the powers of the sultans and the traditional Javanese nobility. Further territories were annexed, the British assumed responsibility for the management of markets and tollgates, and a regressive new land tax was imposed on the peasantry.[79] The return of the Dutch in 1816 offered no respite. Instead, the widespread introduction of cash crops destabilized peasant life, while a cholera outbreak in 1821 further undermined the social fabric.[80]

Successive British and Dutch administrations thus systematically curtailed the territory and authority of the Javanese sultans. The 1812 assault on the Yogyakarta court – 'the Versailles of Java'[81] – moreover remains for Javanese to this day a singularly traumatic humiliation. Dutch moves in 1825 to formally annex Yogyakarta and Surakarta then provided the crowning indignity for the Javanese elite. The immediate causes and course of the ensuing Java War of 1825–30 are less relevant for our inquiry than its magnitude and long-term consequences for Dutch rule in Indonesia. While formally led by a Javanese prince (Dipanagara, now considered an Indonesian national

[75] *Ibid.* [76] *Ibid.*, p. 56.
[77] Marshall, 'British Assessments of the Dutch', p. 9. [78] *Ibid.*
[79] Carey, 'The Origins of the Java War', p. 56.
[80] P. Carey, 'Waiting for the "Just King": The Agrarian World of South-Central Java from Giyanti (1755) to the Java War (1825–30)', *Modern Asian Studies* 20:1 (1986), pp. 106–8.
[81] P. Carey, *The Power of Prophecy: Prince Dipanagara and the End of an Old Order in Java, 1785–1855*, 2nd edn (Leiden: KITLV Press, 2007), p. 1.

hero), the revolt against Dutch rule was broad-based, including in its ranks not only royalty and disaffected aristocrats but also peasants as well.[82] Outwardly millenarian in its elevation of Dipanagara as the mythical Javanese 'just king', the revolt was in essence profoundly conservative in character, seeking to arrest and if possible reverse the challenge to Javanese culture and authority that an expansionist and aggressively standardizing Dutch administration sought to impose.[83]

The immediate human costs of the Java War – 200,000 Javanese killed as well as 8,000 European and 7,000 Indonesian soldiers – were immense.[84] The impact of the war on subsequent colonial administration throughout the Dutch East Indies was proportionately large. While ruthless in dealing with the rebellion's leaders, the insurgency compelled the Dutch to fundamentally dilute their earlier programme of territorial annexation and direct sovereignty. Within Java itself, the post-war period thus witnessed the shift towards a more collaborative system of co-rule alongside the Javanese aristocracy. Dutch colonial authority henceforth extended nominally down to the village level, with villagers forced to dedicate a portion of their lands to the production of cash crops that the Dutch colonial government then exported through a state-owned trading monopoly.[85] This more intrusive model of government nevertheless worked through Javanese regents, who gained both security in office and a percentage of cash crop profits through the new system, and remained thereafter the lynchpin of the colonial order in Java down to its dissolution in 1949.[86]

Beyond Java, the trauma of both the Java War and a roughly coterminous conflict against Wahhabi-style militants in Sumatra impressed on the Dutch the perils of direct rule. These traumas also convinced them of the benefits of preserving and working through 'native' authorities wherever possible. Consequently, as the Dutch extended their authority to the Outer Islands after 1830, they did not reproduce the unitary sovereign state, as mainstream proponents of the interaction–homogenization nexus would anticipate. Instead, the post-VOC Dutch East Indies that gradually emerged 'was not a single entity but a multiplicity of entities: one territory [Java] under direct Dutch rule alongside

82 Carey, 'Waiting for the "Just King"', p. 60. 83 *Ibid.*
84 Ricklefs, *A History of Modern Indonesia*, p. 117.
85 Lieberman, *Strange Parallels*, p. 877.
86 *Ibid.* See also R. Cribb, 'Legal Pluralism and Criminal Law in the Dutch Colonial Order', *Indonesia* 90 (2010), pp. 49–50.

innumerable local states. There was not a single flag but many flags; not a single tariff system but many tariffs; not a single kind of nationality but many different forms.'[87] Localization – albeit a top-down form embodied in strategies of indirect rule and the manipulation of cultural difference to uphold and preserve the colonial order – thereafter succeeded standardization as the Dutch East Indies' foundational way of governing. The Dutch maintained indirect rule beyond Java through customized contracts with allied rulers governing no less than 282 'native states' that collectively comprised approximately half of the Dutch East Indies' territory.[88] Like the 'ramshackle, leopard-spot structure' of the VOC that had preceded it,[89] albeit on a larger and more robust scale, this system helped Batavia maintain a network of fortified commercial entrepôts throughout the island chain without assuming the costs, responsibilities and dangers of direct rule.[90] The chief consequence was the reproduction of heteronomous patterns of authority across South-East Asia's largest and most populous colonial empire.

The ideological crises that shook *ancien régime* Europe may indeed have 'hit Java with the force of an Asian tsunami',[91] as Europeans tried to impose more direct and rationalized forms of territorial sovereignty onto indigenous societies. But as the floodtide receded, it left behind it a renewed diversity of polities, now yoked loosely to the Batavian centre through overlapping webs of European and local authority that reinforced rather than superseded an earlier heteronomy.

The 1857 Indian 'Mutiny' and the reconfiguration of diversity in the British Raj

While the Dutch explicitly opted to integrate rather than eradicate diversity in managing their empire as early as 1830, the British wholeheartedly embraced this approach only following the catastrophic Indian 'Mutiny' in 1857. In the lead-up to the 'mutiny', local revolts against the Raj were reasonably common. But these earlier flare-ups

[87] E. Locher-Scholten, *Sumatran Sultanate and Colonial State: Jambi and the Rise of Dutch Imperialism, 1830–1907* (Ithaca, NY: Cornell University Press, 2004), p. 34.

[88] Cribb, 'Legal Pluralism', p. 63.

[89] Lieberman, *Strange Parallels*, p. 863.

[90] Locher-Scholten, *Sumatran Sultanate and Colonial State*, pp. 255–66.

[91] Carey, *Power of Prophecy*, p. xiii.

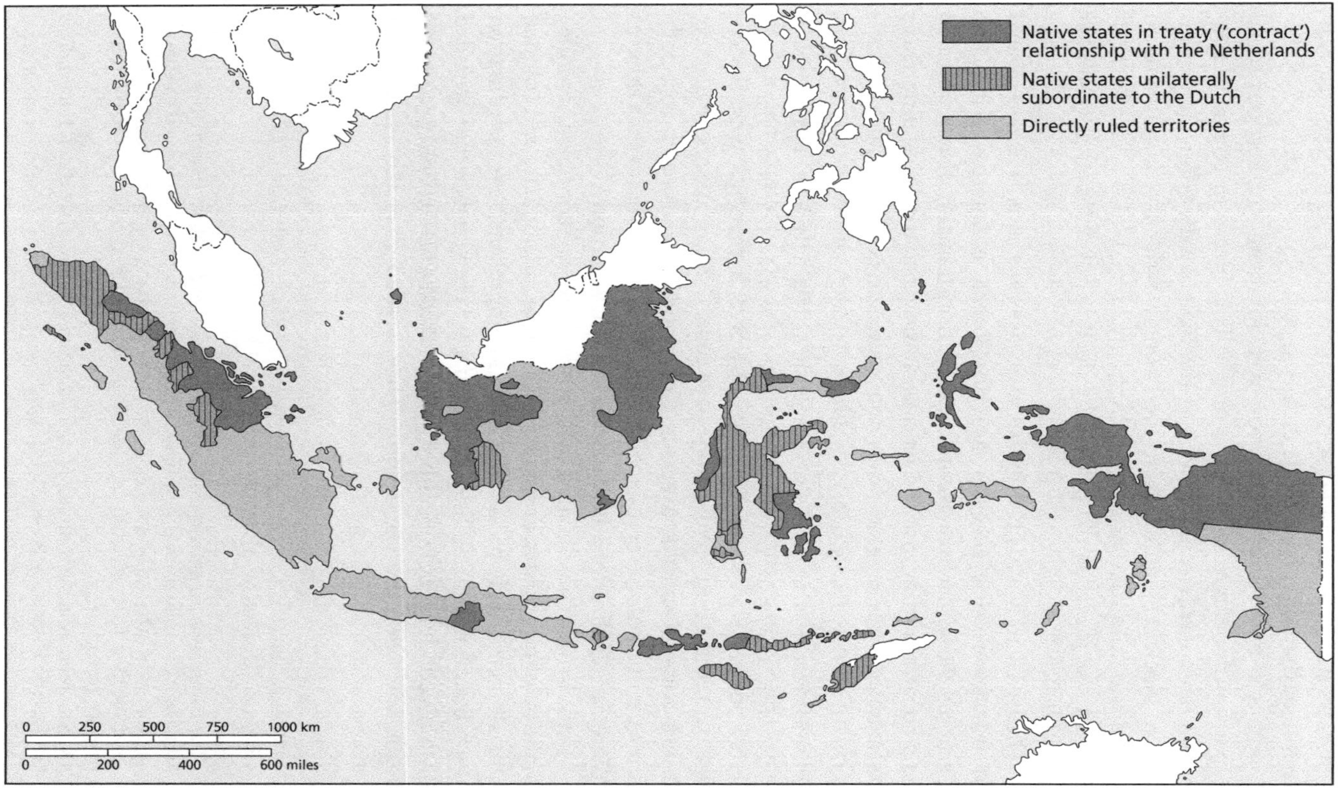

Figure 5.1 The Dutch East Indies, 1909.

generally stayed local, and dissipated more easily across the vast subcontinent than did comparable disturbances in Java.[92] After 1818, the company's huge war debts moreover inhibited further territorial expansion for the next twenty years.[93] This hiatus in company conquests temporarily removed one of the main catalysts for indigenous revolt. Notwithstanding their increasingly strident commitment to liberal and utilitarian principles, company officials also typically moderated these ideals as the practical exigencies of colonial government demanded.[94]

These caveats aside, EIC officials were generally equally as determined to transform local societies as their Dutch counterparts in Java. Certainly, by the late nineteenth century, British imperial identity rested on a conviction that vast and possibly unbridgeable cultural differences distinguished white rulers from non-white subjects.[95] But in the Raj's formative early decades, a very different vision of liberal imperialism, founded on radical universalism, fired the imaginations of colonial officials. This vision celebrated the assumed plasticity of human nature, and rested on the belief that all peoples, however 'barbarous', were susceptible to reform and 'civilization' over time.[96] More specifically, many British colonial officials averred: 'Contemporary European, especially British, culture alone represented civilization. There was no such thing as "Western" civilization; there existed only "civilization".'[97]

As the British consolidated their power in the subcontinent, a motley coalition of merchants, evangelical Christian missionaries and colonial officials increasingly pressed for India's comprehensive transformation along liberal utilitarian lines. Reflecting on the violence that attended Britain's conquest of India, liberals denounced a 'barren and precarious hegemony' won by the sword. They argued that the violence of

92 C. A. Bayly, 'Two Colonial Revolts: The Java War, 1825–30, and the Indian "Mutiny" of 1857–59', in C. A. Bayly and D. H. A. Kolff (eds.), *Two Colonial Empires* (Dordrecht: Martinus Nijhoff, 2013), p. 113.

93 *Ibid.*

94 The company's pragmatic willingness to accommodate local sensitivities during the Raj's consolidation is best illustrated by the fact that it continued to pay an annual tribute to the Mughal emperor as the company's nominal suzerain as late as 1843. See T. R. Metcalf, *Ideologies of the Raj* (Cambridge University Press, 1994), p. 50.

95 K. Mantena. *Alibis of Empire: Henry Maine and the Ends of Liberal Imperialism* (Princeton University Press, 2010), pp. 1–2.

96 Metcalf, *Ideologies of the Raj*, p. 34.

97 *Ibid.*

conquest could be redeemed only though the introduction of liberal institutions and ideas to the Indian people.[98] More generally, a merchant–missionary alliance railed against an unholy trinity of Oriental Despotism, Protectionism, and Idolatry, and celebrated a virtuous counter-constellation of Responsible Government, Free Trade and Protestant Christian Piety as the only possible antidote to India's supposed corruption.[99] These convictions expressed themselves in colonial policy in multiple ways. They included the replacement of Persian by English as the official language of administration, the termination of tribute payments to the Mughal emperor, the establishment of new and more intrusive systems of taxation and finally the annexation of the 'native' territories of indigenous rulers who died without heir.[100] These and other policies collectively amounted to a crash course in modernization. Grounded in liberal understandings of private property and direct state sovereignty, this programme constituted an assault on the more fluid and heteronomous arrangements according to which South Asia had been governed for centuries. As such, it was bound to inspire fierce local resistance, as it did with the revolt of the company's Bengal army in Meerut, north of Delhi, on 10 May 1857.

As with the Java War, the Indian rebellion's causes were complex, and shared with it key common themes. Both revolts encompassed aristocratic and princely resistance to colonial interference, targeted especially against the threat of territorial annexation.[101] Both also involved a millenarian ideological backlash against the spectre of Protestant Christian cultural 'pollution'.[102] And both finally contained aspects of agrarian peasant rebellion, entailing popular resistance to hardships stemming from commercialization and the exactions of the colonial taxation regime.[103] Like the Java War, however, the Indian rebellion is relevant here chiefly because it represents a comparable critical juncture, in which anti-colonial violence forced Europeans to readjust the ideology and practice of colonial rule to accommodate local polity diversity.

While not as deadly as the Java War (estimates of fatalities are 100,000 Indians and 11,000 British killed), the Indian rebellion

[98] E. Stokes, *The English Utilitarians and India* (Oxford: Clarendon Press, 1959), p. 44.
[99] *Ibid.*, pp. 34–5. [100] Bayly, 'Two Colonial Revolts', p. 117.
[101] *Ibid.*, p. 115. [102] *Ibid.* [103] *Ibid.*

represented, in both duration and area affected, one of the largest indigenous revolts against European colonial rule in the nineteenth century.[104] Taking over two years to subdue, the rebellion temporarily broke the Bengal army, then Britain's primary instrument of coercion on the subcontinent.[105] The extreme violence attending the British restoration – what some historians have dubbed a 'second conquest' of India – thereafter permanently changed the imprint of imperial power there.[106] Superficially, the crown's direct assumption of power from the East India Company (in November 1858) represented a further step along the path to Weberian state territoriality. But the royal proclamation announcing this change was just as noteworthy for the crown's solemn commitments to respect native princes' territorial rights and autonomy, and for Queen Victoria's oath to uphold the 'ancient rights, usages and customs of India' against the threat of colonial state intervention or Christian proselytization.[107]

Like the Dutch in Java, then, the British reined in their 'anti-feudal' instincts in the aftermath of anti-colonial rebellion, and swapped abortive standardization for top-down localization. After 1857, reformist liberal and utilitarian sentiments yielded to a far more conservative imperial ideology. This outlook stressed the existence of unbridgeable cultural differences separating Indians from Britons, and recommended non-interference as the most prudent policy for dealing with local cultural customs and managing indigenous authority-holders.[108] Given that the annexation of princely territories was one of the rebellion's key triggers, the crown henceforth guaranteed the separate constitutional status and territorial integrity of over 600 'native states' subject to British suzerainty. This policy reflected a more general conviction that '[the] art of ruling native races is a thing of infinite variety not amenable to standardization'.[109] Armed with a raft of censuses, ethnographic reports and political histories, British colonial officials in the decades following the rebellion affirmed India's irreducible

[104] Darwin, *Unfinished Empire*, p. 256; Mantena, *Alibis of Empire*, p. 1.
[105] Darwin, *Unfinished Empire*, p. 250. [106] *Ibid.*, p. 257.
[107] Proclamation by the Queen in Council to the Princes, Chiefs and People of India (published by the governor-general at Allahabad, 1 November 1858). Available at: www.csas.ed.ac.uk/mutiny/confpapers/Queen'sProclamation.pdf (accessed 20 February 2014).
[108] Mantena, *Alibis of Empire*, p. 10.
[109] C. Newbury, *Patrons, Clients, and Empire: Chieftaincy and Over-rule in Asia, Africa, and the Pacific* (Oxford University Press, 2003), p. 73.

heterogeneity, and derided the idea of India itself as a mere 'geographic expression'.[110] When nationalist and pan-Islamist sentiments later threatened to undermine British power, this tendency towards 'divide and rule' merely intensified, Calcutta aligning with conservative Islamic power-holders in the late nineteenth and early twentieth centuries to fend off challenges to imperial authority.[111]

Both the early Dutch and British colonial experiences illustrate the resilience of traditions of heteronomy in the face of reformist European ambitions. In the late eighteenth and nineteenth centuries, European understandings of the nature and purposes of political authority dramatically changed, and began to reflect modern understandings of direct sovereignty, territorial exclusivity, coercive monopoly, legal monism and cultural and administrative standardization. The quickening tempo of geopolitical rivalry – not least the spill-over of European interstate rivalries into the Indian Ocean – introduced an additional homogenizing pressure. But Western efforts to modernize South and South-East Asian polities in accordance with emerging ideals of direct sovereign rule inspired fierce resistance, forcing a partial reversion to an older system of heteronomy and shared sovereignty. This common sequence of reform, resistance and partial European retrenchment should not be read as implying fundamental continuity between the eighteenth and nineteenth centuries. On the contrary, the rise of Western colonial empires was exceptionally violent and disruptive, and permanently changed the distribution and character of power within the Indian Ocean international system. Colonial empires *did* pioneer qualitatively more intrusive and direct practices of power over the territories that they ruled, but this (to Western eyes) more recognizably modern form of sovereignty was interwoven with suzerain systems of rule in both the Dutch East Indies and the British Raj. These suzerain systems consisted of webs of personalized and decentralized alliances linking colonial governments to a fluid constellation of autocratic and aristocratic local clients.[112] In other words, they worked through the region's extant diversity of polity forms rather

[110] Darwin, *Unfinished Empire*, p. 212.
[111] C. A. Bayly, 'Distorted Development: The Ottoman Empire and British India, circa 1780–1916', *Comparative Studies of South Asia, Africa and the Middle East* 27:2 (2007), pp. 341–2.
[112] Bose, *A Hundred Horizons*, pp. 51–2.

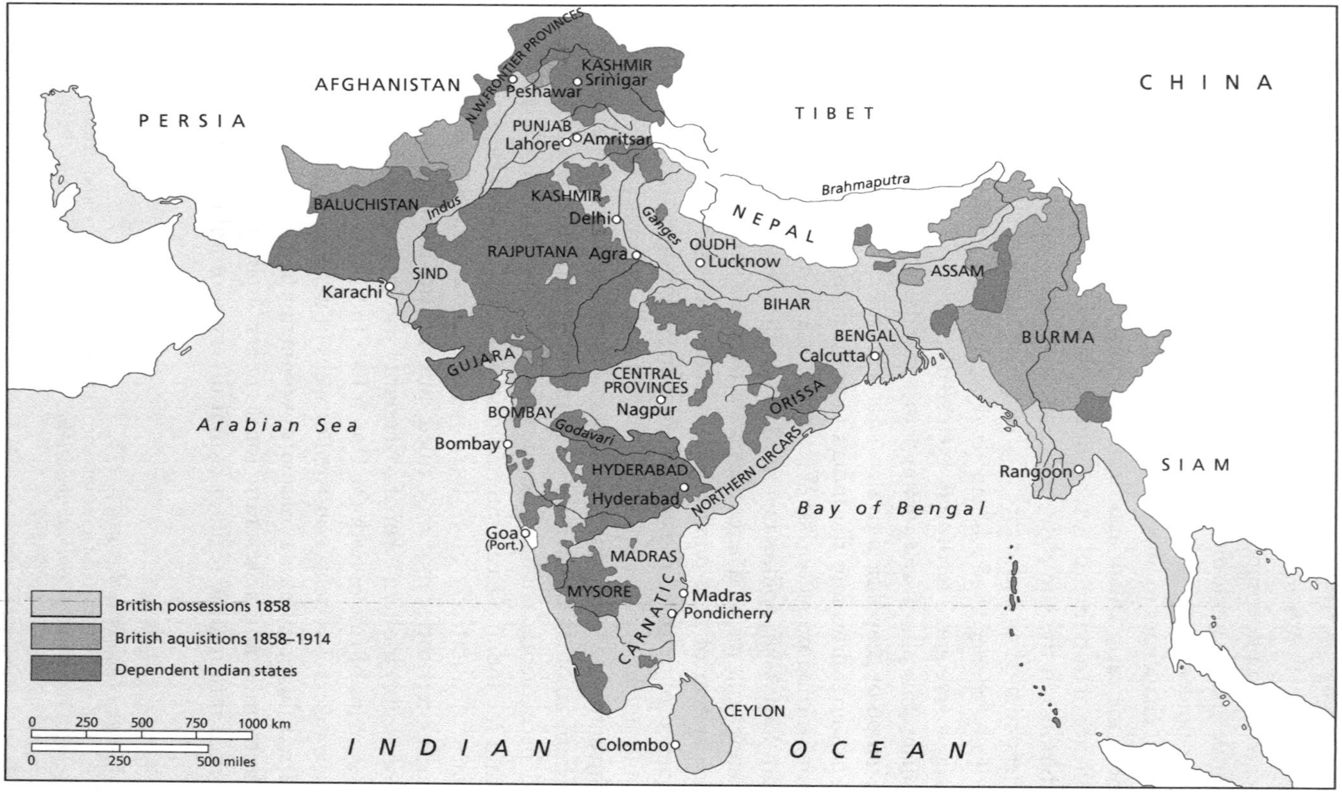

Figure 5.2 British India, 1858–1947.

than against it. Top-down localization – not standardization – was the default mode through which colonial authority expressed itself in both the Dutch East Indies and the British Raj. Critically, this phenomenon was not confined to the South-East and South Asian sub-regions of the Indian Ocean system, nor was it particular to the nineteenth century's middle decades. Rather, it was also evident in the Persian Gulf and East Africa as well, as the long arm of the Raj progressively reached out to drag local polities in these sub-regions into the imperial fold.

The expansion and reconfiguration of diversity in the Indian Ocean to 1900

By the time the Indian rebellion's last cinders were extinguished in late 1859, Britain was indisputably the Indian Ocean's dominant power. This was especially evident in South Asia. There, British dominance was virtually uncontested, save for Afghanistan's defence against company predation in the First Afghan War (1839–42). In South-East Asia, the 1824 London Treaty had meanwhile divided the Malay archipelago between Britain and the Netherlands, the self-styled European 'Lords of the East'.[113] This Anglo-Dutch condominium evolved from London's earlier decision in 1816 to return Dutch territories in the Indonesian archipelago, primarily to strengthen the Netherlands economically against the threat of a resurgent France.[114] The London Treaty codified and stabilized the relationship between Britain and the Netherlands in South-East Asia, and recognized the legitimacy and permanence of British settlements in Penang (established 1784) and Singapore (established in 1819). Thereafter, the British were generally content to leave the bulk of maritime South-East Asia to the Netherlands. British expansion in the Malay archipelago for almost fifty years after the London Treaty was limited to a private empire established by James Brooke (the so-called 'White Raja') in Sarawak in northern Borneo.[115] Elsewhere, in the Persian Gulf and East Africa, Britain's expansionist tendencies were also modest. Would-be expansionists in the British Raj were constrained by the immense costs of

[113] A. Webster, *Gentlemen Capitalists: British Imperialism in South East Asia, 1770–1890* (London: Tauris Academic Studies, 1998).
[114] *Ibid.*, p. 85. [115] *Ibid.*, p. 176.

sustaining the Indian garrison after the rebellion.[116] They were also straitjacketed by successive British governments' hostility to territorial annexation as an expensive and unnecessary indulgence, inimical to advancing Britain's strategic and commercial interests.[117]

Despite Whitehall's hostility to territorial expansion, by 1900 the British Raj extended deep into South-East Asia and the Persian Gulf, and the British had furthermore entrenched themselves as major players in East Africa as well. In 1890 they had blockaded Portuguese Mozambique to force Lisbon to renounce its claims to all the land between Angola and Mozambique, precipitating riots in Portugal in the face of this national humiliation.[118] British rule over white settler colonies in Western Australia and South Africa also ensured that the Indian Ocean was enclosed on all sides by British power by this time. Despite the hard lessons Britain had learned in India concerning the dangers of territorial annexation, British suzerainty was radically extended in the post-rebellion decades to penetrate almost every society along the Indian Ocean littoral. An exhaustive analysis of this expansion is beyond the scope of our inquiry. Instead, the key point of this penultimate section is that rather than the 'new imperialism' of the late nineteenth century replacing an earlier heteronomy, new imperialism in fact crucially depended on and actually expanded such complex authority structures. As the prime examples, the British leveraged and further built upon the region's extant diversity of polity forms to realize imperial interests. The British Raj – a sprawling composite of directly ruled territories and 'native states' concentrated around but not limited to the Indian subcontinent – remained the pivot around which Britain's imperial strategy revolved. But the continued permeability of neighbouring polities in the Persian Gulf, South-East Asia and East Africa allowed the Raj to extend British suzerainty. The late nineteenth-century revival of chartered companies in South-East Asia and East Africa, moreover, provided London with an additional vehicle through which to project influence without assuming the costs and dangers of

116 On the immense costs of sustaining the British Indian army garrison after the rebellion (when a new policy insisted that the proportion of Indian to white soldiers never exceed a two-to-one ratio), see Darwin, *Unfinished Empire*, p. 257.

117 J. S. Galbraith, 'The Charter of the British North Borneo Company', *Journal of British Studies*, 4:2 (1965), p. 102.

118 B. Vandervort, *Wars of Imperial Conquest in Africa 1830–1914* (Bloomington: Indiana University Press, 1998), p. 35.

direct sovereign-territorial rule. Even Germany created a short-lived East African Company to govern territory leased from the sultan of Zanzibar, as well as the German New Guinea Company in 1884.[119]

By the second half of the nineteenth century, and particularly after 1870, both material and ideational pressures again seemingly favoured imperial expansion and sovereign-territorial consolidation in the Indian Ocean international system. At the material level, the spread of industrialization in Western Europe and North America began to corrode Victorian Britain's previously unassailable strength as the world's sole industrial power. The pace of geopolitical competition increased particularly rapidly following the opening of the Suez Canal in 1869 and with the unification of Germany in 1870–71.[120] Coinciding roughly with a global economic downturn, the last third of the nineteenth century saw the advent of the 'new imperialism', as imperial powers sought to monopolize political control over the world's finite territories.[121] The rise of positive international law – with its discriminatory 'standard of civilization' – meanwhile provided for Westerners a moral licence for imperial expansion, as did the emergence of social Darwinism and 'scientific racism'.[122]

This conjunction of geopolitical competition with pro-imperialist ideas bore resemblances to parallel developments that had transformed South and South-East Asia at the time of the revolutionary and Napoleonic wars. But the key difference was that the lessons Europeans had learned from their prior experiences of colonial conquest and administration in Asia were by then conditioning imperial expansion. To repeat: for late Victorian Britain, the art of imperial rule rested on top-down localization rather than standardization. The trauma of the Indian rebellion cautioned against expansive ambitions to culturally transform subject peoples, and additionally warned colonial officials against territorial annexation and the attempted extinction of indigenous sovereignty.

In London in particular, both Tory and Liberal governments proved reluctant imperialists, their aversion to territorial conquest respectively

[119] On the chartered companies, see, generally, S. Cooney, 'Overseas Companies as Transnational Actors During the European Conquest of Africa', *Review of International Studies* 6:2 (1980), pp. 154–79.

[120] E. J. Hobsbawm, *The Age of Empire, 1875–1914* (London: Abacus, 2003), p. 62.

[121] *Ibid.* [122] See, generally, Gong, *The 'Standard of Civilization'*.

reinforced by considerations of fiscal prudence and nascent humanitarian impulses. Conversely, a more ambivalent attitude prevailed in British India, which by the mid-nineteenth century constituted 'the core and cornerstone of British world power'.[123] Within the mid and late Victorian imagination, some even saw the Raj as a new Byzantium, a British 'Eastern Roman Empire' that would synthesize Western and Asian strengths to promote a new era of global security, prosperity and cultural regeneration.[124] The flipside of this expansive vision was an Indo-centric anxiety for the empire's security. This anxiety typically left Raj officials more enthusiastic than their London counterparts about the prospect of defensively expanding the Raj's influence (though not necessarily its direct territorial sovereignty) into neighbouring regions.

In some cases, as in British India's 1885 annexation of Burma, direct territorial conquest was seen as an unavoidable (if undesirable) necessity for securing the empire's defence. But Raj officials preferred to extend their influence by preserving local client rulers and working through existing authority structures wherever possible. Suzerainty, rather than direct territorial sovereignty, was the chief principle through which the Raj sought to expand colonial authority throughout the Indian Ocean region. Legal pluralism and an oligopolistic rather than monopolistic control over the means of violence remained the default way of organizing power in the Raj.

Throughout the Indian Ocean littoral, the Raj braided British suzerainty into the fabric of local polities. This pattern was evident in the Persian Gulf as early as 1853, when the so-called Trucial sheikhdoms signed a Perpetual Maritime Truce through which they permanently allied themselves to Britain, without alienating the sheikhs' residual sovereignty.[125] Initially concluded to help the Bombay Marine suppress piracy in the western Indian Ocean, the agreement was later extended in 1892 to an 'exclusivity agreement', whereby the sheikhdoms were incorporated into the Raj as 'protected' states.[126] This affiliation to the British Empire thereafter remained constant down to the sheikhdoms' incorporation as the United Arab Emirates in 1971. In

[123] H. Luthy, 'India and East Africa: Imperial Partnership at the End of the First World War', *Journal of Contemporary History* 6:2 (1971), p. 66.
[124] *Ibid.*
[125] J. Onley, 'Britain's Informal Empire in the Gulf, 1820–1871', *Journal of Social Affairs* 22:87 (2005), p. 31.
[126] *Ibid.*, p. 32.

South-East Asia, similarly, suzerain and hybrid sovereignty arrangements remained the preferred means for extending British imperial authority. In 1873–4, the British thus introduced a Residency system in the western Malay sultanates.[127] This system, modelled in part on the existing model employed in the Indian Princely States, saw a British Resident exert an 'advisory' role over indigenous rulers, while arrogating to himself extensive powers, including the administration of justice, landownership and control of foreign policy and immigration.[128] Extensive though the Resident's powers were, Residents were compelled to scrupulously maintain the Malay sultans' nominal authority, this being recognized as a vital prerequisite for the preservation of local stability and order.[129]

Late Victorian expansion in the Persian Gulf and South-East Asia thus instantiated a broader process of expanding British suzerainty throughout the Indian Ocean international system. In the latter case, it also spurred the revival of chartered proprietary companies, which would subsequently spearhead imperial Britain's expansion in East Africa. Thus, in 1881, the British parliament granted a charter establishing the British North Borneo Company as a legitimate authority within a recently acquired territorial concession of 17,252,000 hectares of land in what is now the Malaysian state of Sabah.[130] The revived practice of chartering private companies for purposes of imperial expansion was sufficiently noteworthy to seem anachronistic to contemporary observers. Thus, *The Economist* noted:

> The grant of a charter to a new trading company is, in one sense, so remarkable an event, that a reference to the fact is desirable . . . The granting of charters was a thing natural enough when commerce even with the Mediterranean was so uncertain that the 'Levant Company' had to be formed to carry it on. *At the present day, however, such a proceeding seems out of date*, and it is not exactly intelligible why such a charter has been granted. (emphasis added)[131]

The reservations of *The Economist* notwithstanding, the British North Borneo Company proved a precursor rather than a throwback. For at a

127 Webster, *Gentlemen Capitalists*, p. 178. 128 *Ibid.* 129 *Ibid.*, p. 192.
130 Galbraith, 'The Chartering of the British North Borneo Company', p. 122; Webster, *Gentlemen Capitalists*, p. 200.
131 'The British North Borneo Trading Company', *The Economist*, Saturday 19 November 1881 (issue 1995), p. 1428. Quoted in Galbraith, 'The Chartering of the British North Borneo Company', p. 103.

time of escalating strategic competition between the European powers, revived chartered companies provided a useful functional alternative to direct territorial annexation where the latter might prove too costly, too provocative to local actors or too overtly threatening to the inter-imperial balance of power. The charter that brought the Borneo Company into being conferred on it few powers of governance. It was also sustained by the convenient fiction that the company remained subject to the co-suzerainty of the sultans of Brunei and Sulu, even while simultaneously enjoying the protection of the British crown.[132] These qualifiers aside, the company provided a crucial precedent for the revival of chartered proprietary companies – such as the Imperial British East Africa Company and the British South Africa Company – that did claim extensive state-like powers of governance in extending British power to East Africa.[133] These latter companies, the linear descendants of the English East India Company, did not enjoy quite the same freedom from parliamentary supervision as the EIC, if only because by the late nineteenth century the telegraph tethered them far more closely to the metropole than their early modern predecessors. But their late nineteenth-century resurgence nevertheless testified to the enduring diversity of polity forms within the Indian Ocean international system, an observation that was as true in 1900 as it was in the very different world of 1600.

Conclusion

This chapter has demonstrated the remarkable resilience of polity diversity in the Indian Ocean international system across the most important power transition of the past millennium: the East–West power-flip that catapulted the West to global dominance. From the mid-eighteenth century, powerful geopolitical and ideational pressures seemed to presage homogenization in the Indian Ocean international system. Intense military-fiscal pressures *did* work for a time to push both European and local rulers to embrace more centralized and hierarchical models of authority. And Western powers – principally the British and Dutch – *did* briefly seek during this time to impose more modern sovereign statist forms of governance. But the local backlash against these efforts compelled Westerners to rethink the purposes and

[132] *Ibid.*, p. 122. [133] *Ibid.*, p. 125.

methods of colonial rule in their Indian Ocean possessions. More than any other power, it was the British that successfully mobilized Asian resources to build a viable local empire as the Mughals declined. Equally, however, the very alliances and interdependencies that this process of empire-building generated later tempered British aspirations to impose direct sovereign-territorial rule on local societies. So strong were these constraints that when geopolitical and ideational pressures for expansion resurfaced after 1870, the British harnessed regional traditions of shared sovereignty and revived supposedly defunct polity forms (e.g. private chartered companies) to defend and extend their empire.

From the initial surge of regional diversity after 1500, through diversity's expansion and stabilization in the seventeenth and eighteenth centuries, to its hierarchical reconfiguration after 1750, the historical development of the Indian Ocean system repeatedly confounds mainstream IR theories. Where mainstream IR theorists of all stripes anticipate that increased interaction will yield greater unit homogeneity, our study instead reveals the opposite trend in one of the world's most critically important regions. Whereas in Europe heteronomy was replaced by an anarchical system of sovereign states, in the Indian Ocean heteronomy was overlaid by transcontinental empires. Historically, we simply cannot make sense of key questions about the evolution of global order without confronting these fundamental differences. An understanding of the conditions promoting durable diversity is crucial for making sense of both how 'oriental globalization' was possible in the first place, and how Europeans were able (within limits) to hijack this process and eventually subordinate initially wealthier and more populous non-Western societies to Western domination. Equally, confronting the durable diversity of the Indian Ocean system forces a rethink of foundational theoretical assumptions about what international systems are, how their units interrelate, and how they evolve over time. The historical and theoretical implications of our findings are of more general relevance, as discussed in the final part of this book.

Conclusion: Order in diversity

The period after the end of the Second World War saw a massive transfer of political authority from European colonial rulers to local political elites across the Indian Ocean. In line with broader global trends, the regional international system was transformed from one dominated by empires to one exclusively populated by sovereign states. Beginning in South Asia, the British Indian Empire became the new sovereign states of India and Pakistan, with Burma and Ceylon also receiving independence at this time. In South-East Asia, Dutch defeat by the Japanese in 1941–2, a post-war insurgency by nationalists, and the pressure of international opinion produced the new archipelagic state of Indonesia. The 1950s saw the violent expulsion of the French from mainland South-East Asia, together with the British withdrawal from what became Malaysia from 1957–63. After Lisbon refused to cede what it claimed was the metropolitan Portuguese territory of Goa, hastily evacuating the remains of St Francis Xavier and commanding the members of the garrison to die at their posts, Portuguese forces were overwhelmed by an Indian invasion in 1961. In the late 1960s the British government made it clear to the small sheikdoms of the Persian Gulf that it could no longer honour the 1892 treaty of protection, even after local rulers offered to pay the whole cost of British forces in the region, and so the United Arab Emirates, Qatar and Bahrain became sovereign states in the early 1970s. The first Europeans to shape the region's politics were almost the last to leave, with Portugal's presence at the eastern and western ends of the region lasting until the Carnation Revolution of 1974 sapped the government's will to continue the fight against local independence movements. Independence, but not peace, thus came to Mozambique, while East Timor exchanged one set of colonial masters for another with the brutal Indonesian invasion and occupation. By the turn of the twenty-first century, Diego Garcia, detached by Britain from Mauritius at independence in 1968 and then leased to the United States, and the French possessions of Réunion and Mayotte, were the only remnants of the old European imperial order in the region.

The rapid progress of decolonization in the Indian Ocean over a period of just three decades was a far more fundamental shift than the end of the Cold War, and one critically premised on changing beliefs about the legitimacy of empire.[1] Rather than just a shift in alliances, a change in power distribution, or the entrance or departure of new states, it marked the replacement of one kind of dominant polity in the Indian Ocean – empire – with something very different – the sovereign state. The constitution of the regional order for the first time was essentially identical to that in Europe and the rest of the world. Diversity had ended. Political authority was exclusively organized in the form of the sovereign state, a form defined by a strictly bounded separation of international and domestic politics, constituted by recognition by like units according to the principle of sovereign equality. From India's 1.2 billion-strong polity to tiny Djibouti, military force became the legitimate monopoly of the central government. Those that wanted to buck the trend and share sovereignty found the tide running against them. In unsuccessfully trying to convince Britain to retain the Seychelles as a protectorate rather than grant the islands independence as the smallest country in the region, the Seychellois leader mused in 1970: 'My main problem now was how the Seychelles could remain a colony in a world where "colony" was a dirty word ... we were constantly embarrassed by resolutions passed in the United Nations calling for Britain to grant us independence.'[2] Rather than the gradual, cumulative product of growing interaction, this transformation was a radical, discontinuous and unprecedented simplification of the regional international system. For different reasons, local governments and outside commentators quickly acquired habits of thought and practice that denied the preceding centuries of heteronomy in the region, and instead sought to project the novel sovereign state system far back into history.

In contrast, this book is an attempt to recover the lost history of heteronomy, and of the long and relatively recent dominance of diversity in the Indian Ocean system. The broader significance of this point is

[1] Jackson, *Quasi-States*; Philpott, *Revolutions in Sovereignty*; C. Reus-Smit, *Individual Rights and the Making of the International System* (Cambridge University Press, 2013).

[2] J. R. Mancham, *Seychelles Global Citizen: The Autobiography of the Founding President of the Republic of Seychelles* (St Paul, MN: Paragon House, 2009).

that not only was diversity the norm for the greater part of the last five centuries in this region, but the same applied for most other regions of the world for most of history. Thus as well as seeking to bring the previously neglected Indian Ocean region to the attention of International Relations scholars, the thesis put forward also supports those of others arguing that diversity and heteronomy, not like units under anarchy, has been the default condition in the international system. To this end, the Conclusion first summarizes the argument put forward in the preceding chapters, and then seeks to put this thesis in a broader context. What lessons from the Indian Ocean region can be extrapolated to other regions shaped by European colonialism? What are the implications for Europe itself? In what ways does the Indian Ocean's history of durable diversity force us to rethink traditional narratives of the 'rise of the West'? And how do our findings compel IR theorists to revise the discipline's traditional prejudice associating homogeneity and uniformity with order, and heterogeneity and diversity with disorder?

Recapping the argument

Here we briefly review the argument presented in the book before then exploring the extent to which lessons might be drawn for other regions. At the most basic level, we see a fundamental mismatch whereby International Relations theory has mistaken what is exceptional for what is typical, and vice versa. Specifically, the current arrangement of like units, sovereign states, interacting under anarchy has captured by far the greatest share of the field's attention, even though it is a very recent and historically unrepresentative situation. On the other hand, while diverse international systems comprised of unlike units are the norm, they have generally been slighted by the majority of scholars of international politics. Our evidence that diverse orders are in fact the typical condition has of necessity been brief and only suggestive, for the focus has been to explain how such systems arise, operate and endure with specific reference to the Indian Ocean international system. There is a trade-off between depth and breadth in any research design, but the sections below provide some further brief observations on contrasts and parallels with two other regions at around the same time: the Americas before and after the first European contact and the polities of the Eurasian steppe in the early modern period. Each of these sketches shows that polity diversity is the norm, and tends to confirm that growing interaction can undergird a durable diversity.

The positive aims of the book first required a critique of what has gone before, especially the presumption that growing interaction drives growing convergence in the nature of units. Although there are important exceptions, this presumption has been shared across what are otherwise widely differing strands of scholarship. The combination of a step-change increase in interaction within the Indian Ocean region from the turn of the sixteenth century, and a system where diversity expanded, rather than contracting, is thus a profound anomaly for the conventional wisdom. Furthermore, as the most important arena for exchange between West and East for the early modern period, where agents of the Portuguese king and Dutch and English corporate concerns met Asian polities like the Mughal Empire that were far more powerful than any in Christendom, the Indian Ocean is as important for history as it is for theory. Despite this, as noted, this area has been almost completely ignored by IR scholarship, which is disproportionately focused on Europe, and whose lines of inquiry are crucially structured by abstractions and templates derived from European history.

The first goal of the book has been to establish that the Indian Ocean system in the early modern era was populated and constituted by diverse actors. In the 'preciously statist' Portuguese Estado da Índia authority flowed down from the king via a chain of command to the governor and his various agents from East Africa to southern China. Military and naval resources were publicly held. Although in practice the system was riddled with corruption and shirking, and little worked as it should have done, the Portuguese domain in the East was nevertheless a much closer approximation of the sovereign state than either its main African and Asian counterparts or its European company sovereign rivals. The most powerful of the polities of the region, the Mughal Empire, was organized along classically imperial lines, and thus shared pronounced family resemblances with its contemporaries, the Safavid and Ottoman Empires. Here authority was layered and shared with autonomous subordinate polities in a variety of bespoke arrangements premised on the prestige of the Mughals, and especially the emperor himself. The final, corporate form was the public–private hybrids of the Dutch and English East India Companies, combining sovereign prerogatives and extensive military and naval resources with the pursuit of private profit maximization and limited liability for its shareholders. Growing interaction and exchange between these statist, imperial and corporate forms from 1600 did not diminish their fundamental differences.

What, then, explains the rough-and-ready co-existence between these very different forms over a period of centuries, especially given that for most of this period the Europeans were at a huge military and fiscal disadvantage relative to the Mughals and the other empires of the region? As detailed in Chapters 2–4, the answer hinged on a mix of contrasts and congruence. Europeans and local political actors pursued different but compatible goals. The continental empires unsurprisingly sought wealth, power and glory on land, and were often indifferent to maritime affairs. Even the smaller littoral polities of the region, from the Swahili Coast to the Spice Islands, did not share the militarized monopoly trading aims of the Europeans. For their part, the Europeans largely eschewed territorial conquests, instead building and fighting over maritime networks and strategic fortified ports and trading posts. A critical similarity, however, between Africans, Asians and Europeans was the culturally distinct but congruent beliefs regarding the legitimacy of shared and overlapping authority, especially between the Mughals, the company sovereigns and the smaller Indian Ocean galactic polities. The division of territory and sovereign prerogatives was not zero-sum, and so the sort of competitive dynamics and relative gains logic that International Relations scholars generally assume is an inevitable feature of international polities were muted, if not entirely absent. Finally, rather than relying on static institutional parallels, all these actors adopted and adapted disparate practices of localization. While these did not result in the sort of deeply shared values and beliefs sufficient to constitute a common world-view, they did cement the stability of this diverse international system. There was no tendency for these different polity forms to mimic or come to resemble each other. What might have been expected to be the most institutionally successful form, that of the statist Portuguese, came off very much second-best in its confrontation with the Dutch East India Company in the first half of the seventeenth century.

Though this diverse system was eventually transformed, rather than giving way to an anarchical arrangement of sovereign state-like units, empires became the dominant form. The mighty Mughal realm disintegrated as a result of internal fractions and legitimacy crises in the first half of the eighteenth century, while the VOC went broke in 1800 and the EIC was progressively absorbed into the British state over the first half of the 1800s. After an abortive attempt by the British and Dutch to 'rationalize' their South and South-East Asian domains by imposing direct rule, what remained were complex imperial polities that overlaid a congeries of local polities. Rather than being coercively simplified, hundreds of autonomous princes, sultans, sheiks and *prazo*-holders deferred to European imperial authority.

Europe and other regions

Much if not most of the bedrock of International Relations theory is derived from European, especially Western European, historical experience in the modern era. If this book is critical of this focus on one region, why is a study of another, different single region an improvement? For this study of the Indian Ocean, Europe has been an implicit point of comparison for the simple reason that we employ and test explanations developed in the European context. Those studying Europe too rarely return the favour with equivalent implicit comparisons with any other region. Relatedly, too often explanations are developed from and tested against the same historical material. Given that Europe has formed something of a shadow case for this book, to what extent might knowledge of the wider world, and particularly the Indian Ocean, change our perceptions of developments within the European international system?

Building on the pioneering studies of East Asia written by International Relations scholars like Victoria Tin-bor Hui, David Kang and Shogo Suzuki, as well as historians like Peter Lorge, the first insight is to bring into question what have been posited as natural, perhaps even inevitable, causal relationships.[3] For example, Hui and Kang convincingly show that in East Asia balancing behaviour has been the exception rather than the rule (though they posit different reasons as to why this is the case). In contrast to the view that gunpowder weapons transformed European

[3] V. Hui, *War and State Formation in Ancient China and Early Modern Europe*; Lorge, *Asian Military Revolution*; D. C. Kang, *East Asia before the West: Five Centuries of Trade and Tribute* (New York: Columbia University Press, 2012); S. Suzuki, *Civilization and Empire: China and Japan's Encounter with European International Society* (London: Routledge, 2009); A. I. Johnston, 'What (If Anything) Does East Asia Tell Us about International Relations Theory?' *Annual Review of Political Science* 15:1 (2012), pp. 53–78.

war and societies, Lorge argues that this new technology was easily incorporated within existing institutions in East Asia. For all the important differences between East Asia and the Indian Ocean littoral, once again there was very little that could be seen as balancing. Though there was no single actor in the early modern period as materially and culturally dominant as China in East Asia, actors in the Indian Ocean were much more likely to render deference and tribute to powerful entities like the Mughals or the Ottomans, and later the Europeans, rather than forming the sort of balancing coalitions that waged most of the major wars in Europe. From East Africa to South-East Asia, local actors quickly adopted enhanced European gunpowder weapons, but their experience with firearms, *trace italienne* fortifications and drilled infantry forces did not reproduce the state-formation process that took place in Europe.[4]

The fact that what happened in Europe did not happen elsewhere suggests that these sequences did not *have* to happen in Europe. Indeed, the fact that presumed causal mechanisms did not have the effects they 'should' have done in the wider world raises questions about whether these causal inferences are valid even for Europe. As a classic article by Barbara Geddes argues, if A is presumed to cause B in a small sample of cases (e.g. Europe), the fact that A is present in many other cases (e.g. East Asia and the Indian Ocean region) without producing B may bring the whole explanation into question for every case.[5] Tellingly, regional parochialism is a particular problem: one example Geddes discusses is the claim, premised on East Asian cases, that labour repression causes rapid growth. Once scholars look beyond this one region, however, the relationship disappears, as many cases elsewhere have high labour repression but low growth. To the extent that explanations of the development of the Westphalian system of sovereign states in Europe are pitched in terms of necessary or sufficient conditions, a broader comparative view of other regions tends to be fatal for these accounts.[6]

Yet there are reasons to be sceptical of explanations of deep, long-term socio-political change that rely on expectations of necessary or sufficient causes, and deterministic, invariant processes playing out in

[4] Gommans, *Mughal Warfare*; Lorge, *Asian Military Revolution*.

[5] B. Geddes, 'How the Cases You Choose Affect the Answers You Get: Selection Bias in Comparative Politics', *Political Analysis* 2:1 (1990), pp. 131–50.

[6] Johnston, 'What (If Anything) Can East Asia Tell Us?'

different regions and eras.[7] A more likely conclusion may be that in the social world, and perhaps especially in the study of macro-historical trends, there is more than one route to the same destination (the idea of equifinality). If this means that generalizations from Europe to other regions are fraught with uncertainty, the same degree of caution and modesty is appropriate in seeking to extrapolate inferences from the Indian Ocean region to others. The coincidence of different but compatible preferences, culturally distinct but equivalent beliefs regarding shared authority, and practices of localization was one route to durable diversity; we make no claim that it is the *only* basis on which diverse international systems can arise and endure. The aim is not to replace one set of precarious generalizations from one region with another, but rather to sensitize the field to variety, contingency and pluralism. Furthermore, rather than just supplying different testing grounds for extant theory, broadening our horizons also provides opportunities for creating new theory and new concepts, whether it is processes of localization or institutions like the galactic polity or company sovereign.

The fact of diversity per se is definitely not news for students of the European system. For example, the first task of Spruyt's justly celebrated book *The Sovereign State and its Competitors* was to demonstrate the differentiation of trading leagues, city-states and sovereign states. Tilly's incredibly influential work on the subject also presented pre-modern Europe as a menagerie of different political forms.[8] Such diversity may well have been the norm for at least a millennium after the collapse of the Western Roman Empire. Without going into the voluminous debate over the extent to which the Peace of Westphalia did or did not mark a break-point in terms of the dominance of the sovereign state, the persistence of diverse forms in the Indian Ocean region brings into question the teleological and anachronistic tendency to lavish attention on the prototypes of the sovereign state in Western Europe, while ignoring developments in the eastern two-thirds of the continent.

7 J. Mahoney, 'Nominal, Ordinal and Narrative Appraisal in Macrocausal Analysis', *American Journal of Sociology* 104:4 (1999), pp. 1154–96; G. Goertz and J. Mahoney, *A Tale of Two Cultures: Qualitative and Quantitative Research in the Social Sciences* (Princeton University Press, 2012).

8 C. Tilly, 'Reflections on the History of European State-Making', in Tilly, *The Formation of National States in Western Europe*, pp. 3–83; Tilly, 'War Making and State Making as Organized Crime', pp.169–91; Tilly, *Coercion, Capital and European States.*

The strongest power in Europe until at least 1700 was the Ottoman Empire, whose bid for hegemony was checked only by an alliance of most of the other great powers, rather than any institutional or military inferiority vis-à-vis European states.[9] The Habsburg Empire that did most to oppose the Ottoman threat is perhaps even further from the statist model. Despite their pioneering role in military techniques and the financing of war, the United Provinces of the Netherlands, a loose confederation of seven independent polities, hardly fit the model of the centralized state either. While some polities that faithfully conformed to the sovereign state model rose, stereotypically England/Britain and France, others like Spain and Sweden that would seem to conform just as closely nevertheless declined. Revisionists have successfully questioned the conventional 'triumph of Westphalia' account even without considering other regions,[10] but a broader, comparative perspective only strengthens the doubts they raise.

The Americas and the steppe

This book is not a global comparative study of different international systems. But it is appropriate to at least consider the experiences of other regions, here specifically the Americas and the Eurasian steppe. In first presenting a superficial sketch of the Americas it is notable that before the Europeans' arrival, diversity was the norm, with successive empires, tributaries and city-states occupying the political stage. Clearly, with the Spanish conquest there was nothing remotely akin to the 'age of partnership' that some have said described relations between Europeans and locals in the Indian Ocean. In North America from the 1600s, there were more parallels, with a relatively durable mix of chartered companies, statist colonial outposts and indigenous polities. Turning to the second example, the Turkic and Mongol polities of the steppe show marked similarities with each other, many of which also shaped the Mughal Empire, as discussed in Chapter 2. Centuries of interaction with sedentary bureaucratic empires like China and Russia

[9] J. Black. 'A Military Revolution? A 1660–1792 Perspective', in Rogers, *The Military Revolution Debate*, pp. 95–116; Murphey, *Ottoman Warfare*; V. H. Aksan, *Ottoman Wars 1700–1870: An Empire Besieged* (Harlow: Pearson, 2007).

[10] Nexon, *The Struggle for Power in Early Modern Europe*; Osiander, *Before the State*.

had little impact in leading the steppe peoples to adopt outside institutions, however (or vice versa).

The Americas

Meso-America until the sixteenth century presents an example of a 'pristine' regional international system.[11] From the fifteenth century, the Aztec Empire presented some points of similarity with Indian Ocean polities. First, in its adoption of indirect or 'hegemonic' rule, the empire depended on sharing political authority with local rulers. Those defeated in battle were often permitted to retain their dominions as long as they swore allegiance and paid tribute in goods and labour to their new Aztec overlords.[12] These newly subordinated rulers might themselves have vassals, who would then also be brought into the empire with their lieges. This strategy of indirect rule had the advantage of allowing the rapid expansion of the empire and limited administrative costs and the need to garrison newly conquered territories.[13] Broadly similar advantages had recommended a similar strategy of indirect rule to the Mughals and many other empires also.[14] As discussed in Chapter 2, the expansion of the Mughal Empire was also more a matter of incorporating lesser polities than conquest pure and simple. Less favourably, for the Aztecs this hegemonic organization of authority reduced the resources they could extract relative to a strategy of direct rule. Even more importantly it led to successive rebellions and gave the empire as a whole a brittle character. In moments of weakness, vassals would drive a cumulative centrifugal dynamic whereby the empire was vulnerable to quickly dissolving into its constituent units. This vulnerability was ultimately a major contributing

[11] C. Ciofelli-Ravella and T. Landman, 'The Evolution of Maya Polities in the Ancient Mesoamerican System', *International Studies Quarterly* 43:4 (1999), pp. 559–98.

[12] R. Hassig, *Mexico and the Spanish Conquest*, 2nd edn (Norman: University of Oklahoma Press, 2006), pp. 27–8.

[13] G. W. Conrad and A. A. Demarest, *Religion and Empire: The Dynamics of Aztec and Inca Expansionism* (Cambridge University Press, 1984); R. Hassig, *Aztec Warfare: Imperial Expansion and Political Control* (Norman: University of Oklahoma Press, 1988).

[14] On the importance of rule through local intermediaries as a generic feature of empires, see, generally, Nexon and Wright, 'What's at Stake in the American Empire Debate?'

factor to the collapse of the Aztec Empire in 1521 after defeat at the hands of the Spanish and the conquistadors' far more numerous local allies.[15] Though it was the dominant power, the Aztec Empire co-existed with smaller independent polities, other empires like that of the Tarascans, and other peer competitors like the Tlaxacala Confederacy. Conversely, the earlier Mayan international system had lacked empires, but commonly included hierarchical and vassalage relations between confederacies and chiefdoms.[16]

The Americas experienced the intrusion of extra-regional interlopers in the form of the Spanish conquistadors at almost exactly the same time as the Indian Ocean, but there was much less durable diversity. The Spanish established a domain that shared at least some similarities with the Estado da Índia in its statist character, for example in the system of viceroyalties like that in Goa, but with a much more terrestrial than maritime focus.[17] Though the Dutch West India Company briefly held territory in present-day Brazil, it was much less successful than its Eastern counterpart, and it was in any case subordinated to the interests of the Dutch state much more than the VOC.[18] The contrast of the success of the Portuguese and Spanish colonies in the Americas when faced with Dutch corporate predation marks an important point of comparison to the VOC's savaging of the Estado da Índia on the other side of the world at roughly the same time.[19] Many indigenous polities survived beyond the reach of the Iberians, but there was no equivalent of the long-term sustained diplomatic, commercial and cultural interaction on roughly equal terms that occurred in the Indian Ocean. What explains the difference?

Both the Spanish and the local Americans were competing for the same stakes, particularly tribute and control over land, but even more so control of labour. The defeat of the Aztecs and later the Incas had little to do with the institutional superiority of the European state, or even more narrowly the fruits of the early modern European military revolution. The Spanish forces were tiny and vastly outnumbered by

15 Hassig, *Mexico and the Spanish Conquest.*
16 Ciofelli-Ravella and Landman, 'The Evolution of Maya Polities'.
17 W. S. Maltby, *The Rise and Fall of the Spanish Empire* (Houndmills: Palgrave Macmillan, 2009).
18 Boxer, *The Dutch Seaborne Empire.*
19 Winius, *The Fatal History of Portuguese Ceylon.*

their local allies, in the crucial battles comprising something like 1 per cent of the forces arrayed against the Aztecs and the Incas.[20] The technology gap between the Europeans and local forces was much greater than in the Indian Ocean, with Amerindian forces having no gunpowder, horses or even iron weapons. With the important exception of the ships that enabled the Spanish to cross the Atlantic, however, technology as such was not determinative.[21] Instead the catastrophic losses caused by disease, killing up to 95 per cent of the local population, shattered social, political and economic structures and left a prostrate, traumatized population. Here interaction did produce radical convergence as the Spanish (and Portuguese) expanded across the Americas, destroying native Aztec, Inca, Mayan and other polities. Yet the process of homogenization does not correspond with that proposed by constructivist or liberal accounts, and is only an uncertain fit with realism given that micro-organisms rather than battles may have been the most important mechanism in play.

Looking further north, there are more commonalities with the Indian Ocean experience. Chartered companies were much more prominent in European expansion in North America. Although most of these companies proved to be short-lived commercial failures, there were some important exceptions. Primary amongst these was the Hudson's Bay Company, incorporated in 1670, which came to rule over roughly a third of present-day Canada, and traded, allied and fought with local Indian polities and French colonists, while also running its own courts, and sometimes printing its own money.[22] Hudson's Bay even became a shareholder of the English East India Company (it is the only one of the chartered companies to maintain continuous existence to the present, holding an Initial Public Offering in 2012). At the western edge of the continent the Russian American Company was, like the Hudson's Bay Company and many others, explicitly modelled on the successful Indian Ocean precedents. The Russian company once again combined public and private features, seeking profits but also empowered with the independent prerogative to wage war in the charter it received from the tsar.[23]

20 Hassig, *Mexico and the Spanish Conquest.*
21 Black, *War and the World*, p. 38.
22 P. C. Newman, *Empire of the Bay: The Story of the Hudson's Bay Company* (London: Penguin, 1998).
23 O. Matthews. *Glorious Misadventures: Nikolai Rezanov and the Dream of a Russian America* (New York: Bloomsbury, 2013), p. 8.

A truncated era of diversity also arose among European and indigenous polities around the Great Lakes region from the mid-seventeenth to the early nineteenth century. During this time, an accommodation arose between European settlers and indigenous polities 'because for long periods of time in large parts of the colonial world whites could neither dictate to Indians nor ignore them. Whites needed Indians as allies, as partners in exchange, as sexual partners, as friendly neighbors.'[24] Within this context, a 'middle ground' of improvised practices, grounded in 'creative, and often expedient misunderstandings' of each others' values, developed between Europeans and indigenes.[25] Centred particularly on trade and makeshift security alliances, this 'middle ground' faintly echoed the more robust commitment to two-way practices of localization that sustained the Indian Ocean's more durable diversity. But in contrast to the distinct but compatible preferences underwriting the Indian Ocean's diversity, a zero-sum competition for land between settlers and native Americans doomed the so-called 'middle ground' to extinction as a combination of disease and swelling settler numbers conspired to destroy the earlier equilibrium.

Nevertheless, for the period from the beginning of the seventeenth century to the middle of the nineteenth, North America was populated by a diverse range of polities, ranging from European colonies directly ruled from the home country, through to hybrid public–private chartered companies and indigenous local polities (both clearly deviating from the sovereign state model), as well as settler republics. Diversity rested on more fragile foundations than in the Indian Ocean, particularly with respect to relations between European and indigenous polities, which lacked the prior institutional parallels that underpinned long-distance trade throughout Afro-Eurasia. But the early emergence and late persistence of diversity in North America could make it a valuable parallel case.

The steppe

The second shadow case is the collection of Eurasian steppe polities, extending from China to European Russia. Neumann and Wigen argue

[24] R. White, *The Middle Ground: Indians, Empires, and Republics in the Great Lakes Region, 1650–1815* (Cambridge University Press, 1991), p. xxvi.
[25] *Ibid.*

that the relations within this area, and the relations between steppe polities and their sedentary counterparts like China, Persia and Byzantium, have been marginalized in International Relations because of the teleology whereby states represent civilization and progress, whereas nomads represent backwardness and barbarism.[26] Given their Central Asian origins, the Mughals exhibited pronounced legacies of their steppe heritage, from their reliance on cavalry armies and frontiersman to their synthesis of Persian, Turkic and Mongol cultures. The idea of a mobile capital, corresponding with the peregrinations of the emperor, was common to steppe polities. Even when steppe khans built great capital cities, as in the case of the Mongol city of Karakorum, like the Mughal emperors they often spent more of their time roaming across their domains hunting or campaigning.[27] Not surprisingly, steppe polities had a very different relationship to territory than their sedentary counterparts. They lacked fixed borders, with authority instead extending over populations via real and fictive kinship networks, especially those linking rulers to the great figures of Genghis and Timur.[28]

These common elements in the organization of authority within steppe polities did not represent a homogeneous international system along the lines of the contemporary system. Once again, patterns of hierarchy and complexity were notable. At the western extreme of this region the Crimean Tartars are a case in point. Arising from the splintering of the Mongol Golden Horde, from the 1440s these Tartars were led by a khan descended from Genghis. From the 1480s they came under the suzerainty of the Ottoman Empire. This meant that the Tartar khan swore fealty to the sultan, paid an annual tribute (often in Russian, Ukrainian and Polish slaves), promised to make no alliances hostile to the Ottomans, hosted forts and garrisons of Ottoman troops, and committed to provide a substantial military contribution to Ottoman campaigns (sometimes amounting to tens of thousands of light cavalry).[29] However, the khan retained full authority within his own domains, minted coins, received tribute from lesser

26 I. B. Neumann and E. Wigen, 'The Importance of the Eurasian Steppe to the Study of International Relations', *Journal of International Relations and Development* 16:3 (2013), pp. 311–30.

27 S. Soucek, *A History of Inner Asia* (Cambridge University Press, 2000), p. 43.

28 Neumann and Wigen, 'The Importance of the Steppe'.

29 Murphey, *Ottoman Warfare*, p. 43.

Tartar groups to the east, and, when his services were not required by the Ottomans, fought separate wars in return for tribute on behalf of Muscovy and the Polish-Lithuanian Commonwealth. Some khans were removed and exiled to Rhodes for disobeying their Ottoman overlords, while others managed to stay in place despite their defiance. The khan's subordinates themselves showed a similar pattern of alternating deference and insubordination, often embarking on 'private' slave-raiding campaigns even when the khanate was nominally at peace.[30]

At the other extreme of the steppe, what were to become known as the Manchus formed a similar tribal confederacy. In the 1500s the tribes often acknowledged one chieftain as first among equals, who then was recognized as a suzerain ruler by the Chinese emperor. Like the Crimean Tartars, giving deference to one overlord was often combined with receiving tribute from other lesser vassals.[31] Though the Manchus adopted the bureaucratic structures of the Chinese Empire after their defeat of the Ming Dynasty, for some time afterwards they continued to maintain relations with other steppe polities on this more indirect model of suzerainty. In some cases they incorporated defeated rulers who came to acknowledge the authority of the Manchu leader within their rapidly expanding domain in a similar fashion to the Mughals.[32] The result was a mix of hierarchical relations between substantively autonomous polities, in stark contrast to the formal relations of equality obtaining in a system of sovereign states. Just as the western steppe peoples interacted with the very different Russian, Polish-Lithuanian and Ottoman polities, so too those in the east influenced and were influenced by the Sinocentric order. Though some have contested Kang's depiction of a harmonious order centred on consensual deference to the Chinese emperor from rulers in Korea, Vietnam and sporadically in Japan, there is no doubting the strong elements of hierarchy within the Sinocentric system in general.[33]

How much diversity was there between polities of the steppe, and what effect did interactions among them, as well as with counterparts

[30] B. L. Davies, *Warfare, State and Society on the Black Sea Steppe 1500–1700* (London: Routledge, 2007), pp. 6–8, 23–5; Murphey, *Ottoman Warfare*, pp. 150–1.

[31] T. J. Barfield, *The Perilous Frontier: Nomadic Empires and China 221 BC to AD 1757* (New York: Wiley-Blackwell, 1992).

[32] P. Lorge, *War, Politics and Society in Early Modern China 900–1795* (London: Routledge, 2005), p. 140.

[33] Phillips, *War, Religion and Empire*; Kang, *East Asia before the West.*

in Eastern Europe, South Asia and the Sinosphere, have in fostering convergence or durable diversity? Much depends on where the borders are drawn. Though few if any regional systems are hermetically sealed and self-contained, it is much harder to see the steppe as a separate international system. There were pronounced similarities between the Turkic and Mongol tribally based confederacies.[34] But with the exception of conquerors from the steppe like the Manchus, who took over an existing bureaucratic apparatus, sustained interaction with the sedentary empires and proto-states did not induce any fundamental convergence towards the Westphalian ideal.[35] Until at least the middle of the seventeenth century, steppe armies were often able to dominate the standing professional armies of Russia and China, even though the latter had incorporated the innovations of the military revolution, such as drilled infantry equipped with firearms.[36] Though steppe polities were more interested in trade than is commonly realized,[37] economic concerns did not promote isomorphism. Finally, though the peoples of this region variously absorbed Islam and Buddhism, the bases of legitimacy remained genealogical rather than showing any particular convergence with those of the rimlands.

In sum, if the modern European international system is characterized as one constituted by sovereign state-like units whose fundamental tendency was balancing behaviour in the form of coalitional warfare, this has very little purchase elsewhere. Before Europeans intruded into other world regions, diversity seemed to be the default, often in terms of empires and subordinate tributaries and protectorates with shared, overlapping authority. Though something approximating the statist model triumphed in Iberian America, to the north chartered companies played a vital role in European expansion. Centuries of interaction between steppe tribal confederacies and sedentary empires occasionally led to hybrids like the Mughal Empire, or the Yuan and Qing Dynasties in China, but more often did not produce any convergence between the two different worlds. Furthermore, proper attention to Eastern Europe and

34 Soucek, *A History of Inner Asia*.

35 Barfield, *The Perilous Frontier*; Davies, *Warfare, State and Society on the Black Sea Steppe*.

36 C. B. Stevens, *Russia's Wars of Emergence 1460–1730* (Harlow: Pearson, 2007); Davies, *Warfare, State and Society on the Black Sea Steppe*; Lorge, *War, Politics and Society in Early Modern China*; Lorge, *Asian Military Revolution*.

37 Soucek, *A History of Inner Asia*, p. 43.

the Ottomans, as well as the conceptual and historical critiques of revisionists, brings into question this conventional story even on its home ground.

Rethinking the 'rise of the West'

In addition to rethinking the evolution of regional international systems through the lens of durable diversity, our analysis also invites a reassessment of the dynamics of Western imperialism from the sixteenth century. 'Vanguardist' narratives of Western ascendancy, which credit the West as the sole locomotive of modernity, remain tenaciously entrenched. By contrast, our findings reinforce existing revisionist efforts within IR that have contested Western 'vanguardism' in favour of a more 'syncretist' understanding of early modern global history that better incorporates the interplay of Western and local influences.[38] More specifically, our findings speak to three major issues: the early modern global balance of power; the dynamics of Western entry into other world regions; and the institutional means through which this entry was secured.

Today, the resurgence of non-Western powers is evoking significant alarm among many Western observers. This concern is often expressed in a narrative that projects Western power in Asia back to the so-called 'Vasco da Gama' era of European discovery and exploration – precisely the period covered in this study.[39] Stretching the era of Western dominance all the way back to the late fifteenth century is rhetorically useful for those anxious to dramatize the break the nascent revival of contemporary Asian powers supposedly represents. But it is also profoundly misleading, for by artificially inflating the era of Western predominance, commentators obscure a far richer early modern history of more evenly balanced relations between Western and non-Western powers. For, as

[38] On the distinction between vanguardist and syncretist accounts of the modern international system's expansion, see B. Buzan, 'Culture and International Society', *International Affairs* 86:1 (2010), p. 2.

[39] See, for example, C. Bell. *The End of the Vasco da Gama Era: The Next Landscape of World Politics* (Sydney: Longueville Media, 2007); N. Ferguson, *Civilization: The West and the Rest* (London: Penguin, 2011). Ironically, the term 'Vasco da Gama epoch' seems to have originated with the Indian diplomat K. M. Panikkar. See K. M. Panikkar. *Asia and Western Dominance: A Survey of the Vasco da Gama Epoch in Asian History, 1498–1945* (London: Collier Books, 1959).

we have shown, the period down to the mid-eighteenth century was one in which Asia rather than the West predominated, and where Westerners repeatedly had to adapt to local norms and institutional practices in their engagements with indigenous Indian Ocean powers. On the open seas, Westerners did possess military advantages that won them entry into the Indian Ocean international system. But 'In the early modern world, Europeans enjoyed advantages only in seacraft and gunnery; they were waterborne parasites, quick to command trade at the coast or the mouths of great rivers but slow to penetrate inland.'[40] Naval power won the West access to the Indian Ocean system, but not dominance. On land, indigenous powers remained militarily preponderant well into the eighteenth century. It was precisely this balance between European maritime and indigenous land power that made the first wave of early modern globalization possible, and that necessitated infiltration and localization over straightforward expansion and imposition as Westerners' primary strategies for accessing the vast wealth of pre-industrial Asia and Africa.

Throughout Africa and Asia at least, where epidemics did not decimate local populations on contact with Europeans as they did in the New World, Westerners operated as interlopers at the edges of an indigenous maritime trading order. The balance of military and economic power sufficiently favoured locals that it is misleading to characterize the early modern period as one defined by the expansion of Western power. Within the English School especially, expansion has long predominated as the preferred metaphor defining European interactions with the non-European world.[41] But the expansionist notion of a precociously modern Western Prometheus imposing itself on supine indigenous societies does not reflect historical reality. So ubiquitous is the contemporary sovereign state, and so synonymous is it with Western modernity, that it becomes easy to misread the early history of European encounters with non-Western societies as a mere prologue to the later worldwide triumph of Western institutional forms. From there, it is a short step to assuming that the sovereign state ultimately triumphed because of its inherent superiority, and that today's global

[40] R. Drayton, 'Maritime Networks and the Making of Knowledge', in D. Cannadine (ed.), *Empire, the Sea and Global History: Britain's Maritime World, 1763–1833* (London: Palgrave Macmillan, 2007), p. 73.

[41] The *locus classicus* here remains H. Bull and A. Watson (eds.), *The Expansion of International Society* (Oxford University Press, 1984).

order reflects longstanding processes of Western imposition that its superior institutions made possible.

Our analysis faults this reading of history on two counts. First, metaphors of expansion mischaracterize the Western interaction with indigenous actors in the early modern Indian Ocean system. While undeniably aggressive in their novel attempts to monopolize control of major regional sea lanes, Westerners generally employed strategies of insinuation and localization to establish themselves in Indian Ocean polities. That they were able to do so did not stem primarily from institutional advantages *peculiar* to the West, but rather from ideational and institutional congruences (heteronomy) that were *common* to Europeans and their host societies. By 1500, the Old World had seen several alternating periods of Western and (mainly) Eastern dominance, as well as successive waves of hemispheric interaction and integration centred on long-distance trade.[42] It was precisely the existence of these congruent institutions that gave Europeans a toehold in the Indian Ocean region after 1500. Certainly, from the mid-eighteenth century, city-colonies such as Bombay and Madras – themselves the product of indigenous customs of commercial extra-territoriality – became the springboards for large-scale European territorial conquest. And from that point onwards, we can legitimately begin to speak of the coercive expansion of a European-dominated international society. But before 1750, Afro-Asian incorporation rather than Western expansion serves as a more appropriate shorthand for capturing the processes of localization through which Westerners were drawn into the Indian Ocean world.

It would be churlish to deny all Western innovation in accounting for European incorporation into the Indian Ocean international system. Certain Western institutional innovations did prove indispensable in plugging Europeans into an Afro-Asian-dominated global economy. But it was the company sovereigns, not sovereign states, that proved most central to this endeavour. Company sovereigns – in pooling 'patient capital' and mitigating the inevitable principal–agent problems associated with long-distance trade – prevailed over sovereign states as the more efficient Western institutional forms in the Indian Ocean system. The company sovereigns' prominence in this region was particularly

[42] On this point, see, for example, J. Goody, *The Eurasian Miracle* (Cambridge: Polity Press, 2010), p. 1.

conspicuous, and the performance gap between company sovereigns and sovereign states was conversely less pronounced in the Americas. This variance suggests caution is warranted before making absolute generalizations regarding the two institutional forms' relative superiority. These caveats aside, this study has highlighted the company sovereigns' indispensable role in establishing direct Western trade with Indian Ocean polities. Beyond the Indian Ocean context, company sovereigns were equally conspicuous at other pivotal moments in Europeans' relations with the non-Western world. The colonization of North America; the coordination of the transatlantic slave trade; the renewed scramble for colonies in Africa, South-East Asia and the Pacific in the nineteenth century – in each of these moments, it was company sovereigns as much as sovereign states that were at the van of European empire-building.[43]

This study has provided suggestive evidence as to why company sovereigns prevailed over sovereign states within the particular context of the early modern Indian Ocean. But at a moment when the global 'market for force' is again resurgent,[44] it seems especially timely that IR scholars remedy their past neglect of the company sovereigns by according them a prominence in analysing the dynamics of international change commensurate with their historical importance. More generally, the company sovereigns' longevity in global politics, and their centrality as agents of Western imperialism, contradicts readings of European expansion as synonymous with the expansion of the state. It forces us to question not only conventional narratives of the 'rise of the West', but also broader state-centric readings of the past five centuries of global history.

Order in diversity

This book has examined how a condition of durable diversity emerged and persisted in one international system for over three centuries. Our goals have been theoretical revision and historical recovery. We have sought to revise the widespread theoretical expectation among IR

[43] See, for example, Newman, *Empire of the Bay*; Pettigrew, *Freedom's Debt*; and S. R. Bown, *Merchant Kings: When Companies Ruled the World, 1600–1900* (London: Macmillan, 2010).

[44] D. D. Avant, *The Market for Force: The Consequences of Privatizing Security* (Cambridge University Press, 2005).

scholars equating increased interaction with a convergence on common institutional forms. And we have sought to recover the neglected history of a vitally important world region that theorists have until now overlooked.

Beyond these explicit goals, however, our work contests a deeper intuition within International Relations, which implicitly links convergence and homogeneity with order, and conversely associates heterogeneity and institutional diversity with disorder. This implicit preference for homogeneity as a foundation for international order expresses itself with varying degrees of self-consciousness across different theoretical traditions. One example is classical realism's nostalgia for the 'ideological unipolarity' of *ancien régime* Europe. English School anxieties over a feared 'revolt against the West' among post-colonial polities is another. Even contemporary liberal internationalists' insistence on the necessity of global integration through the universalizing forces of state-building, economic liberalization and democracy-promotion represents a different form of the belief in institutional uniformity as a prerequisite for international order.[45]

By examining international relations as they played out in the Indian Ocean before the advent of Western dominance, we have sought to demonstrate how international order was possible among actors that lacked a thick consensus around shared constitutional values, and that furthermore failed to converge on common polity forms despite continuously growing interaction. A mixture of compatible preferences, congruent ideas and institutions, and a shared commitment to accommodation through localization, were sufficient to support the crucial first wave of globalization. Our findings derive from an in-depth analysis of only one case, and further comparative studies are needed to determine whether the forces that sustained durable diversity in the early modern Indian Ocean were also present in other heterogeneous international systems. The sheer historical frequency of heterogeneous international systems nevertheless suggests that the phenomenon of order in diversity is unlikely to be confined to the Indian Ocean alone. For this reason, we hope that this study will spur others to engage in the study of heterogeneous international systems, not only

[45] On the general tendency to equate homogeneity and uniformity with order and heterogeneity and diversity with disorder in IR theory, see I. Clark, *Legitimacy in International Society* (Oxford University Press, 2005), pp. 16–18.

to broaden the field's historical and geographical horizons, but also to gain a more precise understanding of where, when, how and why polity diversity has historically been constitutive of order, rather than subversive of it.

While the presumption equating international order with uniformity remains strong within the field, we also hope to have shown that diverse scholarly traditions already contain abundant resources for exploring and explaining order in diversity. Developing these implicit theories of diversity promises to bring International Relations theorizing into line with work within cognate disciplines from which IR scholarship has previously drawn inspiration. In particular, micro-economics has moved well beyond the outdated theories of the firm associating market competition with firm convergence towards a single most efficient form. Contemporary studies of 'competitive heterogeneity', which seek to explain the durable diversity of firms ostensibly subject to the same competitive pressures, might, for example, provide a useful point of departure for developing modified neorealist explanations for heterogeneous international systems, especially given the tradition's existing intellectual debts to micro-economics.[46] More generally, despite the field's nominal embrace of evolutionary metaphors to describe international systems' historical development, a more thoroughgoing engagement with evolutionary theories derived from the natural sciences might prove fruitful in theorizing the dynamics of heterogeneous international systems.[47] The broad point here is that economists and evolutionary biologists, like those studying international politics, study environments where competitive interaction and the presence of selection effects are the norm. Within these fields, diversity and variation, rather than uniformity and monoculture, are increasingly recognized as constitutive of order, and as being entirely consistent with continuous interaction and competition. International Relations has adapted much of its theoretical inspiration from economists, and a good deal of its metaphors for explaining change from evolutionary

[46] On 'competitive heterogeneity', see, generally, D. G. Hoopes, T. L. Madsen and G. Walker, Guest Editors' introduction to the special issue: 'Why Is There a Resource-Based View? Toward a Theory of Competitive Heterogeneity', *Strategic Management Journal* 24:10 (2003), pp. 889–902.

[47] On the disconnect between theories of change in political science and evolutionary theory, and suggested means for remedying it, see, generally, I. S. Lustick, 'Taking Evolution Seriously: Historical Institutionalism and Evolutionary Theory', *Polity* 43:2 (2011), pp. 179–209.

biologists. As such, the field of International Relations would be well served by heeding the examples of these disciplines in qualifying the presumption linking institutional uniformity with order, and engaging more fully with the long history of stable heterogeneity that has characterized international relations for the great bulk of human history.

We end this book with a strong awareness of the need to further investigate the workings of the diverse international systems that comprise the historical norm, and with a sense of excitement for the huge potential and possibilities for the field of International Relations that are opened up by going beyond the well-trodden paths of Western European history and the contemporary international system. As the first book (to our knowledge) aiming to advance International Relations theory through studying the Indian Ocean international system, we are conscious of barely having scratched the surface of the rich, disparate and fascinating history of this area, and the accompanying potential theoretical insights that might be gleaned from a more comprehensive engagement with this history. Given that both scholarly, scientific principles and the law of diminishing returns argue for broadening our horizons to new and largely untapped regions and histories, International Relations could and should be on the threshold of a new era of empirical and theoretical advancement. In revealing how order in diversity emerged and endured in the Indian Ocean international system, we hope to have made a catalytic contribution to advancing this larger project.

Bibliography

Abu-Lughod, J. L., *Before European Hegemony: The World System A.D. 1250–1350* (Oxford University Press, 1989).

Acharya, A., 'How Ideas Spread: Whose Norms Matter? Norm Localization and Institutional Change in Asian Regionalism', *International Organization* 58:2 (2004), pp. 239–75.

Whose Ideas Matter? Agency and Power in Asian Regionalism (Ithaca, NY: Cornell University Press, 2009).

Adams, J., 'Principals and Agents, Colonials and Company Men: The Decay of Colonial Control in the Dutch East Indies', *American Sociological Review* 61:1 (1996), pp. 12–28.

Aksan, V. H., *Ottoman Wars 1700–1870: An Empire Besieged* (Harlow: Pearson, 2007).

Alam, M. and Subrahmanyam, S., 'Introduction'. in M. Alam and S. Subrahmanyam (eds.), *The Mughal State 1526–1750* (Delhi: Oxford University Press, 1998), pp. 1–35.

Alavi, S., 'The Makings of Company Power: James Skinner in the Ceded and Conquered Territories, 1802–1840'. in J. Gommans and D. Kolff (eds.), *Warfare and Weaponry in South Asia* (Delhi: Oxford University Press, 2003), pp. 275–310.

Andrade, T., *Lost Colony: The Untold Story of China's First Great Victory over the West* (Princeton University Press, 2011).

Anghie, A., *Imperialism, Sovereignty and the Making of International Law* (Cambridge University Press, 2007).

Asher, C. B. and Talbot, C., *India before Europe* (Cambridge University Press, 2006).

Avant, D. D., *The Market for Force: The Consequences of Privatizing Security* (Cambridge University Press, 2005).

Balabanlilar, L., 'Lords of the Auspicious Conjunction: Turco-Mongol Imperial Identity on the Subcontinent', *Journal of World History* 18:1 (2007), pp. 1–39.

Barbour, R., 'Power and Distant Display: Early English "Ambassadors" in Mughal India', *Huntington Library Quarterly* 61:3/4 (1998), pp. 343–68.

Barendse, R. J., 'Trade and State in the Arabian Seas: A Survey from the Fifteenth to the Eighteenth Century', *Journal of World History* 11:2 (2000), pp. 173–225.

Barfield, T. J., *The Perilous Frontier: Nomadic Empires and China 221 BC to AD 1757* (New York: Wiley-Blackwell, 1992).

'The Shadow Empires: Imperial State Formation along the Nomad–Chinese Frontier', in S. Alcock (ed.), *Empires: Perspectives from Archaeology and History* (Cambridge University Press, 2001), pp. 10–41.

Barnett, M. and Duvall, R., 'Power in International Politics', *International Organization* 59:1 (2005), pp. 39–75.

Barua, P., 'Maritime Trade, Seapower, and the Anglo-Mysore Wars, 1767–1799', *The Historian*, 73:1 (2011), pp. 22–40.

Bassett, D. K., 'Early English Trade and Settlement in Asia, 1602–1690', in P. Tuck (ed.), *The East India Company, 1600–1858*, vol. IV: *Trade, Finance and Power* (London: Routledge, 1998), pp. 1–26.

Bayly, C. A., *Imperial Meridian* (London: Longman, 1989).

Indian Society and the Making of the British Empire (Cambridge University Press, 1991).

'Knowing the Country: Empire and Information in India', *Modern Asian Studies* 27:1(1993), pp. 3–43.

'The First Age of Global Imperialism, c.1760–1830', *Journal of Imperial and Commonwealth History* 26:2 (1998), pp. 28–47.

'"Archaic" and "Modern" Globalization in the Eurasian and African Arena, c. 1750–1850', in A. G. Hopkins (ed.), *Globalization in World History* (London: Pimlico, 2002), pp. 47–73.

'Distorted Development: The Ottoman Empire and British India, circa. 1780–1916', *Comparative Studies of South Asia, Africa and the Middle East* 27:2 (2007), pp. 332–44.

'The British Military-Fiscal State and Indigenous Resistance: India 1750–1820', in *The C. A. Bayly Omnibus* (Oxford University Press, 2009), pp. 322–54.

'Two Colonial Revolts: The Java War, 1825–30, and the Indian "Mutiny" of 1857–59', in C. A. Bayly and D. H. A. Kolff (eds.), *Two Colonial Empires* (Dordrecht: Martinus Nijhoff, 2013), pp. 111–35.

Beaujard, P., 'The Indian Ocean in Eurasian and African World Systems before the Sixteenth Century', *Journal of World History* 16:4 (2005), pp. 411–65.

Bell. C., *The End of the Vasco da Gama Era: The Next Landscape of World Politics* (Sydney: Longueville Media, 2007).

Bentley, J. H., *Old World Encounters: Cross-Cultural Contacts and Exchanges in Pre-Modern Times* (New York: Oxford University Press, 1993).

'Seas and Ocean Basins as Frameworks of Historical Analysis', *Geographical Review* 89:2 (1999), pp. 215–24.

Benton, L., 'Colonial Law and Cultural Difference: Jurisdictional Politics and the Formation of the Colonial State', *Comparative Studies in Society and History* 41:3 (1999), pp. 563–88.

'The Legal Regime of the South Atlantic World, 1400–1750: Jurisdictional Complexity as Institutional Order', *Journal of World History* 11:1(2000), pp. 27–56.

'Legal Spaces of Empire: Piracy and the Origins of Ocean Regionalism', *Comparative Studies in Society and History* 64:4 (2005), pp. 700–24.

'From International Law to Imperial Constitutions: The Problem of Quasi-Sovereignty, 1870–1900', *Law and History Review* 26:3 (2008), pp. 595–619.

A Search for Sovereignty: Law and Geography in European Empires 1400–1900 (Cambridge University Press, 2010).

Benton, L., and Ross, R. J. (eds.), *Legal Pluralism and Empires, 1500–1850* (New York University Press, 2013).

Berman, H., *Law and Revolution: The Formation of the Western Legal Tradition* (Cambridge, MA: Harvard University Press, 1983).

Bethencourt, F., 'Political Configurations and Local Powers', in F. Bethencourt and D. Curto (eds.), *Portuguese Oceanic Expansion, 1400–1800* (Cambridge University Press, 2007), pp. 193–250.

Biedermann, Z., 'Portuguese Diplomacy in Asia in the Sixteenth Century: A Preliminary Overview', *Itinerario* 29:2 (2005), pp. 13–37.

Black, J., *War and the World: Military Power and the Fate of Continents* (New Haven, CT: Yale University Press, 1998).

Rethinking Military History (London: Routledge, 2004).

'A Wider Perspective: War Outside the West', in G. Mortimer (ed.), *Early Modern Military History1450–1815* (Houndmills: Palgrave Macmillan, 2004), pp. 212–26.

'A Military Revolution? A 1660–1792 Perspective', in C. J. Rogers (ed.), *The Military Revolution Debate: Readings in the Military Transformation of Early Modern Europe* (Boulder, CO: Westview, 2005), pp. 95–116.

'On Diversity and Military History', in D. A. Yerxa (ed.), *Recent Themes in Military History: Historians in Conversation* (Columbia: University of South Carolina Press, 2009), pp. 22–5.

Blake, S., 'The Mughals as a Patrimonial-Bureaucratic Empire', *Journal of the Royal Asiatic Society* 39:1 (1979), pp. 77–99.

Blussé, L. and Gaastra, F., 'Companies and Trade: Some Reflections on a Workshop and a Concept', in L. Blussé and F. Gaastra (eds.), *Companies and Trade: Essays on Overseas Trading Companies During the Ancien Régime* (Leiden University Press, 1981), pp. 3–16.

(eds.), *Companies and Trade: Essays on Overseas Trading Companies During the Ancien Régime* (Leiden University Press, 1981).
Boulding, K. E., 'Towards a Pure Theory of Threat Systems', *American Economic Review* 53:2 (1963), pp. 424–34.
Bose, S., *A Hundred Horizons: The Indian Ocean in an Age of Global Empire* (Cambridge MA: Harvard University Press, 2009).
Bown, S. R., *Merchant Kings: When Companies Ruled the World, 1600–1900* (London: Macmillan, 2010).
Boxer, C. R., *The Dutch Seaborne Empire 1600–1800* (New York: Alfred Knopf, 1965).
The Portuguese Seaborne Empire 1415–1825 (London: Hutchinson, 1969).
Branch, J., *The Cartographic State: Maps, Territory, and the Origins of Sovereignty* (Cambridge University Press, 2014).
Brenner, W. J., 'In Search of Monsters: Realism and Progress in International Relations Theory after September 11', *Security Studies* 15:3 (2006), pp. 496–528.
'The British North Borneo Trading Company', *The Economist*, 19 November 1881 (issue 1995), p. 1428.
Bull, H. and Watson, A. (eds.), *The Expansion of International Society* (Oxford: Clarendon Press, 1984).
Butel, P., *The Atlantic* (London, Routledge, 1999).
Buzan, B. and. Lawson, G., 'The Global Transformation: The Nineteenth Century and the Making of Modern International Relations', *International Studies Quarterly* 57:3 (2013), pp. 620–34.
Buzan, B. and Little, R., 'The Idea of "International System": Theory Meets History', *International Political Science Review* 15:3 (1994), pp. 231–55.
International Systems in World History: Remaking the Study of International Relations (Oxford University Press, 2000).
Caldwell, I. and Henley, D., 'Introduction: The Stranger Who Would be King – Magic, Logic and Polemic', *Indonesia and the Malay World* 36:105 (2008), pp. 163–75.
Canfield, R. L., 'Introduction: The Turko-Persian Tradition', in R. L. Canfield (ed.), *Turko-Persia in Historical Perspective* (Cambridge University Press, 1991), pp. 1–34.
Cannadine, D. (ed.), *Empire, the Sea and Global History: Britain's Maritime World, 1763–1833* (London: Palgrave Macmillan, 2007).
Carey, P., 'The Origins of the Java War (1825–1830)', *English Historical Review* 91:358 (1976), pp. 52–78.
'Waiting for the "Just King": The Agrarian World of South-Central Java from Giyanti (1755) to the Java War (1825–30)', *Modern Asian Studies* 20:1 (1986), pp. 59–137.

The Power of Prophecy: Prince Dipanagara and the End of an Old Order in Java, 1785–1855, 2nd edn (Leiden, KITLV Press, 2007).

Casale, G., *The Ottoman Age of Exploration* (Oxford University Press, 2011).

Charney, M. W., *Southeast Asian Warfare 1300–1900* (Leiden: Brill, 2004).

Chaudhuri, K. N., *The Trading World of Asia and the English East India Company: 1660–1760* (Cambridge University Press, 1978).

'The English East India Company in the 17th and 18th Centuries: A Pre-Modern Multinational Organization', in L. Blussé and F. Gaastra, *Companies and Trade: Essays on Overseas Trading Companies During the Ancien Régime* (Leiden University Press, 1981), pp. 29–47.

Trade and Civilisation in the Indian Ocean: An Economic History from the Rise of Islam to 1750 (Cambridge University Press, 1985).

Asia before Europe: Economy and Civilization of the Indian Ocean from the Rise of Islam to 1750 (Cambridge University Press, 1990).

'Reflections on the Organizing Principle of Pre-Modern Trade', in J. D. Tracy (ed.), *The Political Economy of Merchant Empires: State Power and World Trade 1350–1750* (Cambridge University Press, 1990), pp. 421–42.

Ciepley, D., 'Beyond Public and Private: Toward a Political Theory of the Corporation', *American Political Science Review* 107:1 (2013), pp. 139–58.

Ciofelli-Ravella, C. and Landman, T., 'The Evolution of Maya Polities in the Ancient Mesoamerican System', *International Studies Quarterly*, 43:4 (1999), pp. 559–98.

Cipolla, C. M., *Guns, Sails, and Empires: Technological Innovation and the Early Phases of European Expansion* (New York: Pantheon, 1965).

Clark, H. R., 'Maritime Diasporas in Asia before Da Gama: An Introductory Commentary', *Journal of the Economic and Social History of the Orient* 49:4 (2006), pp. 385–94.

Clark, I., *Legitimacy in International Society* (Oxford University Press, 2005).

Clulow, A., 'European Maritime Violence and Territorial States in Early Modern Asia, 1600–1650', *Itinerario* 33:3 (2009), pp. 72–94.

Collier, D. and Mahon, J. E., 'Conceptual "Stretching" Revisited: Adapting Categories in Comparative Analysis', *American Political Science Review* 87:4 (1993), pp. 845–55.

Conrad, G. W. and Demarest, A. A., *Religion and Empire: The Dynamics of Aztec and Inca Expansionism* (Cambridge University Press, 1984).

Cooley, A. and Spruyt, H., *Contracting States: Sovereignty Transfers in International Relations* (Princeton University Press, 2009).

Cooney, S., 'Overseas Companies as Transnational Actors During the European Conquest of Africa', *Review of International Studies* 6:2 (1980), pp. 154–79.

Corn, C., *The Scents of Eden: A History of the Spice Trade* (New York: Kodansha, 1999).

Cribb, R., 'Legal Pluralism and Criminal Law in the Dutch Colonial Order', *Indonesia* 90 (2010), pp. 47–66.

Crowder, M. 'Indirect Rule: French and British Style', *Africa* 34:3 (1964), pp. 197–205.

Curtin, P. D., *Cross-Cultural Trade in World History* (Cambridge University Press, 1984).

Death by Migration: Europe's Encounter with the Tropical World in the Nineteenth Century (Cambridge University Press, 1989).

Dale, S., 'India under Mughal Rule', in D. Morgan and A. Reid (eds.), *The New Cambridge History of Islam*, vol. III: *The Eastern Islamic World, Eleventh to Eighteenth Centuries* (Cambridge University Press, 2010), pp. 266–314.

Darwin, J., *Unfinished Empire: The Global Expansion of Britain* (London: Penguin, 2012).

Davies, B. L., *Warfare, State and Society on the Black Sea Steppe 1500–1700* (London: Routledge, 2007).

de Silva, C., 'Beyond the Cape: The Portuguese Encounter with the Peoples of South Asia', in S. B. Schwartz (ed.), *Implicit Understandings: Observing, Reporting, and Reflecting on the Encounters Between Europeans and Other Peoples in the Early Modern Era* (Cambridge University Press, 1995), pp. 295–322.

de Vries, J., 'The Limits of Globalization in the Early Modern World', *Economic History Review* 63:3 (2010), pp. 710–33.

DiMaggio, P. J. and Powell, W. W., 'The Iron Cage Revisited: Institutional Isomorphism and Collective Rationality in Organizational Fields', *American Sociological Review* 48:2 (1983), pp. 147–60.

(eds.), *The New Institutionalism in Organizational Analysis* (University of Chicago Press, 1991).

Dirks, N. B., *The Scandal of Empire: India and the Creation of Imperial Britain* (Cambridge, MA: Harvard University Press, 2009).

Disney, A. R., *A History of Portugal and the Portuguese Empire*, vol. II (Cambridge University Press, 2009).

Downing, B., *The Military Revolution and Political Change: Origins of Democracy and Autocracy in Early Modern Europe* (Princeton University Press, 1992).

Donnelly, J., 'Sovereign Inequalities and Hierarchy in Anarchy: American Power and International Society', *European Journal of International Relations* 12:2 (2006), pp. 139–70.

'Rethinking Political Structures: From "Ordering Principles" to "Vertical Differentiation" – and Beyond', *International Theory*, 1:1 (2009), pp. 49–68.

Duncan, T. B., 'Niels Steensgaard and the Europe–Asia Trade of the Early Seventeenth Century', *Journal of Modern History* 47:3 (1975), pp. 512–18.

Dunne, T., 'Society and Hierarchy in International Relations', *International Relations* 17:3 (2003), pp. 303–20.

Elliott, J. H., 'A Europe of Composite Monarchies', *Past and Present* 37:1 (1992), pp. 48–71.

Elster, J., 'Rational Choice History: A Case of Excessive Ambition', *American Political Science Review* 94:3 (2000), pp. 685–95.

Ertman, T., *Birth of the Leviathan: Building States and Regimes in Medieval and Early Modern Europe* (Cambridge University Press, 1997).

Evans, P., Rueschemeyer, D. and Skocpol, T. (eds.), *Bringing the State Back In* (Cambridge University Press, 1985).

Ewans, M., *European Atrocity, African Catastrophe: Leopold II, the Congo Free State and its Aftermath* (London: RoutledgeCurzon, 2002).

Faruqi, S. S., 'The Malaysian Constitution, the Islamic State and Hudud Laws', in K. S. Nathan and N. H. Kamali (eds.), *Islam in Southeast Asia: Political, Social and Strategic Challenges for the 21st Century* (Singapore: ISEAS, 2005), pp. 256–77.

Fazal, T. M., *State Death: The Politics and Geography of Conquest, Occupation, and Annexation* (Princeton University Press, 2007).

Ferguson. N., *Civilization: The West and the Rest* (London: Penguin, 2011).

Ferguson, Y. H. and Mansbach, R. W., *Polities: Authority, Identities, and Change* (Columbia: University of South Carolina Press, 1996).

Fernández–Armesto, F., *Before Columbus: Exploration and Colonization from the Mediterranean to the Atlantic, 1229–1492* (Philadelphia: University of Pennsylvania Press, 1987).

'The Stranger Effect in Early Modern Asia', *Itinerario* 24:2 (2000), pp. 80–103.

Pathfinders: A Global History of Exploration (New York: W. W. Norton, 2007).

Finlay, R., 'The Treasure Ships of Zheng He: Chinese Maritime Imperialism in the Age of Discovery', *Terrae Incognitae* 23:1 (1991), pp. 1–12.

Fisch, J., 'Law as a Means and as an End: Some Remarks on the Function of European and Non-European Law in the Process of European Expansion', in W. J. Mommsen and J. A. De Moor (eds.), *European Expansion and Law: The Encounter of European and Indigenous Law in 19th and 20th Century Africa and Asia* (Oxford: Berg, 1992), pp. 15–38.

Fisher, M. H., 'Indirect Rule in the British Empire: The Foundations of the Residency System in India (1764–1858)', *Modern Asian Studies* 18:3 (1984), pp. 393–428.

Flores, J., 'The Sea and the World of the *Mutasaddi*: A Profile of Port Officials from Mughal Gujarat (c. 1600–1650)', *Journal of the Royal Asiatic Society* (3rd series), 21 (2011), pp. 55–71.

Flynn D. O. and Giraldez, A., 'Born with a "Silver Spoon": The Origin of World Trade in 1571', *Journal of World History* 6:2 (1995), pp. 201–21.

Foltz, R., *Religions of the Silk Road: Premodern Patterns of Globalization* (London: Palgrave Macmillan, 2010).

Freeman, D. B., *The Pacific* (London: Routledge, 2009).

Gaastra, F., 'The Shifting Balance of Trade of the Dutch East India Company', in L. Blussé and F. Gaastra (eds.), *Companies and Trade: Essays on Overseas Trading Companies During the Ancien Régime* (Leiden University Press, 1981), pp. 47–69.

Galbraith, J. S., 'The Chartering of the British North Borneo Company', *Journal of British Studies* 4:2 (1965), pp. 102–26.

Geddes, B., 'How the Cases You Choose Affect the Answers You Get: Selection Bias in Comparative Politics', *Political Analysis* 2:1 (1990), pp. 131–50.

Glete, J., *Warfare at Sea, 1500–1650: Maritime Conflicts and the Transformation of Europe* (London: Routledge, 2000).

War and State in Early Modern Europe: Spain, the Dutch Republic and Sweden as Fiscal–Military States, 1500–1660 (London: Routledge, 2002).

Goertz, G. and Mahoney, J., *A Tale of Two Cultures: Qualitative and Quantitative Research in the Social Sciences* (Princeton University Press, 2012).

Gommans, J., *Mughal Warfare: Indian Frontiers and the High Road to Empire 1500–1700* (London: Routledge, 2002).

Gommans, J. and Kolff, D. (eds.), *Warfare and Weaponry in South Asia 1000–1800* (Delhi: Oxford University Press, 2003).

'Introduction', in J. Gommans and D. Kolff (eds.), *Warfare and Weaponry in South Asia, 1000–1800* (Delhi: Oxford University Press, 2003), pp. 1–22.

Gong, G., *The 'Standard of Civilization' in International Society* (Oxford: Clarendon Press, 1984).

Goody, J., *The Eurasian Miracle* (Cambridge: Polity Press, 2010).

Griffiths, J., 'What is Legal Pluralism?' *Journal of Legal Pluralism and Unofficial Law* 18:24 (1986), pp. 1–55.

Gross, L., 'The Peace of Westphalia', *American Journal of International Law* 42:1 (1948), pp. 20–41.

Grygiel, J., *Great Powers and Geopolitical Change* (Baltimore, MD: Johns Hopkins University Press, 2011).

Hall, P. A. and Soskice, D. A., *Varieties of Capitalism: The Institutional Foundations of Comparative Advantage* (Oxford University Press, 2001).

Halliday, F., 'International Society as Homogeneity: Burke, Marx, Fukuyama', *Millennium: Journal of International Studies*, 21:3 (1992), pp. 435–61.

Hannigan, T., *Raffles and the British Invasion of Java* (Singapore: Monsoon Books, 2013).

Hanson, V. D., *Why the West Has Won: Carnage and Culture from Salamis to Vietnam* (London: Faber & Faber, 2002).

Hasan, F., 'Conflict and Cooperation in Anglo-Mughal Trade Relations During the Reign of Aurungzeb', *Journal of the Economic and Social History of the Orient* 34:4 (1991), pp. 351–60.

'The Mughal Fiscal System in Surat and the English East India Company', *Modern Asian Studies* 27:4 (1993), pp. 711–18.

State and Locality in Mughal India: Power Relations in Western India c. 1572–1730 (Cambridge University Press, 2004).

Hassig, R., *Aztec Warfare: Imperial Expansion and Political Control* (Norman: University of Oklahoma Press, 1988).

Mexico and the Spanish Conquest, 2nd edn (Norman: University of Oklahoma Press, 2006).

Henley, D., 'Conflict, Justice and the Stranger-King Roots of Colonial Rule in Indonesia and Elsewhere', *Modern Asian Studies* 38 (2004), pp. 85–144.

Hingley, R., 'Cultural Diversity and Unity: Empire and Rome', in S. Hales and T. Hodos (eds.), *Material Culture and Social Identities in the Ancient World* (Cambridge University Press, 2009), pp. 54–75.

Hinkkanen, M.-L. and Kirby, D., *The Baltic and the North Seas* (London: Routledge, 2000).

Hobsbawm, E. J., *The Age of Empire, 1875–1914* (London: Abacus, 2003).

Hobson, J., *The Eastern Origins of Western Civilization* (Cambridge University Press, 2004).

The Eurocentric Conception of World Politics: Western International Theory, 1760–2010 (Cambridge University Press, 2012).

Hobson, J. and Sharman, J. C., 'The Enduring Place of Hierarchy in World Politics: Tracing the Social Logics of Hierarchy and Political Change', *European Journal of International Relations* 11:1 (2005), pp. 63–98.

Hoopes, D. G., Madsen, T. L. and Walker, G., Guest Editors' introduction to the special issue: 'Why Is There a Resource-Based View? Toward a Theory of Competitive Heterogeneity', *Strategic Management Journal*, 24:10 (2003), pp. 889–902.

Hopkins, A. G., 'Introduction: Globalization – An Agenda for Historians', in A. G. Hopkins (ed.), *Globalization in World History* (London: Pimlico, 2002), pp. 1–10.

Hsueh, V., *Hybrid Constitutions: Challenging Legacies of Law, Privilege and Culture in Colonial America* (Durham, NC: Duke University Press, 2010).

Hui, V. T., *War and State Formation in Ancient China and Early Modern Europe* (Cambridge University Press, 2005).

Jha, M. K., 'The Mughals, Merchants and the European Companies in 17th Century Surat', *Asia Europe Journal* 3:2 (2005), pp. 269–83.

Isaacman, A., *Mozambique: The Africanization of a European Institution: The Zambezi Prazos, 1750–1902* (Madison: University of Wisconsin Press, 1972).

Isaacman, A. and Isaacman, B., '*Prazeros* as Transfrontiersmen: A Study in Social and Cultural Change', *International Journal of African Historical Studies* 8:1 (1975), pp. 1–39.

Israel, J. and Chaudhuri, K. N., 'The English and Dutch East India Companies and the Glorious Revolution of 1688–9', in J. Israel (ed.), *The Anglo-Dutch Moment: Essays on the Glorious Revolution and its World Impact* (Cambridge University Press, 1991), pp. 407–38.

Jackson, R. H., *Quasi-States: Sovereignty, International Relations and the Third World* (Cambridge University Press, 1990).

James, L., *Raj: The Making and Unmaking of British India* (London: St Martin's Griffin, 2000).

Jeffrey, R., 'The Politics of Indirect Rule: Types of Relationships among Rulers, Ministers and Residents in a "Native State"', *Journal of Commonwealth and Comparative Politics* 13:3 (1975), pp. 261–81.

Jervis, R., *System Effects: Complexity in Political and Social Life* (Princeton University Press, 1997).

Johnston, A. I., 'What (If Anything) Does East Asia Tell Us about International Relations Theory?' *Annual Review of Political Science* 15:1 (2012), pp. 53–78.

Jones, E., *The European Miracle: Environments, Economies and Geopolitics in the History of Europe and Asia* (Cambridge University Press, 2003).

Kang, D. C., 'The Theoretical Roots of Hierarchy in International Relations', *Australian Journal of International Affairs* 58:3 (2004), pp. 337–52.

East Asia before the West: Five Centuries of Trade and Tribute (New York: Columbia University Press, 2012).

Katzenstein, P. J., 'A World of Plural and Pluralist Civilizations: Multiple Actors, Traditions and Practices', in P. J. Katzenstein (ed.), *Civilizations in World Politics* (London: Routledge, 2007), pp. 1–72.

Kian, K. H., 'How Strangers Became Kings: Javanese–Dutch Relations in Java, 1600–1800', *Indonesia and the Malay World* 36:105 (2008), pp. 293–307.

Klein, P. W., 'The Origins of Trading Companies', in L. Blussé and F. Gaastra (eds.), *Companies and Trade: Essays on Overseas Trading Companies During the Ancien Régime* (Leiden University Press, 1981), pp. 17–28.

Krasner, S. D., 'Westphalia and All That', in J. Goldstein and R. Keohane (eds.), *Ideas and Foreign Policy: Beliefs, Institutions and Political Change* (Ithaca, NY: Cornell University Press, 1993), pp. 235–64.

Sovereignty: Organized Hypocrisy (Princeton University Press, 1999).

Lake, D. A., 'Anarchy, Hierarchy and the Variety of International Relations', *International Organization* 50:1 (1996), pp. 1–33.

'New Sovereignty in International Relations', paper presented at the 98th American Political Science Association Conference, Boston, 29 August–1 September, 2002.

Hierarchy in International Relations (Ithaca, NY: Cornell University Press, 2009).

Lane, F. C., 'The Economic Consequences of Organized Violence', *Journal of Economic History* 18:4 (1958), pp. 401–17.

Profits from Power: Readings in Protection Rents and Violence-Controlling Enterprises (Albany, NY: State University of New York Press, 1979).

Lawson, P., *The East India Company: A History* (New York: Longman, 1993).

Lefevre, C., 'Europe–Mughal India–Muslim Asia: Circulation of Political Ideas and Instruments in Early Modern Times', in A. Fluchter and S. Richter (eds.), *Structures on the Move: Technologies of Governance in Transcultural Encounter* (Heidelberg: Springer, 2012), pp. 127–45.

Lewis M. W. and Wigen, K. E., *The Myth of Continents: A Critique of Metageography* (Berkeley: University of California Press, 1997).

Lieberman, V., *Strange Parallels: Southeast Asia in Global Context, c. 800–1830* (Cambridge University Press, 2009).

Liu, X., 'The Silk Road: Overland Trade and Cultural Interactions in Eurasia', in M. Adas (ed.), *Agricultural and Pastoral Societies in Ancient and Classical History* (Philadelphia: Temple University Press, 2001), pp. 151–79.

Locher–Scholten, E., 'Dutch Expansion in the Indonesia Archipelago around 1900 and the Imperialism Debate', *Journal of Southeast Asian Studies* 25:1 (1994), pp. 91–111.

Sumatran Sultanate and Colonial State: Jambi and the Rise of Dutch Imperialism, 1830–1907 (Ithaca, NY: Cornell University Press, 2004).

Lorge, P., *War, Politics and Society in Early Modern China 900–1795* (London: Routledge, 2005).

The Asian Military Revolution: From Gunpowder to the Bomb (Cambridge University Press, 2008).

Loth, V. C., 'Armed Incidents and Unpaid Bills: Anglo-Dutch Rivalry in the Banda Islands in the Seventeenth Century', *Modern Asian Studies* 29:4 (1995), pp. 705–40.

Lustick. I. S., 'Taking Evolution Seriously: Historical Institutionalism and Evolutionary Theory', *Polity* 43:2 (2011), pp. 179–209.

Luthy, H., 'India and East Africa: Imperial Partnership at the End of the First World War', *Journal of Contemporary History* 6:2 (1971), pp. 55–85.

Mahoney, J., 'Nominal, Ordinal and Narrative Appraisal in Macrocausal Analysis', *American Journal of Sociology* 104:4 (1999), pp. 1154–96.

Maloni, R., 'Europeans in Seventeenth Century Gujarat: Presence and Response', *Social Scientist* 36:3/4 (2008), pp. 77–80.

Maltby, W. S., *The Rise and Fall of the Spanish Empire* (Houndmills: Palgrave Macmillan, 2009).

Mancham, J. R., *Seychelles Global Citizen: The Autobiography of the Founding President of the Republic of Seychelles* (St Paul, MN: Paragon House, 2009).

Mancke, E., 'Early Modern Expansion and the Politicization of Oceanic Space', *Geographical Review* 89:2 (1999), pp. 225–36.

Mantena. K., *Alibis of Empire: Henry Maine and the Ends of Liberal Imperialism* (Princeton University Press, 2010).

March, J. G. and Olsen, J. P., *Rediscovering Institutions: The Organizational Basis of Politics* (New York: The Free Press, 1989).

Marshall, P. J., 'British Expansion in India in the Eighteenth Century: A Historical Revision', *History* 60:198 (1975), pp. 28–43.

'Western Arms in Maritime Asia in the Early Phases of Expansion', *Modern Asian Studies* 14:1 (1980), pp. 13–28.

'British Assessments of the Dutch in Asia in the Age of Raffles', *Itinerario* 12:1 (1988), pp. 1–16.

'The British in Asia: Trade to Dominion, 1700–1765', in P. J. Marshall and A. Low (eds.), *The Oxford History of the British Empire*, vol. II: *The Eighteenth Century* (Oxford University Press, 1998), pp. 487–507.

Marx, K., Lenin, V. I. *et al.*, *The Civil War in France: The Paris Commune* (New York: International Publishers, 1988).

Matthews. O., *Glorious Misadventures: Nikolai Rezanov and the Dream of a Russian America* (New York: Bloomsbury, 2013).

McNeill, W. H., *The Pursuit of Power: Technology, Armed Force and Society since AD 1000* (Oxford: Blackwell, 1982).

The Rise of the West: A History of the Human Community (University of Chicago Press, 1992).

Merritt, H. P., 'Bismarck and the German Interest in East Africa, 1884–1885', *Historical Journal* 28:1(1978), pp. 97–116.

Metcalf, T. R., *Ideologies of the Raj* (Cambridge University Press, 1994).

Meyer, J. W., Boli, J., Thomas, G. M. and Ramirez, F. O., 'World Society and the Nation-State', *American Journal of Sociology* 103:1(1997), pp. 144–81.

Meyer, J. W. and Rowan, B., 'Institutionalized Organizations: Formal Structure as Myth and Ceremony', *American Journal of Sociology* 83:2 (1977), pp. 340–63.

Mostert, T., 'Chain of Command: The Military System of the Dutch East India Company 1655–1663', master's thesis, Department of History, University of Leiden, 2007.

Mulich, J., 'Microregionalism and Intercolonial Relations: The Case of the Danish West Indies, 1730–1830', *Journal of Global History* 8:1 (2013), pp. 72–94.

Murphey, R., *Ottoman Warfare 1500–1700* (New Brunswick, NJ: Rutgers University Press, 1999).

Nadri, G. A., *Eighteenth Century Gujarat: The Dynamics of its Political Economy, 1750–1800* (Leiden: Brill, 2009).

Neumann, I. B. and Wigen, E., 'The Importance of the Eurasian Steppe to the Study of International Relations', *Journal of International Relations and Development* 16:3 (2013), pp. 311–30.

Newbury, C., 'Patrons, Clients and Empire: The Subordination of Indigenous Hierarchies in Africa and Asia', *Journal of World History* 11:2 (2000), pp. 227–63.

Patrons, Clients, and Empire: Chieftaincy and Over-rule in Asia, Africa, and the Pacific (Oxford University Press, 2003).

Newman, P. C., *Empire of the Bay: The Story of the Hudson's Bay Company* (London: Penguin, 1998).

Nexon, D. H., *The Struggle for Power in Early Modern Europe: Religious Conflict, Dynastic Empires, and International Change* (Princeton University Press, 2009).

Nexon, D. H. and Wright, T., 'What's at Stake in the American Empire Debate', *American Political Science Review* 101:2 (2007), pp. 253–71.

Nightingale, C. H., 'Before Race Mattered: Geographies of the Early Modern Color Line in Early Colonial Madras and New York', *American Historical Review* 113:1 (2008), pp. 48–71.

North, D. C., 'A Transactions Cost Theory of Politics', *Journal of Theoretical Politics* 2:4 (1990), pp. 355–67.

Institutions, Institutional Change and Economic Performance (Cambridge University Press, 1990).

'Institutions, Transaction Costs, and the Rise of Merchant Empires', in J. Tracy (ed.), *The Political Economy of Merchant Empires: State Power and World Trade 1350–1750* (Cambridge University Press, 1990), pp. 22–40.

North, D. C. and Thomas, R. P., *The Rise of the Western World: A New Economic History* (Cambridge University Press, 1973).

Oliver, R. A. and Atmore, A., *Medieval Africa, 1250–1800* (Cambridge University Press, 2001).

Olson, M., *Power and Prosperity: Outgrowing Communist and Capitalist Dictatorships* (New York: Basic Books, 2000).

Onley, J., 'Britain's Informal Empire in the Gulf, 1820–1871', *Journal of Social Affairs* 22:87 (2005), pp. 29–45.

The Arabian Frontier of the British Raj: Merchants, Rulers and the British in the Nineteenth Century Gulf (Oxford University Press, 2008).

Osiander, A., *Before the State: Systemic Political Change in the West from the Greeks to the French Revolution* (Oxford University Press, 2007).

Owen IV, J. M., *The Clash of Ideas in World Politics: Transnational Networks, States, and Regime Change, 1510–2010* (Princeton University Press, 2010).

Panikkar, K. M., *Asia and Western Dominance: A Survey of the Vasco da Gama Epoch in Asian History, 1498–1945* (London: Collier Books, 1959).

Parker, G., *The Military Revolution: Military Innovation and the Rise of the West, 1500–1800* (Cambridge University Press, 1988).

Pearson, M. N., 'Merchants and States', in J. D. Tracy (ed.), *The Political Economy of Merchant Empires: State Power and World Trade 1350–1750* (Cambridge University Press, 1990), pp. 41–116.

Port Cities and Intruders: The Swahili Coast, India and Portugal in the Early Modern Period (Baltimore, MD: Johns Hopkins University Press, 1998).

The Indian Ocean (London: Routledge, 2003).

'Islamic Trade, Shipping, Port States, and Merchant Communities in the Indian Ocean, Seventh to Sixteenth Centuries', in D. Morgan and A. Reid (eds.), *The New Cambridge History of Islam*, vol. III: *The Eastern Islamic World, Eleventh to Eighteenth Centuries* (Cambridge University Press, 2010), pp. 315–65.

Peers, D. M., 'War and Public Finance in Early Nineteenth Century British India: The First Burma War', *International History Review* 11:4 (1989), pp. 628–47.

'Gunpowder Empires and the Garrison State: Modernity, Hybridity and the Political Economy of Colonial India, circa 1750–1860', *Comparative Studies of South Asia, Africa and the Middle East* 27:2 (2007), pp. 245–58.

'Revolution, Evolution or Devolution: The Military and the Making of Colonial India', in W. Lee (ed.), *Empires and Indigenes: Intercultural Alliance, Imperial Expansion and Warfare in the Early Modern World* (New York University Press, 2011), pp. 81–106.

Perdue P., *China Marches West: The Qing Conquest of Central Asia* (Cambridge, MA: Harvard University Press, 2005).

Pettigrew, W. A., *Freedom's Debt: The Royal African Company and the Politics of the Slave Trade 1672–1752* (Chapel Hill: University of North Carolina Press, 2013).

Phillips, A., *War, Religion and Empire: Transformation of International Orders* (Cambridge University Press, 2011).

Philpott, D., *Revolutions in Sovereignty: How Ideas Shaped Modern International Relations* (Princeton University Press, 2001).

Pollock, S., *The Language of the Gods in the World of Men: Sanskrit, Culture and Power in Premodern India* (Berkeley: University of California Press, 2006).

Posen, B. R., 'Nationalism, the Mass Army, and Military Power', *International Security* 18:2 (1993), pp. 80–124.

Prakash, O., 'The Dutch East Indian Company in Bengal: Trade Privileges and Problems, 1632–1712', *Indian Economic Social History Review* 9:3 (1972), pp. 273–4.

'Europeans, India and the Indian Ocean in the Early Modern Period', *South Asia: Journal of South Asian Studies* 19: supplement 1 (1996), pp. 15–25.

Prange, S. R., 'Scholars and the Sea: A Historiography of the Indian Ocean', *History Compass* 6:5 (2008), pp. 1382–93.

Prestholdt, J., 'Portuguese Conceptual Categories and the "Other" Encounter on the Swahili Coast', *Journal of Asian and African Studies* 36:4 (2001), pp. 383–92.

Reid, A., 'Islam in Southeast Asia and the Indian Ocean Littoral, 1500–1800: Expansion, Polarisation, Synthesis', in D. Morgan and A. Reid (eds.), *The New Cambridge History of Islam*, vol. III: *The Eastern Islamic World, Eleventh to Eighteenth Centuries* (Cambridge University Press, 2010), pp. 427–69.

Remmelink, W., 'Expansion Without Design: The Snare of Javanese Politics', *Itinerario* 12:1 (1988), pp. 111–28.

Resende-Santos, J., *Neorealism, States, and the Modern Mass Army* (Cambridge University Press, 2007).

Reus-Smit, C., 'Struggles for Individual Rights and the Expansion of the International System', *International Organization* 65:2 (2011), pp. 207–42.

Individual Rights and the Making of the International System (Cambridge University Press, 2013).

Richards, J. F., 'The Islamic Frontier in the East: Expansion into South Asia', *South Asia: Journal of South Asian Studies* 4:1(1974), pp. 91–109.

The Mughal Empire (Cambridge University Press, 1996).

Ricklefs, M. C., *Jogjakarta under Sultan Mangkubumi, 1749–1792: A History of the Division of Java* (London: Oxford University Press, 1974).

A History of Modern Indonesia since c. 1300 (Stanford University Press, 1993).

War, Culture and the Economy in Java, 1677–1726 (London: Allen and Unwin, 1993).

Robertson, R., *The Three Waves of Globalization: A History of a Developing Global Consciousness* (London: Zed Books, 2003).

Rogers, C. J. (ed.), *The Military Revolution Debate: Readings on the Military Transformation of Early Modern Europe* (Boulder, CO: Westview, 1995).

Rogowski, R., *Commerce and Coalitions: How Trade Affects Domestic Political Alignments* (Princeton University Press, 1990).

Roper, L. and Ruymbeke, B. (eds.), *Constructing Early Modern Empires: Proprietary Ventures in the Atlantic World, 1500–1750* (Leiden: Brill, 2007).

Roy, K., 'Military Synthesis in South Asia: Armies, Warfare and Indian Society, c.1740–1849', *Journal of Military History* 69:3 (2005), pp. 651–90.

'The Hybrid Military Establishment of the East India Company in South Asia: 1750–1849', *Journal of Global History* 6:2 (2011), pp. 195–218.

Roy, T., *The East India Company: The World's Most Powerful Corporation* (New Delhi: Penguin, 2012).

India in the World Economy: From Antiquity to the Present (Cambridge University Press, 2012).

'Rethinking the Origins of British India: State Formation and Military-Fiscal Undertakings in an Eighteenth Century World Region', *Modern Asian Studies* 47:4 (2013), pp. 1125–56.

Rudolph, L. I. and Hoeber Rudolph, S., 'Federalism as State Formation in India: A Theory of Shared Sovereignty', *International Political Science Review* 31:5 (2010), pp. 553–72.

Ruggie, J. G., 'Territoriality and Beyond: Problematizing Modernity in International Relations', *International Organization* 47:1 (1993), pp. 139–74.

Russell-Wood, A. J. R., *The Portuguese Empire, 1415–1808: A World on the Move* (Baltimore, MD: Johns Hopkins University Press, 1992).

Sapra, R., 'A Peaceable Kingdom in the East: Favourable Early Seventeenth Century Representations of the Moghul Empire', *Renaissance and Reformation* 27:3 (2003), pp. 5–36.

Scammell, G. V., 'Indigenous Assistance in the Establishment of Portuguese Power in Asia in the Sixteenth Century', *Modern Asian Studies* 14:1 (1980), pp. 1–11.

Sen, T., 'The Formation of Chinese Maritime Networks to Southern Asia, 1200–1450', *Journal of the Economic and Social History of the Orient* 49:4 (2006), pp. 421–53.

Shaffer, L., 'Southernization', *Journal of World History* 5:1 (1994), pp. 1–21.

Maritime Southeast Asia to 1500 (New York: M. E. Sharpe, 1996).

Sharman, J. C., 'International Hierarchies and Contemporary Imperial Governance: A Tale of Three Kingdoms', *European Journal of International Relations* 19:2 (2013), pp. 189–207.

Siddiqi, M., *The British Historical Context and Petitioning in India* (New Delhi: Aakar Books, 2005).

Sood, G. D. S., 'Circulation and Exchange in Islamicate Eurasia: A Regional Approach to the Early Modern World', *Past and Present* 212:1 (2011), pp. 113–62.

'Sovereign Justice in Precolonial Maritime Asia: The Case of the Mayor's Court in Bombay, 1726–1798', *Itinerario* 37:2 (2013), pp. 46–72.

Soucek, S., *A History of Inner Asia* (Cambridge University Press, 2000).

Spruyt, H., *The Sovereign State and its Competitors* (Princeton University Press, 1994).

'Diversity or Uniformity in the Modern World? Answers from Evolutionary Theory, Learning and Social Adaptation', in W. R. Thompson (ed.), *Evolutionary Interpretations of World Politics* (New York: Routledge, 2001), pp. 110–32.

Steensgaard, N., *Carracks, Caravans and Companies: The Structural Crisis in the European–Asian Trade in the Early 17th Century* (Lund: Studentlitteratur, 1973).

'Companies as a Specific Institution in the History of European Expansion', in L. Blussé and F. Gaastra (eds.), *Companies and Trade: Essays on Overseas Trading Companies During the Ancien Régime* (Leiden University Press, 1981), pp. 245–64.

Steinberg, P. E., *The Social Construction of the Ocean* (Cambridge University Press, 2001).

Stern, P., '"A Politie of Civil and Military Power": Political Thought and the Late Seventeenth-Century Foundations of the East India Company-State', *Journal of British Studies* 47:2 (2008), pp. 253–83.

The Company-State: Corporate Sovereignty and the Early Modern Foundations of the British Empire in India (Oxford University Press, 2011).

Stevens, C. B., *Russia's Wars of Emergence 1460–1730* (Harlow: Pearson, 2007).

Stokes, E., *The English Utilitarians and India* (Oxford: Clarendon Press, 1959).

Strang, D., 'Anomaly and Commonplace in European Political Expansion: Realist and Institutional Accounts', *International Organization* 45:2 (1991), pp. 143–62.

Streusand, D. E., *Islamic Gunpowder Empires: Ottomans, Safavids, and Mughals* (Boulder, CO: Westview Press, 2010).

Subrahmanyam, S., 'The Mughal State: Structure or Process? Reflections on Recent Western Historiography', *Indian Economic and Social History Review* 29:3 (1992), pp. 291–321.

'Of *Imârat* and *Tijârat*: Asian Merchants and State Power in the Western Indian Ocean, 1400–1750', *Comparative Studies in Society and History* 37:4 (1995), pp. 750–80.

'Written on Water: Designs and Dynamics in the Portuguese *Estado da India*', in S. E. Alcock (ed.), *Empires: Perspectives from Archaeology and History* (Cambridge University Press, 2001), pp. 42–69.

'Taking Stock of the Franks: South Asian Views of Europeans and Europe', *Indian Economic and Social History Review* 42:1 (2005), pp. 69–100.

'A Tale of Three Empires: Mughals, Ottomans, and Habsburgs in a Comparative Context,' *Common Knowledge* 12:1 (2006), pp. 66–92.

'Holding the World in Balance: The Connected Histories of the Iberian Overseas Empires 1500–1640', *American Historical Review* 112:5 (2007), pp. 1359–85.

Mughals and Franks: Explorations in Connected History (Oxford University Press, 2012).

The Portuguese Empire in Asia 1500–1700 (London: Blackwell-Wiley, 2012).

Subrahmanyam, S. and Thomaz, Luís Filipe F. R., 'Evolution of Empire: The Portuguese in the Indian Ocean During the Sixteenth Century', in J. D. Tracy (ed.), *The Political Economy of Merchant Empires: State Power and World Trade 1350–1750* (Cambridge University Press, 1990), pp. 298–331.

Subramanian, L., 'Banias and the British: The Role of Indigenous Credit in Processes of Imperial Expansion in Western India in the Second Half of the Eighteenth Century', *Modern Asian Studies* 21:3 (1987), pp. 473–510.

Suzuki, S., *Civilization and Empire: China and Japan's Encounter with European International Society* (London: Routledge, 2009).

Tagliacozzo, E., 'Trade, Production and Incorporation: The Indian Ocean in Flux, 1600–1900', *Itinerario* 26:1 (2002), pp. 75–106.

Tambiah, S. J., 'The Galactic Polity: The Structures of Traditional Kingdoms in Southeast Asia', *Annals of the New York Academy of Sciences*, 293 (1977), pp. 69–97.

'What did Bernier Actually Say? Profiling the Mughal Empire', *Contributions to Indian Sociology* 32:2 (1998), pp. 361–86.

Teschke, B., *The Myth of 1648: Class, Geopolitics, and the Making of Modern International Relations* (London: Verso, 2003).

Therborn, G., 'Globalizations: Dimensions, Historical Waves, Regional Effects, Normative Governance', *International Sociology* 15:2 (2000), pp. 151–79.

Thompson, W. R., 'The Military Superiority Thesis and the Ascendancy of Western Eurasia in the World System', *Journal of World History* 10:1 (1999), pp. 143–78.

Thomson, J., *Mercenaries, Pirates and Sovereigns: State-Building and Extraterritorial Violence in Early-Modern Europe* (Princeton University Press, 1994).

Thornton, J. K., *Warfare in Atlantic Africa 1500–1800* (London: Routledge, 1999).

'The Portuguese in Africa', in F. Bethencourt and D. R. Curto (eds.), *Portuguese Oceanic Expansion, 1400–1800* (Cambridge University Press, 2007), pp. 138–60.

Tilly, C., 'Reflections on the History of European State-making', in C. Tilly (ed.), *The Formation of National States in Western Europe* (Princeton University Press, 1975), pp. 3–83.

'War Making and State Making as Organized Crime', in P. Evans, D. Rueschemeyer and T. Skocpol (eds.), *Bringing the State Back In* (Cambridge University Press, 1985), pp. 169–92.

Coercion, Capital and European States, AD 990–1992 (Oxford: Blackwell, 1992).

Trust and Rule (Cambridge University Press, 2005).

Tracy, J. D., 'Introduction', in J. D. Tracy (ed.), *The Political Economy of Merchant Empires: State Power and World Trade 1350–1750* (Cambridge University Press, 1990), pp. 1–21.

(ed.), *The Rise of Merchant Empires: Long Distance Trade in the Early Modern World 1350–1750* (Cambridge University Press, 1990).

Tucker, E., 'Seeking a World Empire: Nadir Shah in Timur's Path', in J. E. Woods (ed.), *Historiography of Post-Mongol Central Asia and the Middle East* (Wiesbaden: Harrassowitz, 2006), pp. 332–42.

Vail, L., 'Mozambique's Chartered Companies: The Rule of the Feeble', *Journal of African History* 17:3 (1976), pp. 389–416.

Van Leur, J. C., *Indonesian Trade and Society: Essays in Asian Social and Economic History* (The Hague: W. van Hoeve, 1955).

Vandervort, B., *Wars of Imperial Conquest in Africa 1830–1914* (Bloomington: Indiana University Press, 1998).

Vigneswaran, D., 'A Corrupt International Society: How Britain Was Duped into its First Imperial Conquest', in S. Suzuki, Y. Zhang and J. Quirk (eds.), *International Orders in the Early Modern World* (London: Routledge, 2013), pp. 166–207.

Vink, M., 'From Port City to World-System: Spatial Constructs of Dutch Indian Ocean Studies, 1500–1800', *Itinerario* 28: 2 (2004), pp. 45–116.

Wallerstein, I., *The Modern World System*, vol. I: *Capitalist Agriculture and the Origins of the European World-Economy in the Sixteenth Century* (New York: Academic Press, 1974).

The Modern World System, vol. II: *Mercantilism and the Consolidation of the European World-Economy, 1600–1750* (New York: Academic Press, 1980).

Waltz, K., *Theory of International Politics* (New York: McGraw Hill, 1979).

Wang, Z., *Tang China in Multipolar Asia: A History of Diplomacy and War* (Honolulu: University of Hawaii Press, 2013).

Ward, K., *Networks of Empire: Forced Migration in the Dutch East India Company* (Cambridge University Press 2008).

Washbrook, D., 'India, 1818–1860: The Two Faces of Colonialism', in A. Porter (ed.), *The Oxford History of the British Empire*, vol. III: *The Nineteenth Century* (Oxford University Press, 2001), pp. 395–421.

Webster, A., *Gentlemen Capitalists: British Imperialism in South East Asia, 1770–1890* (London: Tauris Academic Studies, 1998).

White, R., *The Middle Ground: Indians, Empires, and Republics in the Great Lakes Region, 1650–1815* (Cambridge University Press, 1991).

Wills Jr., J. E., "Was There a Vasco da Gama Epoch? Recent Historiography', in A. Disney and E. Booth (eds.), *Vasco da Gama and the Linking of Europe and Asia* (Oxford University Press, 2000), pp. 350–60.

Wilson, J. E., 'Early Colonial India Beyond Empire', *Historical Journal* 50:4 (2007), pp. 951–70.

Winius, G. D., *The Fatal History of Portuguese Ceylon: Transition to Dutch Rule* (Cambridge, MA: Harvard University Press, 1971).

Wolters, O. W., *History, Culture, and Region in Southeast Asia* (Singapore: Southeast Asia Program Publications, 1982).

Index

CAMBRIDGE STUDIES IN INTERNATIONAL RELATIONS

126 *Thomas Risse, Stephen C. Ropp and Kathryn Sikkink (eds.)*
The persistent power of human rights
From commitment to compliance

125 *K. M. Fierke*
Political self-sacrifice
Agency, body and emotion in international relations

124 *Stefano Guzzini*
The return of geopolitics in Europe?
Social mechanisms and foreign policy identity crises

123 *Bear F. Braumoeller*
The great powers and the international system
Systemic theory in empirical perspective

122 *Jonathan Joseph*
The social in the global
Social theory, governmentality and global politics

121 *Brian C. Rathbun*
Trust in international cooperation
International security institutions, domestic politics and American multilateralism

120 *A. Maurits van der Veen*
Ideas, interests and foreign aid

119 *Emanuel Adler and Vincent Pouliot*
International practices

118 *Ayşe Zarakol*
After defeat
How the East learned to live with the West

117 *Andrew Phillips*
War, religion and empire
The transformation of international orders

116 *Joshua Busby*
Moral movements and foreign policy

115 *Séverine Autesserre*
The trouble with the Congo
Local violence and the failure of international peacebuilding

114 *Deborah D. Avant, Martha Finnemore and Susan K. Sell*
Who governs the globe?

113 *Vincent Pouliot*
International security in practice
The politics of NATO–Russia diplomacy

112 *Columba Peoples*
Justifying ballistic missile defence
Technology, security and culture

111 *Paul Sharp*
Diplomatic theory of international relations

110 *John A. Vasquez*
The war puzzle revisited

109 *Rodney Bruce Hall*
Central banking as global governance
Constructing financial credibility

108 *Milja Kurki*
Causation in international relations
Reclaiming causal analysis

107 *Richard M. Price*
Moral limit and possibility in world politics

106 *Emma Haddad*
The refugee in international society
Between sovereigns

105 *Ken Booth*
Theory of world security

104 *Benjamin Miller*
States, nations and the great powers
The sources of regional war and peace

103 *Beate Jahn (ed.)*
Classical theory in international relations

102 *Andrew Linklater and Hidemi Suganami*
The English School of international relations
A contemporary reassessment

101 *Colin Wight*
Agents, structures and international relations
Politics as ontology

100 *Michael C. Williams*
The realist tradition and the limits of international relations

99 *Ivan Arreguín-Toft*
How the weak win wars
A theory of asymmetric conflict

98 *Michael Barnett and Raymond Duvall*
Power in global governance

97 *Yale H. Ferguson and Richard W. Mansbach*
Remapping global politics
History's revenge and future shock

96 *Christian Reus-Smit*
The politics of international law

95 *Barry Buzan*
From international to world society?
English School theory and the social structure of globalisation

94 *K. J. Holsti*
Taming the sovereigns
Institutional change in international politics

93 *Bruce Cronin*
Institutions for the common good
International protection regimes in international security

92 *Paul Keal*
European conquest and the rights of indigenous peoples
The moral backwardness of international society

91 *Barry Buzan and Ole Wæver*
Regions and powers
The structure of international security

90 *A. Claire Cutler*
Private power and global authority
Transnational merchant law in the global political economy

89 *Patrick M. Morgan*
Deterrence now

88 *Susan Sell*
Private power, public law
The globalization of intellectual property rights

87 *Nina Tannenwald*
The nuclear taboo
The United States and the non-use of nuclear weapons since 1945

86 *Linda Weiss*
States in the global economy
Bringing domestic institutions back in

85 *Rodney Bruce Hall and Thomas J. Biersteker (eds.)*
The emergence of private authority in global governance

84 *Heather Rae*
State identities and the homogenisation of peoples

83 *Maja Zehfuss*
Constructivism in international relations
The politics of reality

82 *Paul K. Ruth and Todd Allee*
The democratic peace and territorial conflict in the twentieth century

81 *Neta C. Crawford*
Argument and change in world politics
Ethics, decolonization and humanitarian intervention

80 *Douglas Lemke*
Regions of war and peace

79 *Richard Shapcott*
Justice, community and dialogue in international relations

78 *Phil Steinberg*
The social construction of the ocean

77 *Christine Sylvester*
Feminist international relations
An unfinished journey

76 *Kenneth A. Schultz*
Democracy and coercive diplomacy

75 *David Houghton*
US foreign policy and the Iran hostage crisis

74 *Cecilia Albin*
Justice and fairness in international negotiation

73 *Martin Shaw*
Theory of the global state
Globality as an unfinished revolution

72 *Frank C. Zagare and D. Marc Kilgour*
Perfect deterrence

71 *Robert O'Brien, Anne Marie Goetz, Jan Aart Scholte and Marc Williams*
Contesting global governance
Multilateral economic institutions and global social movements

70 *Roland Bleiker*
Popular dissent, human agency and global politics

69 *Bill McSweeney*
Security, identity and interests
A sociology of international relations

68 *Molly Cochran*
Normative theory in international relations
A pragmatic approach

67 *Alexander Wendt*
Social theory of international politics

66 *Thomas Risse, Stephen C. Ropp and Kathryn Sikkink (eds.)*
The power of human rights
International norms and domestic change

65 *Daniel W. Drezner*
The sanctions paradox
Economic statecraft and international relations

64 *Viva Ona Bartkus*
The dynamic of secession

63 *John A. Vasquez*
The power of power politics
From classical realism to neotraditionalism

62 *Emanuel Adler and Michael Barnett (eds.)*
Security communities

61 *Charles Jones*
E. H. Carr and international relations
A duty to lie

60 *Jeffrey W. Knopf*
Domestic society and international cooperation
The impact of protest on US arms control policy

59 *Nicholas Greenwood Onuf*
The republican legacy in international thought

58 *Daniel S. Geller and J. David Singer*
Nations at war
A scientific study of international conflict

57 *Randall D. Germain*
The international organization of credit
States and global finance in the world economy

56 *N. Piers Ludlow*
Dealing with Britain
The Six and the first UK application to the EEC

55 *Andreas Hasenclever, Peter Mayer and Volker Rittberger*
Theories of international regimes

54 *Miranda A. Schreurs and Elizabeth C. Economy (eds.)*
The internationalization of environmental protection

53 *James N. Rosenau*
Along the domestic–foreign frontier
Exploring governance in a turbulent world

52 *John M. Hobson*
The wealth of states
A comparative sociology of international economic and political change

51 *Kalevi J. Holsti*
The state, war, and the state of war

50 *Christopher Clapham*
Africa and the international system
The politics of state survival

49 *Susan Strange*
The retreat of the state
The diffusion of power in the world economy

48 *William I. Robinson*
Promoting polyarchy
Globalization, US intervention, and hegemony

47 *Roger Spegele*
Political realism in international theory

46 *Thomas J. Biersteker and Cynthia Weber (eds.)*
State sovereignty as social construct

45 *Mervyn Frost*
Ethics in international relations
A constitutive theory

44 *Mark W. Zacher with Brent A. Sutton*
Governing global networks
International regimes for transportation and communications

43 *Mark Neufeld*
The restructuring of international relations theory

42 *Thomas Risse-Kappen (ed.)*
Bringing transnational relations back in
Non-state actors, domestic structures and international institutions

41 *Hayward R. Alker*
Rediscoveries and reformulations
Humanistic methodologies for international studies

40 *Robert W. Cox with Timothy J. Sinclair*
Approaches to world order

39 *Jens Bartelson*
A genealogy of sovereignty

38 *Mark Rupert*
Producing hegemony
The politics of mass production and American global power

37 *Cynthia Weber*
Simulating sovereignty
Intervention, the state and symbolic exchange

36 *Gary Goertz*
Contexts of international politics

35 *James L. Richardson*
Crisis diplomacy
The Great Powers since the mid-nineteenth century

34 *Bradley S. Klein*
Strategic studies and world order
The global politics of deterrence

33 *T. V. Paul*
Asymmetric conflicts
War initiation by weaker powers

32 *Christine Sylvester*
Feminist theory and international relations in a postmodern era

31 *Peter J. Schraeder*
US foreign policy toward Africa
Incrementalism, crisis and change

30 *Graham Spinardi*
From Polaris to Trident
The development of US Fleet Ballistic Missile technology

29 *David A. Welch*
Justice and the genesis of war

28 *Russell J. Leng*
Interstate crisis behavior, 1816–1980
Realism versus reciprocity

27 *John A. Vasquez*
The war puzzle

26 *Stephen Gill (ed.)*
Gramsci, historical materialism and international relations

25 *Mike Bowker and Robin Brown (eds.)*
From cold war to collapse
Theory and world politics in the 1980s

24 *R. B. J. Walker*
Inside/outside
International relations as political theory

23 *Edward Reiss*
The strategic defense initiative

22 *Keith Krause*
Arms and the state
Patterns of military production and trade

21 *Roger Buckley*
US–Japan alliance diplomacy 1945–1990

20 *James N. Rosenau and Ernst-Otto Czempiel (eds.)*
Governance without government
Order and change in world politics

19 *Michael Nicholson*
Rationality and the analysis of international conflict

18 *John Stopford and Susan Strange*
Rival states, rival firms
Competition for world market shares

17 *Terry Nardin and David R. Mapel (eds.)*
Traditions of international ethics

16 *Charles F. Doran*
Systems in crisis
New imperatives of high politics at century's end

15 *Deon Geldenhuys*
Isolated states
A comparative analysis

14 *Kalevi J. Holsti*
Peace and war
Armed conflicts and international order 1648–1989

13 *Saki Dockrill*
Britain's policy for West German rearmament 1950–1955

12 *Robert H. Jackson*
Quasi-states
Sovereignty, international relations and the third world

11 *James Barber and John Barratt*
South Africa's foreign policy
The search for status and security 1945–1988

10 *James Mayall*
Nationalism and international society

9 *William Bloom*
Personal identity, national identity and international relations

8 *Zeev Maoz*
National choices and international processes

7 *Ian Clark*
The hierarchy of states
Reform and resistance in the international order

6 *Hidemi Suganami*
The domestic analogy and world order proposals

5 *Stephen Gill*
American hegemony and the Trilateral Commission

4 *Michael C. Pugh*
The ANZUS crisis, nuclear visiting and deterrence

3 *Michael Nicholson*
Formal theories in international relations

2 *Friedrich V. Kratochwil*
Rules, norms, and decisions
On the conditions of practical and legal reasoning in international relations and domestic affairs

1 *Myles L. C. Robertson*
Soviet policy towards Japan
An analysis of trends in the 1970s and 1980s